A COLOURFUL
VIEW FROM THE TOP

A COLOURFUL VIEW FROM THE TOP

*Twenty-One Extraordinary
Stories of Leaders of Colour
Achieving Excellence in Business*

Curated by Jonathan Mildenhall

CONSTABLE

CONSTABLE

First published in Great Britain in 2023 by Constable

3 5 7 9 10 8 6 4 2

A CIP catalogue record for this book
is available from the British Library.

ISBN: 978-1-40871-579-6 (hardback)

Typeset in Object Sans by Hewer Text UK Ltd, Edinburgh
Printed and bound in Great Britain by Clays Ltd, Elcograf, S.p.A.

Papers used by Constable are from well-managed
forests and other responsible sources.

Constable
An imprint of
Little, Brown Book Group
Carmelite House
50 Victoria Embankment
London EC4Y 0DZ

An Hachette UK Company

www.hachette.co.uk

www.littlebrown.co.uk

This book is dedicated to all leaders of today and tomorrow, particularly those from minority backgrounds. To the leaders that have navigated their way to the top of business and culture, thank you for being a beacon of inspiration for the next generation of talent. And to the rising stars who dare to dream, we salute you as you carve your own paths and create a better future.

CONTENTS

The Experiment

JONATHAN MILDENHALL

◆

Hello,

If you're reading this, chances are you're thinking about a career decision that will change your life.

I've had many of those moments in my life; ones that led me to Manchester Metropolitan University; ones that led me to a Senior Vice President position at the Coca-Cola Company, which was, at the time in 2006, the most valuable brand on the planet; and, ones that led me to the Chief Marketing Officer position at Airbnb in 2014, which ultimately became the most valuable and influential travel brand in the world. But before I get into the details and share some of the highlights, let me start by taking you right back to the beginning.

Owning my difference

During the 1960s, my mum had five sons to three different men. My beautiful mum is white, my two older brothers are white, and my two younger brothers are white. Born in 1967, I'm the child of a brief encounter my mum had with my Nigerian father, a handsome, dark-skinned and tall man, who had emigrated from Nigeria a few years earlier. So, not only did I grow up the only Black person in my primary family, but I also grew up on a predominantly white, poverty-stricken council estate in north Leeds. As a child, I faced abuse in different parts of my life: sometimes at home, occasionally in the classroom, often on the streets, and always in the playground. It was awful. That said, I don't blame anyone specifically – racism was (indeed, it still is) a huge part of British culture.

The late '60s and '70s was an era when Britain generally was struggling to come to terms with mass immigration from places like India, Pakistan, the Caribbean and West Africa. The racism these Black and brown communities experienced was brutal. There was a large and growing population of hard-core racists, with policies based on the idea of 'Keeping Britain White'. The highest-profile group at the time was the National Front party. Founded the year I was born, in 1967, it reached the height of its electoral support during the mid-1970s, when it was the UK's fourth largest party in terms of share of votes. The National Front (NF) was very active in Leeds. I remember being given National Front party flyers too many times, whilst being spat on by angry, hateful NF supporters as I left school. The leaflets were designed to stoke fear of or in Black people. They worked: each time, I was left a terrified little boy. One flyer I remember showed two illustrations of the human brain. One was supposedly the brain of a white man, the other the brain of a Black man. The white man's brain was some twenty per cent larger. The headline read, 'proof, Black men are stupid, they have smaller brains!' I kept a bunch of those leaflets, hidden out of sight from my brothers and my mum. I guess I wanted to find ways to understand if any of the claims were true, so I kept them for later study.

Although extreme in their rhetoric, the NF party didn't occupy a niche opinion. Surveys conducted in the mid-1960s revealed that four out of five British people felt that 'too many immigrants had been let into the country'. The British media played a role too; broadly speaking this was a time when Black communities were communities to either fear or ridicule. Take British TV, for example. Each weekend I would sit with my white family, and oddly laugh at the portrayal of Black people on shows like *The Black and White Minstrel Show* or sitcoms like *Love Thy Neighbour*. Imagine the discomfort of being the only Black child in a room with your white family laughing about the Black people you saw on TV. The pain was made worse by knowing these shows, and others, would generate a fresh batch of racial abuse that I would have to endure at school as I was the only Black kid in my entire year. Although I loved school, I never liked Mondays. In short, I hated being Black because I hated being a target of hateful speech, ignorant humour or physical abuse. For me, all of these media portrayals of minorities not only affected how others saw me but also impacted how I saw myself. Was I a joke? Was I someone to be frightened of? Was I less intelligent than everyone in my class? For a time, I really didn't know the right answer to these important questions. Honestly, before puberty, I would have given anything to be the same colour as everybody else in my family.

I've tried not to let individual incidents impact my broader sense of self and mental wellbeing. My mum played a huge role in this. When I was about five years old, she taught me a very powerful lesson about the difference between character and packaging.

One day, I came home from school very upset. As per usual, my mum was there, ready to comfort me. Some of the kids in school had called me a range of names. I didn't know their exact meanings, but the vitriol, ridicule and anger in their tones made me feel that what they were saying was meant to harm me. And it had the desired effect. I was distraught.

Through my tears I told my mum all the names the kids in school had called me: 'blackie', 'sambo', 'nigger' and 'paki'. I remember asking her if there was anything she could do to make me look more like her, more like my brothers, to make me white! Holding me close to her bosom, my mum comforted me and told me the most powerful truth, even to this day, I have ever heard. She said, 'Jonathan, everywhere you go there will be stupid, ignorant people who might dislike you because of the colour of your skin, or the way you talk or even because of the clothes you wear. Most of the time, it is because they don't like people who are different. But you, Jonathan, have something most people will never have – and that is your beautiful character that shines like sunshine; you light up every room and when people get to know you, they cannot help but really like you. It's what's inside of you, Jonathan, that people love, and your job is to let the inside of Jonathan shine brighter and brighter every day. They may call you names, but they can never, ever take away your character. Your character and your energy, Jonathan, will serve you more than you can possibly understand right now.'

I often look back on that moment as a real turning point in my own self-awareness and understanding of what makes a human being, as well as on what basis I want to be judged. For the longest time I wanted to blend in and be part of the crowd, but as I grew older and started to realise the impact I could have on people, I began to realise that my mum was right. It is in fact my difference that makes me unique; it is my energy that people are drawn to, my character that people grow to trust, my creativity that people get inspired by – and it is the colour of my skin that, honestly, helps people remember me.

The process of fully accepting myself took twenty-five years. Now aged fifty-five, the one thing I absolutely know for sure is that my mum was right: my character and my energy have taken me further than any other aspect of my being.

Dealing with bad advice

In my late teens, I went to Manchester Polytechnic, now called Manchester Metropolitan University, to study General Business and Finance. I was very suspicious of the course, but I followed some poor advice: 'You should go to business school so you can become an accountant.' This is what happens when someone with good intentions fails to consider your personality when they offer career advice.

Due to a lack of enthusiasm, I struggled to concentrate on the course and I failed several of the finance modules. I hadn't failed at anything before and I was terrified that I would get kicked off the course. Meanwhile, I was also discovering and coming to terms with my sexuality. I was left with two fears: I didn't want to fail and I didn't want to be gay.

I sat down with the career advisor at Manchester Met and I was completely honest with her. I told her that I was struggling with the degree but didn't want to get suspended. I wanted to be proactive in finding a solution. She responded with a sense of delight and confidence and said that with a triad, like mine, of personality, energy, and character, I should pursue a career in marketing. 'Jonathan, I can see it now; you were born to become a great marketer', she said.

At the time, I stared at her perplexed. But my confusion didn't hold her back. I had no clue what marketers did, yet she spoke with so much assurance that I started to wonder why I hadn't received that advice earlier and I dreaded the thought that I had just wasted a year pursuing a course that seemed to zap my energy. But there was a solution. She proposed that I swap some of the finance modules and replace them with marketing modules, one of which was in advertising.

In my first advertising tutorial, I started to learn how advertising and marketing underpin business, but there was still some hesitation and doubt. The professor introduced us to the three principal disciplines of an advertising agency. He talked about creative people who fill blank pieces of paper with scripts and concepts, and I remember thinking, 'God, that sounds extremely hard!' Next, he introduced us to strategic planning. He explained that these people directly interact with consumers and use data to figure out what the strategy should be. To my novice ears and without any reference points, that sounded rather boring. Unfortunately, Spotify Wrapped wasn't a thing back then and I had little understanding of how data could be communicated in powerful, interesting and inspiring ways. Finally, he went into account management. He mentioned technical terms like 'the hub of the agency making sure the creative teams are inspired and clear and working on time, on budget . . . managing all of these different relationships to get the work done . . . dealing with client relationships'. And ping, it was like a lightbulb went on in my head.

I had an epiphany. This was what I wanted to do. I knew it instantly. This was my second year at Manchester Met and I'd found my true focus, which I might not have done if I hadn't been so unhappy with my original choices.

Right after that first tutorial and the lightbulb moment, I went back to my career advisor with this renewed sense of purpose and passion. I had found my calling and I wanted to pursue it right away. I thanked her for her advice and promised her that I would work incredibly hard and eventually get a job working for an advertising agency in London. I could barely sit still.

She clasped her hands, lowered her voice and said, 'Jonathan I need to explain some things to you. The advertising industry is very white; it's very middle class; and they only actually recruit from Oxford and Cambridge.'

In the space of a single sentence, she had respectfully told me that my paternal background, socio-economic background, and academic background were going to prevent me from pursuing this ideal career path. I walked out of her office and thought back to the advice from my mum all those years ago. I was determined to prove my advisor wrong and own my difference.

Giving it my all

My career advisor had unlocked something in me and there was no turning back. I had a healthy obsession with researching this new-found industry. With all of my research, I steadily cultivated it into a passion. I researched all the top London advertising agencies, their clients, their leaders, who invested the most in graduate training, campaign awards and different approaches to bringing a campaign to life. By the time I was ready to apply to different agencies, I was sure that I was armed with all of the knowledge and nuance, and this endowed me with the confidence I needed. This also allowed me to relax into the interview and allow my character to shine through.

Despite everything my teams have achieved at Coca-Cola, Airbnb, and TwentyFirstCenturyBrand, one of my proudest life moments is still when I went back to my career advisor, aged twenty-one, eighteen months after our initial conversation, and told her that I got a job at one of the leading advertising agencies in the world, McCann Erickson London, now called McCann London. I had done it. I was about to be the first ethnic minority to join McCann Erickson on their graduate training programme.

When they offered me the role at McCann Erickson, they told me I was their 'experiment'. They said 'there's something special about you, Jonathan. You come from a Polytechnic university, you are working class, you're from Leeds. We don't know if you will fit in with our culture and clients, but there's something about you that is truly special and we have all agreed to experiment with it and see where it takes us. How does that sound?'

At the time I was grateful for their honesty and their invitation to 'experiment'. It almost released me from the pressure to perform and from the instinct to try and hide aspects of my background so that I could fit in and have a greater chance of being a success. I even called my mum and said, 'I got accepted mum, but it is as an experiment. If it doesn't work out, I'll have to find something else to do. At least they are giving me a chance!' For me, there was something very powerful and empowering about how they framed it. Positioning it as an experiment gave license for both parties to fail. When both parties have that license, the pressure of failure disappears and the opportunity for success emerges. Thirty years later, and I think it is very fair to say their experiment was a success. It paid off. And now I make a habit of putting talent experimentation forward. Just because someone hasn't done something doesn't mean that they cannot do something. McCann Erickson hired me because of the potential that they saw in me. I now hire on that premise too. I ask myself the question, 'how far can this individual go?' The resume only tells me where they have been, not where they can go. I'm a great example of a pretty ugly resume, as far as academic and intern experience goes, being overlooked by the good folks at McCann Erickson in favor of my potential. Once you experience this, you have an ongoing obligation to pay it forward.

I have enjoyed a fruitful and rewarding career in the advertising and marketing industry. Among other accolades, in 2017, Forbes ranked me in the top ten most influential Chief Marketing Officers in the world. I have helped build hundreds of billions of dollars' worth of value through the work that I do and the teams I partner with. My calendar is full of meetings with prominent business leaders, entrepreneurs, celebrities, investors, philanthropists and journalists. I have travelled the world, visiting over sixty countries. I've been to the finals of the FIFA World Cup and the opening ceremonies of the Beijing and London Olympics. I took my mum to the latter and honestly it was another one of the proudest moments of my career. From a council estate in Leeds to a VIP box at the opening of the London Olympics with my mum. It was a surreal moment for both of us.

Thankfully, I am in a position now where, if my husband and I invest our wealth wisely, we will have created generational wealth meaning that our children's children will have the financial resources to get a brilliant start in life in terms of education, empowerment and choices. That means a lot to me.

Yet, the issue of positive representation is still burning, especially in business. The upper levels of industry just don't represent the rich diversity of talent across race, sexuality, religion, (dis)abilities, and socioeconomic backgrounds that the world has to offer. We need more experiments; we need more opportunities for companies and aspiring professionals to experiment with risks they may have never previously considered. There isn't a month that goes by where I don't experiment with myself, pushing myself into experiences I have never had, seizing responsibilities I have never taken up before.

But the most satisfying experiments I do today involve offering young folks who think they can't, opportunities to prove to themselves that they can. I couple this with building teams of deep and robust diversity, and then I stand back and watch the creativity run wild. It isn't easy or passive work. Experimenting with talent is hard, active work for any leader but it truly is the most rewarding work of my career.

A Colourful View From the Top

When I reflect on my life, I have numerous moments of incredulity. It could have been very easy for me to have taken a different path. I haven't had positive role models who look like me in such close proximity since my days as a high school athlete. Don't get me wrong, I don't think for one minute this has held me back in terms of my achievements and the impact my work has had on the brands and businesses I have served. That said, I know that if I had been able to follow others who looked like me then I would have arrived here quicker as I wouldn't have endured impostor syndrome for as long as I did. I would have known that I belonged. Nonetheless, when I look back on my life, I still always have a tremendous sense of pride. I made it all the way to the top of my industry and now I do my part to ensure that it is a fairer and more inclusive place for women and minorities.

However, the change we need to see is still happening at a pace so slow I know it will take a couple of generations of professionals before all industries fairly reflect the communities they serve. In 2020, during the aftermath of the murder of George Floyd, my co-founder, Neil Barrie and I were brainstorming on what actions we at TwentyFirstCenturyBrand could take to help address the challenges of systemic racism in the US and here in the UK. We wanted to make sure that we did something positive that leveraged our own expertise.

We knew how stories can shift culture and that we needed to tell more stories about outstanding Black and brown executives who have achieved extraordinary success across a number of professions where the top achievers are predominantly white and male. It was Neil's idea to publish a series of books. I loved his idea, the title *A Colourful View From the Top* instinctively flashed into my mind, and this book was born.

Two and a half years later, here I am writing the introduction. This powerful book is made up of the personal life stories and reflections of twenty-one people who have each defied gravity, societal biases, and prejudice to climb their way to the very top of their chosen profession. To ensure we uncovered new names it was important to us that each executive built their reputation purely off the back of their chosen profession. Because of this we avoided celebrity business people who have built businesses on the back of popular fame. Whilst we truly respect and deeply admire such talent, we were committed to promoting emerging names alongside some iconic names I have no doubt you will be familiar with.

When you start out with a project like this, your greatest fear is that you won't be able to persuade the people you want to feature to actually agree and put in the time to tell their stories. I'm so heartened to tell you that that has not been our experience and we are very grateful to have an amazing collection of world-class leaders who have so generously given their time and truth.

The stories you are about to read are utterly inspiring, captured so beautifully via interviews conducted over the past two years. These Black and brown luminaries have all become heroes to me. They have a number of traits in common:

- None of them understand the meaning of 'no'. They have all faced challenges, insecurities, doubts, disappointments, setbacks and failures. But these are just more reasons to get back up and try harder next time. Tell them 'no' and they'll tell you they can.

- They all work extremely hard and smart, and take great pride in pushing themselves to be the very best executive, creator, entrepreneur or industry leader they can be.

- If the world they want to see doesn't exist, then they will literally create it, build it or shape it into being. They are all united in this conviction.

- None of them enjoy the current status quo in terms of diversity in business and all of them spend a lot of time and energy ensuring their companies, industries or organisations are making it a whole lot easier for the next generation of Black and brown talent to enter the workforce and be set up for ongoing success.

- They are united by their passion to create the world they want to see.

This brings me to you, the reader. This book is specifically targeted towards young people who are either thinking about what career to choose or who are starting out in their chosen profession. The community of *A Colourful View From the Top* all hope that this book inspires you to dream bigger than you ever thought possible. Why? Because our collective future on this planet is dependent on people like you climbing all the way to the top so that you can help make a more balanced, more inclusive and fairer world for all. You might not think, right now, that you have what it takes to succeed – I didn't when I was starting out. But the one thing I know for sure is that incredible things do happen when you believe. We hope this book will stoke your sense of belief in what it is you can become, and the gifts you have the potential to give to the world.

Before you go any further, take another good look at the cover which represents all twenty-one of our heroines and heroes. There's a lot going on there: pride, focus, willingness to learn and a streak of defiance too. But most of all, there's inspiration. You're looking at someone who has been inspired to set out on their own hero's journey.

We dearly hope that these twenty-one stories help inspire yours too. This book is designed to serve as a wisdom companion on your journey: it's packed with extraordinary stories, life lessons and daily affirmations.

With love and untethered encouragement,

Jonathan Mildenhall

A COLOURFUL

VIEW FROM THE TOP

'The Polymath'

AMALI DE ALWIS MBE

◆

After finishing school, Amali studied manufacturing engineering at Birmingham University, then, in what appeared to be a radical shift, switched to the London College of Fashion at the University of the Arts London. She graduated with a degree in Product Design and Development with a specialism in shoe design. After a successful spell at the venerable British shoemakers Clarks, Amali took another equally dramatic change of tack and entered the corporate world. She upskilled as a quantitative researcher at TNS Global and then joined PwC, first as a 'Research Manager' and then moved across to be a 'Thought Leadership Manager'. She was so highly regarded that she was seconded to the World Economic Forum in Geneva to undertake a project that looked at the relationship between trust and business performance. Amali and her team then presented the insights from the research at the Forum's annual meeting in Davos.

However, it didn't take her too long to realise she could have a stronger positive impact on society away from conventional corporate life and she found her true calling in empowering others in business and tech. She joined Code First: Girls (CFG) in 2015 as its first CEO. CFG is a not-for-profit company dedicated to closing the gender gap in the tech industry. It has become the largest provider of in-person free coding courses for women and non-binary people in the UK. The organisation prides itself on creating a safe, empowering and nurturing environment for its members to learn coding skills. It also helps large corporate companies to recruit and retain diverse tech talent. Under Amali's leadership, CFG had tremendous growth and was teaching more women to code each year than any computer science undergraduate degree program in the UK. Following Amali's time at CFG, she joined Microsoft as Managing Director of Microsoft for Startups in the UK where she spent a number of years supporting startups operating in the 'B2B SaaS' (business-to-business software-as-a-service) sector to scale and grow. Most recently, Amali returned to mission-focused entrepreneurship by joining Subak as CEO. Subak is a data cooperative and the world's first accelerator focused on not-for-profit climate data startups.

Outside of her day job, Amali sits on several boards, and is currently on the board of Ada, National College for Digital Skills; the Raspberry Pi Foundation; and Unboxed 2022. She was a founding member at Tech Talent Charter, was named as 'The Most Influential Woman in UK IT' by Computer Weekly and was awarded an MBE in 2019 in the New Year's Honours list for Services to Diversity and Training in the Tech Industry.

Make the most of whatever life gives you

I was a curious kid who asked a lot of questions, and, thankfully, had family members who would answer a lot of those questions for me. Also I'm asthmatic, so as a kid I used to have to carry a little bag of my asthma medications with me, which was brilliant because it doubled as my 'MacGyver' bag (referencing the main character from the 1980s TV series *MacGyver*, an adventurer who could construct any lifesaving gadget from the contents of his pockets). I'd put in pen knives, compasses, bits of string ... *everything* I could find that enabled me to go on adventures. That was something I really loved; the idea of exploring and building new things. My mother trained as a tailor and my dad was a doctor so they made or *did* things – so for me, whether it was doing crafts or building mechanical things out of stuff I could find or little radios out of electronic kits, I didn't really mind. I just liked the idea of finding, building, and making things. As a kid, I was a *maker,* and I guess it began with my MacGyver bag.

Don't be put off by a name

The main reason I chose to study engineering at university was because it felt like the natural place for me to exercise my innate curiosities. It also felt like the only pathway that would allow me to couple abstract creativity with practical creation. However, I soon realised that the building blocks of engineering exist in other professions. If we look back to some of the 'Renaissance man' type characters, like da Vinci and Copernicus, it is so clear that they were not confined to one profession. They exercised their plural interests and pursued the most relevant outlets. They were painters, artists and illustrators; they designed and built things; they were polymaths. There's a connection between the creativity and technology that I think is really important, especially when we talk about what sorts of jobs exist for girls and what sorts of jobs exist for boys, and how we incorrectly stereotype people as more likely to be creative or mathematical based on gender. In reality, creativity, maths and logic apply across lots of different sectors. For example, you can have artists who are fantastic engineering thinkers and then engineers who are artistic and creative.

One of the other mistakes we often make is assigning a job as technical or creative based on a stereotype of an industry. For example, when I did manufacturing engineering, I remember taking drafting classes where we had to draw exploded diagrams of components which gave an exaggerated view of all the different parts, the different angles, the measurements and all of the component parts. Then, when I moved to my degree in shoe design, I had to do the exact same style of drawings. The only difference was that I was drafting shoes instead of car parts. I was completing these incredibly technical drawings on how these things would fit together, including the measurements and angles involved. It got me thinking about how we have these two industries, of which people may say, 'Oh yes, fashion design is all for women . . . and engineering is for men'. But we miss the key point: both industries require the same skillset. The issue is that we view these careers through a gendered lens which often means we pigeon-hole highly capable people and don't give them the chance to

5

explore and apply incredibly valuable skillsets to different kinds of industries.

The method matters

Initially, I was convinced that switching from engineering to shoe design would be a complete paradigm shift. At the time, it was difficult to envision what a career as an engineer would look like. It didn't feel enticing, appealing, or inspiring. On the other hand, shoe design captivated me from the very beginning. Shoe design seemed to capture the magic of creativity in a way that engineering didn't, at least in the way I was taught. I now know that that is not the case, but as a twenty-year-old, I couldn't see the connection. The irony was that six months into my 'radical paradigm shift', I started to recognise the similarities in my engineering degree and shoe design degree. The content was different, and we were designing different products, but the methods were the same. It felt quite profound. Unfortunately, for my bank account, that epiphany came too late. I had to rebuy some of the textbooks I had given away when I left my engineering degree. That was when I realised that I was doing the same degree that I had just dropped; it was just under the guise of a different name. Whether one is manufacturing airplane propellers or shoes, they both go through the same process: research, design, prototype, test, iterate and then they get shipped off to the consumer.

Given that the process is the same, it was quite remarkable to note how differently we were taught. My shoe design professors taught in such a different way to my engineering professors. Engineering was mostly exam based, which I always struggled with as memorising formulas is not the way my brain works. Shoe design, on the other hand, was coursework based, and so included research, analysis, design thinking, and market strategy. We would then implement all of our research and actually design, build and make the product. That was much more fulfilling for me.

It was no surprise that I then went on to become a quantitative researcher because that's the way that I understand the world. The way I find answers is by examining what's around me and asking structured questions, undertaking analysis, and then formulating a solution to whatever the problem might be. I learn things better through 'doing', and this was something we took into CFG. Software roles are *practical* jobs – no software developer goes into work and their boss turns to them and asks, 'Ah, do you remember, what was the X function of this or that?' That's not how a developer works. A developer thinks about problems, works with other people, unpicks the problem and tries different approaches based on other work. It's often a case of, 'Oh, that doesn't work, let's correct this, chop this bit out, take this bit from here. Oh, did you have this bit? We can put that into it as well . . .' It's an iterative and often highly collaborative job.

This is how we designed the courses at CFG. There were no exams, we just got people to build things and to replicate the type of environment they would have as a software developer. We wanted to create a world where they would get to work closely with others, to see their work in practice, and build on each other's products to continue to improve things – a practical way of building. This approach allowed our members to open doors they previously thought might be closed to them. They realised that the types of skills they had were, in fact, very much aligned with the roles they thought they wouldn't have access to, be competent at or enjoy.

Of course, like anything else in life, people have got to want the change in order to look beyond what has been accepted for so long. From having run CFG, I know there is no shortage of women and non-binary people who want that change. We were regularly oversubscribed; by the time I left the organisation we were already halfway to our original goal of delivering coding courses for twenty thousand young women, and some of our courses that were for thirty people would get anything from 150 to 200 applications. When we bought in a new chief exec, the company continued to thrive and grow having now taught over seventy thousand young women to code. The continued success of CFG shows that given the right environment, with the right methods of communication and delivery, you absolutely can build the right pipeline to achieve your goals. This in turn creates a hugely supportive community of current cohorts and supportive alumni.

It's not too late to make that career change

I'm very fortunate with my family in the way that they always believed in what I wanted to do and would support me whatever that was. There was never an expectation that because I was a girl, I would follow a certain path. Early on in my life, I had this understanding that the world saw things in a gendered way, but it didn't stop me from doing what I wanted to do. It didn't matter to me that my interests were more 'boyish' than 'girly'. I enjoyed going on adventures and building things, and if that was 'boyish', so what? I did it anyway.

With CFG, I was aware not everyone came from such supportive environments; there were so many people who had been told, 'This isn't the right thing for you', 'You can't do this' or 'This isn't the kind of thing that people like you do'. That played a big part in my thinking. Whenever anyone asked me about CFG I would tell them it's for people who missed the boat a long time ago. Whether it's around training or upskilling, having different methods to get into new fields and careers avoids the narrative that if you haven't made a start, it's too late.

For me, it's just not the way the world is going. So many people have multiple careers in their lives and *we have to* get used to this idea of cycling people into new careers and helping them reframe what they do, to upskill and more. This is pertinent for diversity, too, as it involves making sure we enable everybody to have the chance to do something incredible regardless of where they're coming from. There's still a way to go in this respect, but I do believe it is better than it was twenty years ago when I was coming out of university.

The idea of CFG was to facilitate that change for people – you could be working in a shop, then the coding course would at least give you access to another world. When I first came into the company, they had just run a pilot with thirty students and so wanted to build a few different hypotheses based on the result. One of the big hypotheses included the idea that the current gender imbalance in the industry was not an *interest* issue – of course women could be interested in working in coding and technology – rather, it was an *access and knowledge* issue. What we needed to provide was access to cheap or no-cost coding education, a network and a support structure to help this demographic through their journey. We would need to connect them to employers too, those who cared about supporting more people from underrepresented backgrounds.

While a vital part of what we were doing was helping employers to meet these individuals who were looking to develop their careers, we also had to help the employers create better environments for people who were switching careers, or perhaps didn't have an engineering background. That whole idea of how to successfully help people who were moving to a new career, in a way that gave them the skills but also supported them through that switch, was the primary hypothesis we tested with CFG. We were really, really delighted to find that our methods worked: our hypotheses were proven correct.

A little while ago a young woman stopped me in the middle of High Street Kensington and asked, 'Are you Amali?' She was a CFG alumnus who had secured a role at McKinsey & Co as a digital analyst and was now working as a senior manager at Depop. She was a brilliant example of the young women who hadn't thought technology was accessible to them. This was our aim – to provide the opportunity into that world, with the support, training and knowledge needed to allow them to make that move.

Sometimes it's best to look outside the mainstream to get what you want

My research skills from my stint at PwC were incredibly handy when we built the strategy for CFG's 2020 campaign. Naturally, I went digging for data. I pulled UCAS data on applications for computer science degrees and realised that CFG had more young women enrolled on a coding course that year than the total number of women that had enrolled on a computer science degree. At that time, we were a six-person not-for-profit operation, and that statistic, for me, was extraordinary. From a resourcing standpoint, it sounded impossible; however, it just reiterated that when you have the right team working towards the right mission, anything is possible.

I do a lot of work with universities and, while they have come a long way, the big advantage of CFG was that there was no baggage – we were able to think outside the box and action it, offering what a traditional education institute wouldn't be able to. Universities couldn't have a course that required no exams, had no entry criteria and didn't need to have a certificate issued at the end which was nationally recognised as a specific benchmark. We could afford to throw the playbook out and take a behavioural insight approach to getting people into these careers.

For example, we partnered with British telecoms provider, BT, to help them recruit and retain young women into their engineering and tech roles. They already had great graduate programmes, brilliant apprenticeship programmes and were already doing everything which one would think would help people get access to those roles. Yet they were still struggling to recruit female talent. We created a four-month boot camp, designing the curriculum in line with BT's specific technology needs: whatever languages they were working in, everything was aligned with their business. Not only did we provide the training needed, but it was practical and there were no exams. We had a community of tens of thousands of young women of employable age, who had done an introductory course and were looking to develop in the technology sphere. Nobody else in the UK had that pool of people which could be tapped into – we were able to combine forces and make it work.

A lot of universities wouldn't have been able to do the same, as they are primarily formal education institutions. It's difficult for them to cover everything from education to community support to employability, which is something CFG could do. We didn't have any ties to anything – we were never meant to be a formal education institution; we were just meant to help get women and non-binary people into coding in whatever way possible.

I was never surprised that CFG expanded to become this all-embracing operation, because we had a simple goal: we wanted to support more women in the tech industry. The first strategy I set for CFG used a 'human design process', in which you start with understanding. I had many conversations with previous students, current students, potential students, instructors and employers, to understand questions I had around the industry and potential recruits. Why do they need us? What is the problem? What is the job to be done? We took our findings and developed an understanding of the landscape to find the crux of our mission.

Once we had landed on that mission, we then went through an exercise to discover exactly how to achieve it. If we were to think about the thousand and one different ways that you could help more women and non-binary people into the tech industry, what would those ways be? You could run training courses, offer scholarships at universities, pay people to join companies, train the corporates to be able to hire people from underrepresented genders, work with policy makers in government to make this a priority . . . but there was more to be done. More than just supporting people who were at university; another aspect was supporting women and non-binary people who were career switching. This was why we thought about the employability side, too, so we worked with employers and provided advisory work around recruitment and retention, problem solving why they were struggling to recruit. We were never about just wanting to teach women and non-binary people how to code – we thought about the bigger picture.

Find a way to carve a new path

I'm a firm believer that when something isn't working for you, you have the power to carve a new path for yourself. Change can be difficult, but it's always possible – if you want something to happen, it may not always be easy, but it might just take a little bit of time. In CFG we supported women who were single mums and supporting themselves, women who were trying to upskill from careers where they didn't feel challenged, women who were responsible for elderly parents and more. There have been all these types of obstacles that they have managed to move beyond. Bill Gates is quoted as saying 'Most people overestimate what they can do in one year and underestimate what they can do in ten years' – I think that's really true. Change doesn't happen overnight.

When I think about some of the incredible people I've seen going through those various career and life changes, I realise that they just take little steps every day and then suddenly, four years later, they're in a completely different scenario to where they were. That's hard earned. I would always encourage anyone who's feeling daunted about making a change: you can do it. It will take time and it will take effort, but find people who will support you in that journey and go on from there.

Flexibility is the way forward

Mobility is becoming a bigger part of normal working life. I believe there's been a huge change in how companies view their employees as well, in response to them believing they no longer owe their employees as much loyalty. I worked for Clarks early on in my career, a very old-school company; people used to stay at that company for a lifetime, from when they were first working to all the way through their adult life. The company often got involved with their employee's families and were looking at something that wasn't just the bottom line.

That sort of approach would be unusual in today's landscape: staff turnover has become far more commonplace as companies have become more competitive, more selective and – some would argue – more efficient. Their aim is to find the top talent to fill their job vacancies, looking at profitability, making sure people keep training and that fresh blood is consistently brought into the company. But the flip side of this is that people can't be offered loyalty. In response, those same people ask, 'If the company can't offer me loyalty, why should I offer them my loyalty? Why wouldn't I go and find a new company who can offer me better terms?'

The covid pandemic has been an incredibly self-reflective period; people have been thinking hard about how they spend their time, asking 'What do I want to spend my days doing?' For people living in a position of privilege (and I consider myself one of these) where they're not struggling to put a roof over their heads, if given the opportunity to look for new job roles that suit their lifestyles more, or make them feel more valued, why wouldn't they take it? We're all living longer, too, and the idea of doing the same job for sixty or seventy years is becoming a less popular one. I think people just want a bit more variety.

Remember your worth

It's not always easy to step into a society that has not been designed to accommodate or recognise you. It is even more difficult when that social system suffers from gender discrimination and belittles one's value, intelligence, and contribution based on their gender. I've spoken to a lot of the young women who have completed our courses, as well as our instructors who are female, and there has been some bad behaviour in the field. However, following a lot of work on different fronts, a new system is emerging, and the industry is going through a redesign to nurture and accommodate talent and hard work in all its forms.

Something I used to say repeatedly at CFG was that there's no such thing as a non-tech business these days; *every* single business needs *somebody* with technology experience and skills. As a result, developers are in high demand and salaries can be significant. But what if a new employee doesn't feel comfortable, or if the company doesn't create a good work environment? This issue isn't just affecting women either – it's affecting people from different ethnic backgrounds, people with a different sexual orientation and other marginalised groups. Thankfully, the good thing is that there will always be other companies out there who will treat you better – again, you can carve a new path for yourself. Vote with your feet – if you're finding a situation doesn't work for you, don't get stuck. You have the power to move away from it.

This is especially relevant at junior level. Some people would argue that if you stay within a company, you can eventually change it. But it's not the job of a junior developer to change the culture of the company she works in – rather, it's the job of the company to fix those issues. To be the driver of change is an unfair expectation to be put on somebody who is early in their career, and even more so for female developers in their first role. Too often, telling management of the various problems and issues in the company is something that lands on their shoulders. I wholly believe this is a responsibility that should rest with the company.

For a new, young developer, try to make sure you get support. It may not always be easy in your immediate environment, so look for it elsewhere, including your wider network: peers in other companies or people you've studied with. If you find in any way your situation is making you deeply unhappy, do move: you have great skills and great experiences, and they are transferable.

The remarkable thing is that coding used to be a women's world

I'm currently on the board of Ada: The National College for Digital Skills, which is named after Ada Lovelace, who was a fascinating character born in 1815 as the daughter of Lord and Lady Byron. Her mother and father divorced and Lord Byron died when she was very young. She was encouraged to pursue mathematics by her mother who very much tried to move Ada away from anything she thought would be related to arts or poetry, as a counterbalance to her father.

She considered herself more than just a mathematician, interested in theology and phrenology (the study of people's skulls which supposedly linked abilities and characteristics to different features of the skull). She worked very closely with Charles Babbage who created this machine called the 'analysis engine', which many people today consider the first computer. Ada saw potential in this invention and suspected it could be developed into something more than a calculating machine. She saw the possibility for it to write sets of instructions and developed one of the first machines that had the idea of memories, so that you could carry things over and calculate sums based on what was in that memory. Ada was a real pioneer of coding and writing algorithms and is someone we hold up as an example to Code First: Girls' young women.

Ada is just one of many incredible women who have worked within computing and software. There was also Dame Stephanie Shirley who was one of Britain's early tech pioneers; she built computers and wrote code for the Post Office in the 1950s. She also set up a computing company that used to do punch-card programming for companies and built a business that was almost entirely staffed by women, many of whom were writing programmes at their kitchen tables onto cards.

It's true that women were the early computers – calculating was considered a sort of manual work that women coming out of typing pools were allowed to do. It wasn't until more money and power was assigned to computing and technology sectors that women started being pushed out of the field. Dame Stephanie has talked about how a new pay band had to be set up at the Post Office when men started getting interested in computing – management realised they couldn't put them into the same pay band as women because it was so low. They even created a new job *term* for men so they could keep women at a lower level of pay.

This is not just about technology – this is thinking about women's worthiness to be paid and their value to society. This is why the retelling of these stories around women in the field is so important, and one of the reasons why I'm involved with this project and others. But it isn't just about women either; it's about people from different ethnic backgrounds or different gender backgrounds. History is written by the victor and there's a tendency to airbrush out the events that don't fit with the narrative around success.

Women have made up half of the population of the earth since humanity began, yet if you were to look through all of our historical texts, you'd assume that women were only roughly about a tenth of the population because we only have access to half of the story. There are so many examples of narratives that must be rewritten so we no longer forget women from history.

The confidence will come

Confidence is an *outcome*, it's not an *input*. When you do something, the act of having done it – having learned from that experience – makes you feel more confident.

This is important to keep in mind when doing anything new. Whether it's learning to code, going to a new country or starting a new career, you will never arrive at it with confidence. The question is, can you move forward without it? And, importantly, can you be provided with an environment that will help you to build confidence over time? That community element – the scaffolding to help you build your confidence – is a critical part, so it's important you find that environment.

Lessons

Curiosity is one of the most powerful traits as a precursor to success. For young Amali this came early, as did her ability to turn her weakness, asthma, into a strength – remember her MacGyver bag.

Understand that there are many ways to learn. It doesn't all have to be about texts, revising and exams. If you don't like theoretical learning, look for practical and/or vocational ways to learn.

Don't let pre-conceived notions or stereotypes restrict you. If you don't like the box you have been put in, draw and label another box that feels more right for you, or better yet, rub out all of the boxes and exist in the blank canvas.

Professional reinvention can be an effective strategy to build success and stay relevant.

Don't ever underestimate the power of your long-term potential.

Affirmation: Today I will ask myself, what do I want to spend my days doing?

'The Beacon'

IMRAN AMED MBE

As founder, CEO and Editor-in-Chief of *The Business of Fashion*, Imran Amed is a leading authority on the global fashion industry, bringing together his years as a management consultant with his passion for fashion and creativity. Imran was born and raised in Calgary, Canada. He went to McGill University in Montreal where he studied business and earned an MBA from Harvard Business School. After graduating, Imran worked at the global consultancy McKinsey & Company. For more than a decade, he was an associate lecturer at Central Saint Martins College of Art & Design, one of the world's leading art colleges.

Today, *The Business of Fashion* (*BoF*) boasts more than one and a half million unique visitors per month, and has more than six million followers on social media. His global team spans London, New York, Los Angeles, Paris and Milan, and manages market-leading products and services including *BoF Professional* (a subscription membership which is the world's largest community of fashion professionals), *BoF Careers* (a global marketplace for fashion talent), *BoF VOICES* (an annual invitation-only gathering for leading thinkers and innovators from inside and outside fashion), and the *BoF 500* (the authoritative annual index of the people shaping the global fashion industry). Recently, *BoF* launched *The Business of Beauty* to provide the same kind of authoritative journalism to serve the global beauty community, and *BoF Insights*, a data and analysis think tank for the fashion, luxury and beauty.

Since founding *BoF* in 2007, Imran has earned several accolades. In 2014, he was the youngest ever recipient of the Desautels Management Achievement Award at McGill University. In 2015, he was named Honorary Professor of Fashion Business at the Glasgow Caledonian University. In 2017, he was appointed by Queen Elizabeth II as Member of the Order of the British Empire (MBE) for services to the fashion industry. In 2018, Imran was awarded an honorary doctorate from Central Saint Martins College of Art & Design.

He has also been named in Fast Company's annual list of the 'Most Creative People in Business', *British GQ's* list of the '100 Most Influential Men in Britain', *Indian GQ*'s list of the '50 Most Influential Global Indians' and *Wired UK*'s list of the '100 most influential figures in Britain's Digital Economy'.

A family history spanning continents and cultures

I grew up as a Shia Isma'ili Muslim in Calgary, Canada. Our forebears left India for East Africa in the nineteenth century during the time of the British Empire. Many of them initially came to Kenya, Uganda and Tanzania as labourers and eventually settled down in mercantile communities, setting up small businesses as shop owners.

My father was born in Kisumu, Kenya. His mother had only a third-grade education. She worked hard as a seamstress to raise six children on her own after her husband died. My father was only eight years old at the time of his death.

My mother was born in Moshi, Tanzania in the foothills of Mount Kilimanjaro. She grew up with her parents, two sisters and two brothers in a small two-room house. My grandfather was a respected leader in the Isma'ili community, and so his faith played an important role in shaping her values.

After East African countries gained independence from their colonisers, our community began to face an increasingly hostile environment. In 1972, the dictator Idi Amin suddenly ordered eighty thousand South Asians in Uganda to leave. So began the migration of Isma'ilis from East Africa to Western countries, including Canada, whose prime minister, Pierre

Trudeau, created a special programme to house them as refugees.

My parents met at the University of Nairobi. They were the first in their respective families to graduate with university degrees. They followed the migration wave and left everything they knew to immigrate to Canada. When they arrived in Calgary in the middle of the winter in December 1974, my mum was five months pregnant.

They had big dreams for me. They moved to Canada so I could have a good education and the financial security and psychological safety that would bring. The day I was born, my father apparently said to mum, 'this boy will go to Harvard', so there were always high expectations for what I would achieve.

Their own educational qualifications were not recognised in Canada, so they had to go back to school when they arrived. My dad retrained to get his architectural qualifications and my mum attended the University of Calgary, and eventually became a school teacher.

There's nobody else like you

Over the years, I have experienced Islamophobia, racism, and homophobia – sometimes all at the same time and, on occasion, even from within the Isma'ili community. As someone whose family history spans three continents, I also had to constantly answer questions about where I was 'really from'.

As a young person, I was always the smallest person in the room – something I was constantly made aware of by adults who would ask me if my parents were feeding me enough and by bullies who teased me relentlessly. They would call me 'shrimp' (because I was small), or 'faggot' (because I was effeminate), or 'Paki' (because I was brown). At one point, I was bullied so badly that I had to change schools.

The first person who helped me to understand that my differences were what made me unique was my childhood physician, Dr. Ramji. My parents had taken me to see Dr Ramji because they were genuinely worried that I was not growing fast enough. I remember in a private conversation, Dr Ramji looked at me and said, 'You're totally normal – for you. You don't have to be like everybody else. That's what makes you special. There's nobody else like you.'

Expose yourself to everything. It will help you discover your natural gifts and talents.

My parents championed and believed in me from a young age, and made decisions that were in my best long-term interest. When I was in second grade, my school asked me to do an IQ test. When the results came back and I was classified as 'gifted', I was given the option of going to a different school with a curriculum specifically designed for kids like me. But my mother thoughtfully declined because, as an educator, she felt it was more important for me to be around a diverse group of kids with all kinds of talents. That it would be a much better education. She was right.

My parents still expected me to excel academically. It was assumed I would eventually become a doctor, lawyer or engineer, as is common with a lot of immigrant communities. But, unusually for that time, they also encouraged me to explore my creativity. When I was in fifth grade, my music teacher suggested to my parents that they get my voice professionally trained. I auditioned to join the Calgary Boys Choir. At first, I was rejected, but I tried again the next year and got in.

When my voice changed, I had to leave the choir. One day after speech class, my dad had a twinkle in his eye and said he wanted to show me something. He knew I really missed singing. He walked me down a long hallway to a room with the sounds of a co-ed choir rehearsing. They were singing and dancing and having so much fun. They were called the Youth Singers of Calgary. He asked if I might like to join. I auditioned shortly after that and got in. Over the next few years, I made lifelong friends, met the first people in my life who were openly gay and even sang at the Sydney Opera House in Australia.

I loved the performing arts. I studied voice, public speaking, speech arts and drama until I finished high school. There weren't many people who looked like me in those spaces; getting cast in roles was challenging because of my ethnicity and because I was physically very small. But there was a part of me I could be on stage that I couldn't be anywhere else. I felt alive.

That training has given me so much and is still valuable to this day: strong communication skills; an appreciation of creativity and creative people; how to work in teams to create something together; confidence in expressing myself and comfort in being on stage, which is handy as now I find myself on stages a lot, sometimes in front of thousands of people.

There were plenty of other things I was exposed to when I was younger that I did not enjoy or excel at. Unlike my dad, who was a natural and talented athlete, I had no talent for sports. But because I was able to try so many things, I discovered my own talents early on and developed both my left-brain analytical skills and right-brain creative skills. This balance is essential to the work that I do today. I am forever grateful to my parents for this.

A solid educational foundation will serve you well

For my undergraduate degree, I wanted to study political science, but my dad didn't believe that would offer a clear career path. He was probably right. I was also curious about entrepreneurship, so we settled on a business degree. I was admitted to McGill University in Montreal, a city I loved. I majored in finance and international business, knowing that I wanted to have a global angle to my career one day.

In the beginning, I wasn't sure what I wanted to do with my degree. So I focused on building a strong CV, hoping that it would open doors and give me degrees of freedom in the future. In my final year, I applied for jobs at the top investment banking and management consulting firms. I didn't know much about these companies, nor did I know anyone who worked in these kinds of jobs, but I had learned how prestigious these firms were and that they were a good entry point into the top business schools. The best firms were also globally minded, so there was a chance I could work internationally which I found exciting.

Just getting to the interview stage in these firms was tough. Of four hundred graduating students, perhaps ten would be shortlisted for an interview and perhaps only one or two would be offered a job. I was drawn to McKinsey because it was the most prestigious firm.

The interviews were very rigorous. They tested our problem-solving skills using case studies that we had to solve in real-time. I was offered a chance to do a practice round of five interviews with McKinsey which helped me to learn what the interviews would be like and to meet some people in the firm. I was then shortlisted for the first round of two interviews and then made it to the final round of five interviews. Afterwards, my contact at McKinsey called me back to say the interviewers couldn't agree on whether to offer me a job, so they asked me to come back to Toronto for five more interviews. This made me even more nervous.

In the end, I didn't get the job. I'll never forget when the McKinsey partner finally called to say they *still* weren't sure about me and that they would prefer to make a type II statistical error (false negative) rather than a type I error (false positive). I was pretty devastated. It took them seventeen interviews and they still couldn't decide if I was good enough? It was a big blow to my confidence.

Back then, I thought a label like McKinsey would validate me in the eyes of other people as I was struggling with my sense of self-worth. I desperately wanted to show people that even though I was so different, I could still be successful.

Now that McKinsey was off the table, I felt more unsure about my future. My friends were all moving to New York, London or Toronto, but I decided to accept a job offer at another consulting firm called Braxton Associates (part of Deloitte Consulting). I had been offered other jobs in Toronto but decided to stay in my beloved Montreal to hone my French language skills. This was an example of making a decision with my gut and going against the grain, even though logically the jobs in Toronto were better paid and more prestigious.

There was something I liked about the people at Braxton. They seemed kind and took an interest in me and my career. They were also fun; the Québecois are known for their *joie de vivre* and they seemed to accept my quirks and idiosyncrasies. I felt psychologically safe working there and learned a lot. It was an excellent first professional experience. I have never regretted my decision to stay in Montreal. It was the right decision for me.

After two years, I asked Deloitte for a transfer to the Braxton offices in Paris or London. The managing director explained to me that this would not be possible as my skill set wasn't so special to justify the costs associated with this kind of move. I knew it was time for me to leave Montreal, so I began looking for other international opportunities. Eventually, I received a fellowship to work at a microfinance organisation in Dhaka, Bangladesh. But on the day I was planning to resign, the managing director came to me with unexpected news. He had found a way for me to transfer to London as there was an analyst there who wanted to transfer to North America. We could do a swap.

I was so excited! I turned down the fellowship and moved to London a few months later, not knowing anyone in the city (or that I would still be living in London more than twenty years later). My first project was for a bank in Switzerland, and after that I worked for a telecom company in Norway and a pharmaceutical company in the Netherlands. This international experience was so precious to me, and in each new country I had the chance to learn not just about a new industry, but also about a new culture, which I found very stimulating.

Meanwhile, I was also applying to business schools. I was admitted to the Wharton School of the University of Pennsylvania but hadn't heard back from Harvard Business School about an interview. As with McKinsey, I assumed I didn't get in. Then, while I was making plans to move to Philadelphia, a package arrived from HBS with an admission letter. Another unexpected twist. Somehow, I had gotten in without an interview! Things were starting to go my way. And, I had fulfilled my father's wish for me to go to Harvard which, to this day, I think means a lot to him.

Your differences are your superpowers and this is what gives you a unique point of view

When I arrived at Harvard Business School, many of my classmates came from privileged backgrounds. There were sons of presidents and prime ministers, aristocrats and billionaires. Many students came from elite private schools and Ivy League universities, and worked at companies like McKinsey and Goldman Sachs.

I was still the smallest person and I felt I stood out like a sore thumb. Even my name was ridiculed. Some of the American students called me 'Enron', after the energy company whose disgraced CEO, Jeffrey Skilling, an HBS alumnus, had to resign amid a scandal and was eventually convicted of felony charges. Was it a joke, or simply ignorance or insensitivity? I was never quite sure.

Eventually I found my groove. With my global background and work experience, I was able to find common ground with people across campus. I loved being around so many motivated people who were interested in having an impact on the world.

But at times, HBS was very challenging due to events going on in the wider world. The bursting of the dot com bubble had pushed the economy into a recession and dimmed our job prospects. I thought HBS would be the golden ticket to the creative career I wanted, but this seemed increasingly unlikely.

When the terrorist attacks of 9/11 happened in my second year, things really came to a boiling point. Being a Muslim was a core part of my upbringing, but not something I spoke about with my classmates. And yet, after those heinous attacks, I was forced to reckon with this part of my identity. It was a scary time for people across the country, and that was acutely felt by Muslims on campus. There were Muslims from all over the world – from Turkey, Saudi Arabia, the UAE, India, Pakistan and beyond. Some of them had only been in the United States for a few weeks when we began hearing reports about Islamophobia and racism on campus.

And then one day I witnessed it firsthand. I was in a class called 'The Moral Leader' when a classmate made a really ignorant, Islamophobic comment. He matter-of-factly said that he wasn't surprised by the attacks as Islam teaches its adherents that by killing Jews, they will go to heaven. And then another classmate built on that misinformed comment. She mentioned a Pakistani classmate of ours by name and said that she was worried he would blow her up like suicide bomber.

The professor did not challenge either one of them. Neither did any of the students. I felt my heart beating quickly as the conversation spiralled. I was so upset by what I was hearing that I got up and left the classroom. I stood outside and contemplated going home when I realised that I was the only Muslim in the classroom, and that if I didn't say something, if I didn't correct these ignorant statements, then nobody was going to. It was my responsibility. So I went back in and spoke up.

I was always intimidated speaking in HBS classrooms where everyone was scrutinising what you were saying as in-class participation was a big driver of our grades. I didn't want to say anything stupid. But saying what I needed to say this time was harder than usual, as I was going against the grain of the conversation and would be speaking up as a Muslim when we were, quite literally, being attacked in the media and on the streets.

When I came back into the classroom, everyone's hands went down, and I raised my hand up. When the professor called on me, I spoke for a few minutes and explained to my classmates that a handful of people committing a vicious attack in the name of Islam did not represent more than 1.5 billion Muslims in the world, and that tenets of our faith do not promote this kind of abhorrent violence. After an extended silence, the classroom erupted in applause.

When I went back home, classmates began showing up and calling to see how I was doing. It was a really pivotal moment for me in understanding that true leadership is not always comfortable and often comes from sharing a perspective that others do not have. You just have to have the courage to use your voice. It was the first time in my life when I felt truly proud of being my authentic and powerful self.

This experience also taught me that my differences – my size, ethnicity, sexual orientation, religion and cultural background – together make me better equipped to be a leader in a world that is becoming more and more global and diverse, but also more polarised and divided.

Because of my family history, because I have lived on three continents and worked all around the world, because I speak multiple languages, I am culturally mobile. I am able to navigate different people, places and cultures to bridge divides and foster understanding. This is now a core part of my personal mission and purpose – and a big part of my work at *BoF*. I see it as my responsibility to use my position and my privilege to spark conversations for others who may not have the platform or freedom to do so.

Listen to signals from the universe — they can guide you

After graduating from HBS, I moved to London and ended up working at McKinsey after all, which was not at all part of my plan. In my HBS application, I said I wanted to work in a creative industry, like music or fashion, but given the state of the economy this was not possible. The McKinsey London office had approached me, and after spending a summer there as an associate, they gave me a full-time offer.

My experience at McKinsey had so many positive aspects – smart colleagues, international experience, interesting problems and more money than I had ever imagined I would make. I experienced first-hand the idea of 'global business', working in far flung countries like South Africa and Australia. I loved these parts of the job.

But I also felt stifled and increasingly burnt out. I was working so hard on projects in industries I was not passionate about. And though the people at McKinsey came from so many different backgrounds, the performance evaluation process sometimes made it feel like they were trying to make us all the same.

I was being asked to conform in ways that were at times very painful. I was very different from the mostly straight, white British men in McKinsey boardrooms. In one feedback meeting I was told, "you don't have enough gravitas"', because I looked very young and used my hands a lot when I spoke.

This was the worst feeling because the feedback was about things I couldn't (and shouldn't have to) change. Looking back now, I understand I was feeling pain because this was coded language telling me I could not be myself. This made me feel that no matter what I did, I would never really belong at McKinsey. I knew it was time to leave, but I was not sure how or where to go.

At the end of my second year at McKinsey, I was on a stopover at Delhi airport on my way to Dhaka in Bangladesh to visit a friend when a Sikh man in a turban came over to me. I was feeling tired and stressed, fiddling with my Blackberry. I didn't want to deal with anyone, so I told him I didn't have any money. He told me, 'I don't want your money. I'm on your flight as well. I just want to talk to you.' I finally relented when our flight was delayed by two hours. I had nothing else better to do to pass the time, so why not?

It turns out this man was a kind of seer. He took a piece of paper, wrote down some stuff, crumpled up the paper and put it in my hand. Then he asked me, 'What's your favourite colour?' I said 'blue' because at McKinsey they told me to wear blue shirts to fit in. 'What's your favourite flower?' I said 'lily' because my cousin's wife had lilies in her wedding bouquet. He wrote my name down and put the numbers one to five above the letters in my name. Then he asked, 'Which number do you pick?' I picked three because it was in the middle. Finally, he said, 'Open your hand.'

On that piece of paper, it said 'blue, lily, three'. That's when I really started listening to him. He told me a lot of things about my life, and at the end, he told me I needed to practice meditation.

This was interesting guidance, because in my faith, we practice something called *bandagi* which is a mantra-led silent meditation. My grandfather practiced this meditation every morning before dawn, but I never really learned how to do it. So being told by a random person in the middle of Delhi airport to try meditation was like being struck by a lightning bolt. He helped me to realise that I could take control of my destiny. The changes I wanted needed to start with me.

You are in control of your destiny

I went back to London and asked McKinsey for a three month sabbatical to step back and make a plan for how I would change my life. My identity and sense of self-worth were so wrapped up with McKinsey and my other achievements, that I needed to take time and space to heal myself and visualise the life and career I wanted.

Independently, two friends recommended I take a ten day Vipassana meditation course which involved ten hours of meditation per day with no speaking, reading, writing or looking at anyone else in the eye. It turned out to be the best decision I ever made. It transformed my life.

After Vipassana, I went to see my parents, who had moved back to Nairobi. I told them I was really unhappy, needed to leave my job and make some changes in my life. I told them that I had worked so hard to do everything I needed to do to be successful, but I was not feeling any joy in my life.

I could tell my parents were worried about me and of course I didn't want to disappoint them. But they supported me and said all they wanted was for me to find happiness. And that definitely wasn't becoming a partner at McKinsey.

During that time, I kept reminding myself that this was an opportunity to create the life I had dreamed of.

Pay attention to your childhood obsessions as these may lead you to lifelong passions

Growing up, I was very curious about the fashion industry, not because I was reading *Vogue*. I was more interested in what happened behind the scenes. On the weekends, I would religiously watch a television show called *Fashion File* hosted by my fashion hero, Tim Blanks, who now works with me at *BoF*. I never even imagined a career in fashion was possible for me. The fashion world seemed so far away – and so exclusive.

After my Vipassana course, I tried to meet people in creative industries like music, television and fashion to see if I could find a way of breaking in and applying my business skills. Early on in my search, I met with a fashion CEO who said to me, 'We don't need people like you in this industry.' I wasn't sure exactly what he meant, but it was similar to a lot of the feedback I was getting: that it would be almost impossible for someone like me to break in.

During this time, my HBS classmate Henry Wu came to London and said something to me that I will never forget. He said, 'Imran, I don't know anyone like you. You can do anything!' Just hearing those words from someone at a time when I was feeling so low helped me so much. To have a friend who saw potential in me when I couldn't was really powerful, and gave me the energy and motivation to continue my search.

Eventually, I received a job offer to join a big UK television company, but this just felt like McKinsey in a different form. Something deep down inside kept pulling me towards the fashion industry. I decided to give it a shot. And the more people I told about my interest in working in fashion, the more people I met who could help me.

Eventually, I found my way to new friends like Mesh Chhibber, Margherita Guarino and Bandana Tewari who snuck me into fashion shows and helped me to understand how the fashion industry worked. I turned down the big salary and security that would have come with the TV job and set up a business incubator for young fashion designers.

Once you take the first risk, it becomes easier to take the next one

It was scary to leave a financially secure and prestigious job at McKinsey. I had paid off my student loans and had no other debt, but I still had to scale back my lifestyle if I was going to make my move into fashion, which I knew did not pay nearly as well. I used to live on my own in a big Notting Hill flat, but now I had to share a smaller apartment with a new flatmate, Juan, whom I met in our neighbourhood grocery store. It turned out he was at McGill at the same time as me. We became fast friends and moved in together.

During this time, I also began documenting everything on a private blog, the first kind of social media. I bought a DSLR camera and would take lots of photos and in the evenings, I would write down what I was learning and upload the photos on my blog for my family and friends to follow my journey from McKinsey into fashion.

After eight months, I had to shut the incubator down. The business model we had envisioned was not working. But I had learned so much and felt so connected to my work for the first time in my career; I knew I was on to something. I was on the right path.

While I planned my next steps, I decided to take the password off my blog. I used PowerPoint to take a black and white photo I had taken at a fashion show in New York and turned it into a header on top of which I wrote the words 'The Business of Fashion'. I used an editorial-looking serif typeface because I wanted it to have the gravitas of a trusted newspaper.

Each time I wrote an article, a newsletter would be sent to anyone who had signed up. The first person to sign up was Gentry Lane, a lingerie designer based in Paris. She and a few other early readers began to share feedback on what they were looking to learn about the business of fashion. From the start, I used this feedback from my community to hone *BoF*'s editorial focus.

It felt natural to me to analyse the fashion industry on *BoF* in the same way that I would analyse industries for my clients:

as a business. It turned out this was something that was totally missing from the fashion media landscape.

Become an expert and be known for something

Very soon after founding *BoF*, I started to develop a reputation as a global expert in the business of fashion, in part because there was no one else doing what I was doing, and also because I had a unique combination of skills to offer.

At McKinsey, I was a generalist. I bounced from one industry to another, and covered many different functional areas from organisation design to supply chain analysis, to mergers and acquisitions. This was a great way to build a general business foundation, but at one point they began to advise me to specialise so I could become an expert in something. The challenge was that there were no industries or functional practices at McKinsey that I felt excited about.

Now things were different. I found the fashion industry so fascinating that it became an obsession. I would think about it, read about it and talk about it all the time. Growing up I had always been quite obsessive about my hobbies. I had a stamp collection that I meticulously organised by country, colour and theme. I painstakingly created a monthly display of my Smurfs on my bedroom shelf. And my music collection of records and tapes was impeccably organised too.

Now I was bringing that same obsessiveness to *BoF*. My ability to analyse complex business and market problems, honed through years of studying business and working in consulting, brought a fresh perspective when applied to the fashion industry. I was not a trained writer, by any means, but I was an avid reader, and devoured lots of newspapers and magazines. I worked on improving it every day, step by step. The more I wrote, the better a writer I became.

But as much as I loved writing and posting articles, I also needed to earn a living. I set up my own consulting firm for the fashion industry and called it Amed & Company. I was becoming a real expert. My first client was LVMH, the world's largest luxury goods company which signed me on to a six month contract. Now I could put that obsessiveness to work for my clients as well.

Today, when people are looking for a global expert in the business of fashion, they often think of me and our team at BoF.

Focus on progress over perfection

Ever since I was a child, I have struggled with a desire to be perfect. I have always worked so hard to be the best I could be, constantly striving for excellence, which is not necessarily a bad thing. But striving for perfection can become toxic when you don't allow yourself room to make mistakes, and when you are too hard on yourself.

Lately, I have been thinking more about where this drive for perfection has come from. Because of my challenging experiences growing up, I built a kind of armor around myself. The armor was of perfection and achievement, which I hoped would make up for what I saw as deficiencies. I thought other people would accept me or love me more if I could validate my existence by going to the best schools, winning awards, winning all the time.

Now, every day, I remind myself that I am human and I will make mistakes, and that's okay. I try to focus on improving every day, focusing on progress over perfection.

Tune into your purpose and intuition to make decisions.

Being clear about your purpose, also means feeling more meaningfully connected to your work. And having a sense of purpose is your compass to help you make decisions, no matter how big or small.

Traditional education trains us to focus primarily on logic and rational thinking. But I find it hard to make decisions unless my heart and head are aligned. Sometimes my team gets frustrated with me because I take too long to make a decision. But I always try to take time to find alignment between the two. Other times it becomes clear that there's no alignment between my heart and head, and so I need to understand why – and perhaps that in and of itself is a signal about the decision I need to make.

That signal is called intuition, something I've learned from my purpose and intuition coach, Mory Fontanez. But you need to have healthy habits to clear the internal noise and hear your intuition. You need to sleep, exercise and eat well so you have the clarity to understand your own triggers, neuroses and patterns, and hone in on that all-important signal.

I wish someone had told me how important sleep is when I was younger. I used to average four to five hours of sleep a night. I was so busy trying to achieve that I would wake up and start working right away. If you get enough sleep, you're prepared for anything and you have more clarity, empathy and focus.

Now, I try to check in with myself every day to understand my mind and body, and how I am feeling. Because every day is an adventure, I want to make sure I am physically and mentally prepared to deal with whatever life throws my way!

You can find deeper meaning when your work is in service of others

I find that my own purpose is evolving as I get older and understand myself better. In Islam, there is the concept of Seva, where your purpose can be found in serving others. I grew up with this concept and always knew it, but now that I am older, I understand this more deeply. There is so much ancient wisdom within us and I find myself tapping into that more. Now, I feel my purpose is to help other people find their purpose.

In 2016, we started *BoF VOICES*, our annual gathering for big thinkers, bringing together leaders from fashion and mixing them with the inspiring people shaping the wider world. At *BoF*

VOICES, we aim to have frank conversations about issues that we can help to address by learning from each other, creating a shared understanding and coming up with solutions.

For example, at the very first *BoF VOICES*, the renowned fashion industry casting director, James Scully, shared for the first time in a public forum how models were being abused and disrespected by stylists and photographers. The audience – including CEOs of some of the industry's biggest brands – was shocked when directly confronted with these hard truths. It inspired the industry's two major fashion conglomerates, LVMH and Kering, to co-create a charter for models' rights, together with James, the next year.

Another person who has used the *BoF VOICES* platform to create change is the Irish disability advocate Sinéad Burke who has achondroplasia, a form of dwarfism. I had seen her TED talk and wondered what her views were on the fashion industry, so we contacted her. We found out that she was a *BoF* reader and had always been interested in fashion, but also that the industry had systematically excluded her. In a barnstorming talk, Sinéad highlighted the lack of understanding and inclusion of disabled people in the fashion industry. Following her talk at *BoF VOICES*, Sinéad went on to be the first little person on the cover of British *Vogue* and the first to attend the Met Gala. Sinéad's agency, Tilting The Lens, is now advising companies in fashion and beyond on how to shift systems and structures to create more inclusive environments for disabled people.

These are just two examples of the kind of important changes that have been sparked at *BoF VOICES* and which *BoF* has worked hard to deliver in our mission to open, inform and connect the global fashion industry. It's something that I know the young boy who was so viciously bullied and excluded for his own differences would be proud of.

Lessons

To find your purpose, align your skills and talents with what you love doing. But also remember, purpose is not a fixed state. It's always evolving, just as you are.

Invest in relationships and communities that uplift and inspire you. It's those people who will not only celebrate your successes, but also guide you through uncertain times.

Look after your body to look after your mind. Sleep, eat and live well so you can be the best version of yourself every day.

Don't be too hard on yourself. It's important to reflect on your shortcomings and mistakes, but don't dwell on them. You are only human.

Affirmation: Today, I will trust my intuition and purpose to guide me.

'The Alchemist'

KAREN
BLACKETT OBE

◆

Karen Blackett was dynamite as a young sprinter with an ambition to compete at the Olympic Games. However, Team GB's loss was media and communications' gain as Karen has risen to become the UK President of WPP, connecting the different companies operating within the organisation to help them work together and achieve the most in their fields. It's a role Karen's happy to explain in Marvel Cinematic Universe terms, describing herself as 'the Nick Fury of WPP UK responsible for assembling the talent'. Previously acting as Chief Executive Officer (CEO) of GroupM UK, Karen was responsible for bringing together the talent, businesses, products, and technology to supercharge GroupM's five media agencies: Mindshare, MediaCom, Wavemaker, Essence and m/Six.

In addition to Karen's day job, she is a NED for Diageo, Creative UK and The Pipeline. In 2012, working with the first *The Apprentice* winner Tim Campbell and the National Apprentice Service, Karen launched an apprentice scheme designed to encourage people aged eighteen to twenty-four into the advertising industry through paths outside the traditional graduate routes. Beyond that she has been a Department of International Trade Business Ambassador; was appointed Race Equality Business Champion by Prime Minister Theresa May in 2018 as part of the Race At Work Charter, helping businesses address their equality issues; and in 2017 was appointed Chancellor of the University of Portsmouth, the university she attended.

Karen was awarded an OBE in 2014 for outstanding services to the advertising industry.

A second choice needn't be a compromise . . .

My first love was athletics. If I'd been good enough, I would have had my own successful career and by this time (in 2021) I would have been one of the people on the BBC commentating on all the athletes that have gone to the Olympics. I was just not quite good enough to compete for Team GB at international level as a senior, and after athletics my great passion was advertising. I genuinely was fascinated by advertising. Literally *fascinated*.

As in so many West Indian households of the time we had the 'good room' at the front, where the television was, while the room at the back was where us kids spent most of our time. So, when I was allowed to watch telly in the good room I was fascinated by this box in the corner. I loved the ads as much as the programmes – maybe because they were repetitive, but it was the same on the radio too; I would avidly listen to the ads. I was quite creative as a child, and I would think I could come up with better ideas for certain adverts, or that I could make up better jingles. I absolutely loved it, although I had no idea it was a world in which I could have a career.

As a typical second-generation West Indian, I had 'work hard on your education . . . get your qualifications' drummed into me. It was important I went to university because my mum and dad never got the chance, and once I got there, I studied what I loved – geography. I loved geography because in secondary school I had the most amazing geography teacher; also, at university, geography was full of people who didn't have a clue what they were going to do when they grew up because geography was a bit of everything, That's probably another reason why it suited me.

I was always fascinated by *human* geography and by psychology – what motivates people to pick one thing over another. I studied that and when I finished university I realised this was very relevant in advertising, and that there was a whole industry attached to something I loved anyway. So, I tried to navigate my way into the world of advertising and media. I bought all the trade and industry press, reading interviews with people like Jonathan Mildenhall and trying to answer my own question which was, 'How do you get into this world?'

Resilience is the key to so much

I applied and applied and applied for advertising industry jobs, on the agency side and on the client side, and I got rejection after rejection after rejection. I kept going, though, which I think has a great deal to do with the competitive streak that drove me on in athletics. I was determined to get into advertising just like I used to be determined not to be beaten on the track, where, literally, I wasn't going to give up at the first hurdle.

My parents taught me a lot of things, but what they embedded in my DNA was *resilience*. My mum and dad came over to the UK from Barbados in 1961, separately, when they were both nineteen years old. My mum came to train as a nurse, which she did in Edgware, then got a job in the Royal Berkshire Hospital in Reading. My dad came over with his cousin, and he worked as a bus conductor for London Transport (now Transport for London) for a year, before he got an apprenticeship with the GPO (now BT) to become an electrical engineer. I cannot imagine what it was like for them sixty years ago. Still teenagers, they left a tiny island 21 miles long, 14 miles wide – which was all they knew – to get on a plane to somewhere where the climate is different, the food is different ... The people, the housing, how everybody talks; everything is different, and this is without taking into account what they would have faced in terms of acceptance. Yet, because they'd made that decision to come here to build a better life, they were determined to do so. The resilience that must have been baked into them to keep going is absolutely extraordinary.

As I said, I can't imagine it, but it was something they passed on – and thank God they did because there were loads of rejections. But I wasn't having any of it. I was *determined*, because I had this stubborn competitive streak and I knew this was the world I wanted to get into.

After so many rejections from the more obvious sides of the industry, I saw a job advertised in the *Independent* for a media auditor; they're the ones who analyse an advertising campaign after it has happened. It's the auditors who tell the client whether or not the advertising agency bought the advert well, or if they reached the right target audience – did they control the TV ratings well, did they access the most appropriate programmes? It was an analytical role rather than a creative post, but as part of my geography degree I had done a statistical module, so I felt I understood what this job involved.

It wasn't the job I'd dreamed about in advertising, but after all those rejections I was ready to try a different path. I applied for it and the company saw something in me beyond that particular role – maybe it was my love and enthusiasm for advertising in general – and sent me to a different part of the agency to interview for a role as a media planner and buyer. That was how I got into the industry, and when I look back at it now, I say thank God, they did send me for the other interview because I honestly think I would have been a pretty terrible auditor.

Get comfortable being remarkable

After I'd got the acceptance letter, the thing I remember vividly is thinking *Oh my God! Nine 'til six! Those are really long hours!* I'd been used to doing about fifteen hours a week on my university course, so those agency hours seemed almost impossible. If only I could just work nine 'til six today! I moved in with my sister in south Croydon and remember walking into the agency – a top three agency – on my first day and counting to myself the number of people who were non-white: there was Michelle on reception; my immediate boss, Colin Gillespie; and there was me. And that was it. I remember thinking how strange this was because I was in *London*. Reading was known as mini-Barbados because so many people from that island emigrated there in the sixties, so I was used to seeing Black people around me. I went to university in Portsmouth and while there were fewer people from a Black background in the city, the university attracted students from all over. Now here I am in a city that is far more culturally diverse than anywhere else I've lived; I arrive in the office and the agency is nothing like that. I thought, *God, this is odd.*

However, I was the newbie and I drew on a very good piece of advice my dad had given me. While I was growing up, he would tell us kids, 'You have two ears and one mouth, use them in that proportion.' Listen, learn, see how things are, then when you're ready, when you've got the knowledge, you start to speak. Which is what I did; I looked, and I listened and as I'm a good student I learned how things worked within that agency and the industry in general. I learned so much. I learned about different industry sectors, different client problems, and how I could take one issue and the solution for it and transfer it to another industry sector and a different client.

All of this combined with my competitive nature, because a big part of getting ahead in the advertising industry is the competitiveness – not competing with people within the same four walls as me, but with other agencies. And I like to win! In our industry you win by picking up new clients and new business, which is where I cut my teeth; winning clients and bringing them to the agency.

Another valuable lesson my mum and dad had taught me was to get comfortable being memorable because I was always going to be 'one of a few'. In advertising nearly thirty years ago I was always going to be one of the very few, if not, the only Black person in the room; I was always going to be one of the few women in a room; and I learned I had to get comfortable with this because I was going to stand out. I learned to use that to my advantage, and I celebrated the fact that I was going to be memorable because when you stand out and you speak, people will look to you and listen. That is another reason why I made sure I used my ears before I used my mouth; I had to make sure I was saying something worth listening to, otherwise being memorable works against you.

I had some great bosses as well, bosses that spotted something and essentially, even before the term became popular, they sponsored my career. Maybe they noticed me when I did speak up, but they were so important because they would talk up for me in the rooms I didn't have access to, so once senior members of an agency knew what I was capable of, they would vouch for me. This was so important because I was different to what had gone before in terms of my gender and ethnicity, and without that sponsorship it wouldn't have happened for me. I'm sure I would still be plodding along trying to do my best, hoping that somebody might see that I'm good.

I learned that hope wasn't a strategy, you have to get people behind you, and I think this is why I put so much emphasis on finding where I belonged. I've always believed that there are different reasons for people to move around within an industry. People move around from job to job for money or they move around for titles and experience, but when you can find people that just see your talent, *especially* when you're in the minority in an organisation or in an industry, that is something you should cherish.

Diversity isn't a problem, it's a solution

Our industry still has work to do in terms of making it diverse. Ninety per cent of the industry is based in London, yet the industry is not representative of the makeup of London at all. Only 34 per cent of leaders in the industry are female; one in three of our leaders in the advertising industry were educated in a private school whereas the national average is one in fourteen; and less than 4 per cent of our industry is from an ethnic minority background. Those statistics are from 2019, which was a couple of years ago but as 2020 was a year like no other in which not much will have changed, it is still not a diverse industry. Yet we are trying to grow to be more representative of the UK, which is such a beautiful fruit salad of people.

In 2020 I spent time trying to talk to people in the UK, some of my bosses and colleagues, about George Floyd, saying this is just as relevant here, this isn't just a US thing, and people just started getting into gear. They really did! Suddenly people were saying, 'Do you know what? You're right. Our histories may be very different but what happened there happened here twenty-nine years ago with Stephen Lawrence, continues to happen and actually we need to do more.' That's a wonderful thing, that the industry's realised it has to do more.

What the advertising industry has been doing recently to be more representative is amazing. Some brilliant forward-thinking brands and organisations have really pushed the agenda and not simply because it's about doing things for altruistic reasons. This is something I've banged on about since God was a boy – diversity isn't a problem to fix, it's a *solution*, the solution to growth. This is something that made the continued lack of diversity in the industry all the more remarkable.

Look at your audience. Look at where your *growth audience* is going to come from; it's going to come in the shape of the country's demographic as it changes. There's a brilliant quote from the book *East of Eden* (1952), written by John Steinbeck, that goes: 'If a story is not about the hearer, he will not listen. And here I make a rule – a great and interesting story is about everyone or it will not last.' If you're creating brand stories and they're overlooking a significant section of the public, that same section is just going to check out. They're not going to listen to you. I believe there is this awakening, that these organisations have realised that if they want to future-proof themselves and continue to grow they'd best understand modern Britain, which does not look like it did in Enoch Powell's days. (The former Conservative MP was famously critical of mass immigration, and made the inflammatory, notorious 'Rivers of Blood' speech in 1968.) Modern Britain has changed, and companies and their agencies need to start reflecting authentic consumer insight in their brands. I believe that's what we're starting to see.

A brilliant study has been done of ethnic minority audience purchasing power in the UK. In 2001, when a census was taken, ethnic minority purchasing power was £32 billion. In 2011, the next time the census was done, and that survey was carried out again, that audience had a purchasing power of £300 billion. You can imagine what that is in 2021, when we get the data back from the census. It's going to be *huge*. And then there are future consumers. One in four kids in primary and secondary school comes from an ethnic minority background, 9 per cent of all under-tens are Muslim . . . this is growth audience here.

This change is happening for a combination of altruistic and commercial reasons. As a society we want to see organisations actually doing good for society, so we'll support those companies with philanthropic and socially concerned ideologies. At the same time consumers are perfectly happy to buy from brands that make money for the sake of making money, but if the only thing they make is money then consumers are less likely to frequent with you. So, it's clear-cut business sense, it is absolutely future-proofing yourself.

The process is far from perfect. I can still see where somebody has thought about diversity at the end of a creative process and they've just chucked in somebody for casting's sake – that's always so obvious. However, on the plus side I can see more ads and more pieces of content where it's authentic representation, where there's a piece of insight that's authentic to the community or the race that's in that particular piece of work, which is brilliant on the part of brands and organisations.

The wider industry is definitely aware of what needs to be done, which is a huge step. Lloyd's Bank do their amazing Modern Britain survey that looks at the top hundred advertisers and how representative they are in their advertising – *fantastic* piece of work. Then there are organisations like the Advertising Association and the Institute of Practitioners in Advertising, who are our industry bodies, looking out in this respect because they are trying to do more to make sure we all have a job in ten- or fifteen-years' time.

Change won't happen by itself; it needs to be curated

The advertising industry, historically, has been so biased in terms of where we look to find talent. My journey in, which was rejection after rejection after rejection, wasn't helped by the fact I didn't go to the *right* university – I went to a brilliant university, but it wasn't a Russell Group university. Our industry tends to recruit from Oxford, Cambridge, Durham, Edinburgh and Exeter at best, *or* if you're going in on the art side there's a couple of art colleges they tend to recruit from. If our filter is these universities, then we could be missing out on amazing talent, and that is simply self-defeating.

When I got in the position of being a CEO of a media agency, I was determined to avoid that. I was really focused on trying to make sure I have the *best* people working at the agency, and that means looking outside the graduate intake that had become the norm. University isn't an option for everyone, either because they don't want to go or they can't afford to go, so I wanted to make sure we were really discovering the talent that wouldn't have had that opportunity. Another CEO I know, Caroline Norbury, who is at an organisation called Creative UK, has a great saying; she talks about how talent is everywhere, but opportunity is not, and the opportunity for that talent to have a career in our industry definitely wasn't there. So, when I became a CEO, I worked with the amazing Tim Campbell (the first winner of *The Apprentice*) who'd been appointed by the then Mayor of London to get more companies to offer apprenticeships. He introduced me to the right people at the National Apprenticeship Service and we introduced the first ever government-backed apprenticeships for our sector.

For our recruitment process we specifically went into schools that had above-average exam results but also above-average reliance on subsidised school meals, so you had that potential in terms of talent, but not necessarily the opportunity. We had the first intake of apprenticeships in 2012, the scheme has run ever since and in 2021 we took in our first digital academy of people coming into digital roles. We've got a total of a hundred people coming in, who are all between the ages of eighteen and twenty-four and none of them went to university. I think it's amazing and goes to prove you can find the talent – you just need to try a bit harder.

This doesn't just apply to the advertising industry either; so many industries have been holding themselves back by looking for talent in a very narrow recruitment field. If we are really going to build back Britain, post-Brexit, post-pandemic, we have got to be finding, nurturing and growing talent. This means looking a bit harder, because there are people who want to work, people who want to build careers, and companies can't expect them to walk through the doors if they've got no connection with the industry at all. As a sample size of one, I think there wasn't anybody in my family or in my network that knew anything about this industry, so thank God I eventually managed to navigate my way in, but I could so easily have fallen through the cracks.

It's not enough simply to give jobs to this broader intake

Something we as an organisation had to learn was that bringing people in and expecting them to fly simply doesn't happen. I worked with MediaCom's global chief diversity and inclusion officer, Nancy Lengthorn, and we learned from that first round of apprenticeships that there needed to be a big focus on pastoral care so that individuals don't feel like fish out of water when they turn up for work. Because they're not from the same background, they don't have the same cultural keys as the leadership and many of the other people in the industry. Also, we needed to ensure that the people who are *creating* the opportunities, the leaders in the industry, assess this talent differently and remove any bias they may have. So, you must change certain corporate cultures, because one way or another, people assessing people who have a different background to them, and have a different cultural key to them, can make assumptions.

While a great deal was invested in the pastoral care of the individual, a lot of work was also done in terms of leadership and management and giving the new intake allies. We did so much in terms of allyship training, because making this kind of shift is not about the minority, it's about the majority. It will only be once you can change how the majority thinks that you'll be able to get people from all walks of life entering your industry and feeling comfortable once they get there. Otherwise, they won't stay, and the situation becomes like a leaky bucket – no matter how much you put in, in terms of a diverse intake at junior levels, it will never fill up to the senior positions.

I think unconscious bias is a pile of bollocks – really, it's just hygiene and any responsible company should have unconscious bias training as a matter of course, but the real problem with just having that is, it's passive. If a company genuinely wants to create cultural change it's got to be more active than that. It has to get people feeling comfortable talking about subjects they may be uncomfortable talking about – like race. Honest discussions. Otherwise nothing will get done. My team expect to talk about race, they expect to talk about family and parenthood and children, because I bring it to the conversation – we treat it as a business metric, the same way as everything else is.

Somebody who's good at what they do may not naturally be a good leader

I'm a firm believer that leadership can be taught. I've got people who get promoted because they're brilliant at what they do, because they're technically gifted, they're brilliant strategists, they're brilliant planners, brilliant creatives, but to be a great leader means you then have to be able to bring people with you. Sometimes being a leader means you're out in front, sometimes you're in the middle of the pack, sometimes you're behind pushing everyone forward, and I do think that can all be taught and the mistake most businesses make is not teaching it. They simply assume that because somebody is good at their technical role, they're going to be a great leader, and my twenty-eight-odd years of experience tell me that is not the case.

I've had leaders who are very good at the technical side, but they've not been great leaders because what's called their *soft skills* haven't been good enough. Incidentally, I hate the term 'soft skills' as it makes it sound as if they're not important, but these are skills that are vital in leadership and I think the most important is emotional intelligence. You can have somebody with a *huge* IQ, but if that's not matched with an *EQ* in that emotional intelligence, they're not always going to be great leaders. To be a great leader you've got to know how to read people, you've got to make sure people will follow you, you've got to be empathetic, you've got to show vulnerability, and I think all that can be taught.

49

I also believe great leaders are great listeners, so it's back to that thing my dad said, about two ears one mouth. To lead, you need to be a good listener because you have to have your finger on the pulse of what's going on. You can be intuitive, which helps you in being visionary and strategic, but to stay ahead of the game you need to know what's going on around you and that means listening. Use your two ears to learn about what's going on, *then* put it into action with a vision or a strategy which you'll use your mouth to communicate.

Under these circumstances you have to surround yourself with people who will tell you what you need to hear as opposed to what you want to hear, and they'll tell you stuff you really might not want to hear. Listening and then acting on what you've heard is the mark of a good CEO – in fact so is anything other than thinking *I'm the CEO and you should do what I say because of that. Urrrgh!* That's a route to a rapidly disappearing career.

Confidence comes with practice and preparation

I think my failed athletics career put me in good stead for my current career because I used to practice and practice and practice. I would practice my starts for the 100 metres over and over again because I knew I could win the hundred in the first thirty if I got a good start. Likewise, my take-off for the long jump – I would practice and practice because it left me with less to worry about, which in turn made me more confident. As a result, I won't go into a meeting now without having done my research, done my background, got my thoughts together and feel like I've practiced the answers to any and every question I might get asked. You can't do something off the cuff and do it well. Never just walk into a room and start speaking as though you're God! Whatever the situation, make sure you know what the answer is. Then you won't be worried about what's going to get thrown at you, so you can relax which will lead to confidence.

I also think learning from people that have been before you can do your confidence a lot of good in this respect. That's why I'm a massive fan of sponsorship programmes and mentoring programmes because you have somebody that's gone before you and can give you insight. Mentoring is when somebody helps somebody; sponsorship is when they've got skin in the game and they are investing in you to repay them in the future, but in each case they want to see you succeed and will have an active role in your progression.

I am a firm believer in life coaching. I've had a life coach for over eighteen years and in the same way that you physically train and coach your body you should coach your mind. I believe sponsors, mentors and life coaches do that in a way that can help with confidence. If you just go into what is an unfamiliar situation on your own, coming from a totally different background with nobody to be a cheerleader for you, it's going to be incredibly hard.

A life coach can be a great support

My life coach is an ex-athlete and I think that's why we bonded – his name is Adrian Green and he was part of Team GB as a steeplechase runner. When I met him for the first time I thought, *this bloke is not for real. Nobody can be this positive, a radiator of energy 100 per cent of the time. This is all a ruse.* But he is like that 100 per cent of the time, *genuinely*, and he's helped me both professionally and personally.

Professionally, we all have periods when we're racked with self-doubt or don't have the confidence we need or lack self-confidence in who we are. They're the person who reminds you what you're capable of. They tell you about the strings to your bow, how remarkable your assets are, or remind you of similar situations that you've had to navigate and come through unscathed. All of this can be vital, especially if you're nearly always not part of the dominant culture in your professional situations. I've had some personal crises – I'm a single parent, and there was a time when my dad, who is a big influence on me, suddenly died – and Adrian was brilliant, coaching me through it. But it's more a matter of getting me to work through the smaller problems, work out what's important, and prioritise so I get the work/life blend right.

That's one of the biggest things Adrian's done for me, helping me with my work/life blend; then in those moments when I have that lack of self-confidence, he gives me the verbal slap I need to tell me to keep going.

Know your limitations

When it came to athletics, I was *not bad*. I got through the county level, but my friends went on and competed in Team GB while I was not quite there yet. It was a lot different back then because this was before our athletes got lottery funding, so we had to find a way of paying for our coaches and our training. There was a brilliant woman who trained with me at Reading, and she got into Team GB, but she had to maintain her job at the same time. It was just bonkers, especially when I think about all the talent that didn't have the opportunity because of juggling work and training. Now, thank God, they can focus on being athletes.

That wasn't why I didn't make it into Team GB though, because practically everybody was in the same boat. When I got into the seniors and started competing, I knew I wasn't as good as some of the other athletes – I had peaked. I peaked at the 100 metres and the 200, then they tried to make me up to the 400 and *wow* that was hard work! I had all the passion for it, but although I was close to Team GB I just wasn't as good as the athletes that got it. I wasn't destroyed by it or anything like that, because I think it's about *knowing* your limits. Knowing where you can get to and when to pivot is an important part – and can be a really exciting part – of self-discovery.

Lessons

For young Karen passion came early, as did an understanding of failure. After failing to compete for Team GB in athletics, young Karen turned to her second passion: advertising.

Rejection after rejection after rejection can become the norm so you have to build a deep sense of tenacity and resilience. Both will serve you well throughout the ups and downs of your career.

Develop a deep comfort in your differences. Take pleasure and power in being the odd woman/man out.

Hope is not a strategy for success. Practice really does make for perfection.

Build your own team of cheerleaders; this should be made up of those people you trust to speak truthfully and who will hold you accountable for the progress you choose to make.

Affirmation: Today I will remember that impossible is nothing.

'The Courageous'

VALERIE BRANDES

◆

Founder and CEO of Jacaranda Books, Valerie Brandes came to the British publishing business relatively late and by a somewhat circuitous route. Born and raised in London, a career in local government beckoned but after a few years of pushing paper she quit to enrol in an undergraduate degree course at Exeter University studying American and Commonwealth Arts, with her specialist subject being Caribbean literature. Part of the degree was a year studying abroad and as Exeter had no connections with universities in the Caribbean Valerie went to do a year at the University of California, Santa Cruz. That one year turned into twenty and it was with her American family she returned to the UK where she founded Jacaranda Books to address the lack of opportunity in British publishing for bright young authors of colour.

Valerie has built Jacaranda into the UK's premier Black-owned publishing house. Jacaranda recently celebrated ten years in the industry, reprinting ten of their earliest titles in a collection of special tenth anniversary editions. In recognition of Valerie, the *Bookseller* ran a front-page ad and feature interview to highlight Jacaranda's industry leading work. Within ten years the publisher has expanded from a team of two, to a team of nine staff. Jacaranda Books has introduced international voices from Africa, Asia and the Americas to the UK market, including books in translation. The company has published multiple award winners such as Shola von Reinhold's *LOTE* and Celeste Mohammed's *Pleasantview*. Their publishing campaigns like the #Twentyin2020 initiative and the A Quick Ting On non-fiction series have been featured in the *Guardian*, *Metro, Evening Standard,* and many more.

In 2023, having successfully applied for Arts Council funding, Jacaranda will become a National Portfolio Organisation with assured funding through 2023-26. They will also be publishing some of their most promising titles yet with *MANDEM*, an essay collection about Black masculinity and vulnerability; *Stick to My Roots*, the autobiography of Grammy Award nominated reggae pioneer Tippa Irie; and *Finding Home*, a memoir by Alford Gardner, one of the last living passengers of the SS Empire Windrush.

Valerie has twice been named on the Powerlist, an annual roster of influential Black Britons.

Inspiration can come from anywhere

My first job, straight out of school, was as a clerical assistant at what used to be called a QUANGO – a Quasi-Autonomous Non-Government Organisation, which were publicly funded bodies that were not fully controlled by central government and carried out public service duties. I was working for the Social Science Research Committee in their post-graduate training department and part of my job was to sift through the applications for research grants. I used to look through them and see all these amazing research projects all over the world and how people were getting funding for them. I'd be looking at these applications and thinking, *But wait . . . these people are just being given money to go to Borneo or somewhere else exotic!* It blew my mind, and because the requirement was a 2:1 degree I thought that's it, I'm going to university.

I didn't want to be a researcher or even do research, I was simply inspired into thinking there was something else I could do. I got the job at the QUANGO because I really didn't know what I wanted to do when I left school. Get a job, get a boyfriend, get a house . . . I was going to work and coming home and that was my life, but so much time reading those applications and seeing what other people were doing really did open up doors in my imagination.

I went on to the database in the office and I saw Exeter University and I wrote off for their prospectus – at the time you couldn't go on the internet, you had to write off and then wait for a booklet to come through the mail. I don't know why I chose Exeter, but it turned out they had a course that was American and Commonwealth Arts and the Commonwealth side of it was studying the literature of the Caribbean. For me that was *amazing!* One thing I did have when I was growing up was books, we always had books, my dad loved books and what they could do for you. Every week he'd pay the Encyclopedia Britannica salesman who would turn up at our door – that was like my internet. What was so brilliant was you'd go looking in it and on one page it's the breakdown of a spiny fish, on the next page it's a poem written by Wordsworth and then the periodic table! I loved it, just getting my head into all that randomness taught me that everything can be interesting and you shouldn't limit your knowledge. As well, I'm the second youngest of eleven kids and my brothers were always bringing home books and reading them to me or giving them to me, so there were always a lot of books in the house and I loved to read. Now here was the chance to spend all day reading books, studying them, talking about them . . .

There's no reason you shouldn't give it a go

The prospectus for Exeter said you needed three A levels to get in; I only had two but I thought *Why not?* I tried anyway and they invited me for an interview. When I got there I was interviewed by a guy who told me, 'If you come on this course you'll only be the second Black person in twenty years!' That was almost like putting this burden on me and I felt, *You better know what you're signing yourself up for!*

I got in and immediately I felt it was such a leap from how I'd been spending my days up until then, and the sort of life I had never really considered. I was surrounded by all these people who just took everything for granted – like from primary school they were primed to understand their place in the world. When I thought about it, that was just as my community, again from primary school, had been primed to understand our place in the world, but to our detriment: 'You're from Stoke Newington . . . it's a blighted community . . . no-go areas for the police . . . sus laws and all of that stuff.'

Unlike these kids I was meeting at Exeter there was nobody saying to us, 'You can do more, go on!' My dad had passed away when I was seventeen, so then my mum had the sole responsibility of all of the family – eleven kids – and nobody could ask any more of her than that.

Going to that university was a real shock to the system, and I still don't think I really understood myself as a student or what I was trying to do; I didn't have any ambition other than being there! I wasn't even supposed to be there because I didn't have the full qualifications, but I was there and that was great, as long as nobody asked me what I was doing there or why! I was determined to just get on with it and luckily the course was one that really fed me. It let me study books and literature, it was all the theories of literature and critical thinking and all I could think was, *Oh, this is amazing! Who knew that you could look at a book and deconstruct it and talk about it in the ways that we're talking about it on this course?* I grew into the course, and just grew; it was kind of my escape, not even knowing that I was escaping anything.

When I think about growing up in London, and the way so many of us grew up, there really was an absence of anybody pouring anything into you the way things and understandings had been poured into these kids at university. That's not anything lacking in my parents, because they were limited by their situation as well – in fact they did very well because in my family everyone's good in a sense: among my ten siblings there's an accountant, a head teacher, a pharmacist, a business owner ... But I went to a church school from the age of five so it was all about Christianity – be a good person, do unto others, follow these tenets – so you learn how to be a good person, make your bed, keep yourself clean and so on, but that was the extent of it. There was nothing about ambition, or anything about our situation that we're living in that we could see we could improve.

That was the part that I think I struggle with still, especially now in an industry like publishing, where there's so many posh people it's not even funny! And you see how – or so it *seems* – life has been so much easier for them just because of that early pouring in. You get it early enough, it can carry you a long, long way.

Sometimes the second choice can work out for the best

As part of the course I got to spend a year abroad at another university, and I went through this process to try to go to the University of the West Indies – quite naturally I thought because of my West Indian heritage I needed to go to the West Indies. I told the course director that was where I wanted to go, and he told me that they had no links with anybody in the Caribbean, that their connections were with the Universities of New Mexico, Louisiana and California. All I could think of was, *But I want to go to the Caribbean!* He basically said, 'No. You can't. We've no links to anybody in the Caribbean. I've decided you should go to the University of California, Santa Cruz.' *Where*? I'd never heard of Santa Cruz!

When I got there it was incredible. I flew out a week early because my friend was going to Berkeley which is just across the Bay from Santa Cruz and I could spend some time there first. When we drove down the coast to Santa Cruz it was just *Wow!* The university was on the top of a hill and you turned into a gate and as you got further up on to the campus you entered into this whole redwood forest right there on campus, with all these tall trees, and then you got up on to where it was overlooking the ocean.

It's become more amazing as I've got older, but at the time it was almost overwhelming – *I'm a Black girl from Hackney, what the hell am I doing here?* Because there was literally no-one like me, and the first couple of weeks that I was there were really tough. Then there was a massive earthquake! It was so severe, the town of Santa Cruz was really badly hit and entire buildings just collapsed into holes in the ground. Everybody kind of disappeared, most of the students went home to different parts of America but I couldn't go back to London so I was just there in the university for about two weeks waiting to see what would happen. And that's when I met the man who became my husband. During that first week he had stayed behind and he kind of rescued me from the earthquake, took care of me and gave me food to eat. After I had been so negative about going there in the first place, I stayed in California for fifteen years and we've been married for thirty.

Knowledge and understanding equal power

I didn't have any sense of inferiority about myself as a Black person; I had a lot of Black pride. To the extreme when I was young, as I remember at school I had an afro pick with a clenched Black fist as the handle and I was reading *The Autobiography of Malcolm X* and I got punished for it. I was sent to this room at the top of the building, 'the attic' we called it, where you had to sit by yourself and write about why you were a bad person. The teacher told me, 'You've got a chip on your shoulder and you're never going to get anywhere in life with that.' I literally saw a chip like a fish-and-chips chip on my shoulder because I had no idea what the woman was talking about!

Where I did feel inferiority though was in not knowing about the world. I felt I didn't know how anything worked – *nothing*! Like the movie *Moonlight*, one of the things I identified with about that movie is how that young boy is trying to find himself, obviously sexually, but how his early life is drawn is something I fully related to. Like when he's done something wrong and his mother tells him, 'Oh go and pick up a book', but she's never read to him so he doesn't understand what this means. It's this lack of guidance, this lack of *infusion* – it's what I call the 'pouring in', without which there's a lack of knowledge of self or of the world.

The racism, you take it and we all deal with it a different way, but worse in some ways in my mind is this lack of understanding of so many things that would open doors for us, because we've never been properly guided or coached or taught things beyond the very basics of the curriculum. It is all part of the racism story because it goes back to colonialism, why we're lacking in those areas. Once in class there was a discussion about the poem 'The Lady of Shalott' by Tennyson, and I'd never even heard of it. It was not in any way something that I understood or could comprehend. But I *could have*. I had a good brain – if somebody had said to me, 'Let me explain to you about the poems of Tennyson or Shelley', or whatever, I could have learned that, but there was no encouragement like that and I had been all the way through the school system.

I think that's the part I struggle with even now, like in business, feeling like the fundamentals of finance – yeah, I can learn them, but not being exposed to that and not being taught that and understanding that from an early age, it just feels like a deficit all the time. It's not an inhibitor, I will continue to learn and to improve, but it does feel like I'm always operating at this deficit so I move forward by learning as much as I can about everything I can.

However, lack of knowledge can be a positive too . . .

Although I might gripe that no one's poured into me maybe that's exactly the reason why I was able to see the opportunities that presented themselves and I was able to use them, because there's no voice telling me, 'Oh, you can't do that, you haven't got this, you haven't got that.' Maybe if I'd been guided more, I might not have been so adventurous because I would have been much clearer about what the barriers or the parameters were, but as it was I really didn't have any. I didn't have any limits in terms of what I could do because I'd never learned what I could or couldn't do – as the saying goes I didn't know what I didn't know. For years I carried it around as a deficit before I realised it was actually the thing that allowed me to do the most.

My approach to so many new things was, *I'll have a go.* Always much more *Why not?* than *Why?* Quite often there isn't a formal thought behind some of my decisions because if I stopped to think too long I'd probably talk myself out of them. I started Jacaranda Books when I was forty-eight years old, with two kids, not long back from America. I've got a Masters in publishing but thought, *Nobody's going to give me a job – I can't go and be an intern at Penguin for a couple of years!* I knew I had to go and do it for myself, even though I actually had no idea what *it* was! I had a job I hated as an office manager in a publishing company in London and when I gave in my notice everybody said, 'No, no, you can't leave . . . what are you going to do?' and they were trying to give me advice. When I told the Artistic Director there I was starting a company his reply was 'Are you sure?' but he did the logo for me which is the one we still use today.

That was 2011 and Jacaranda began right after New Year in January 2012, the Monday after the holidays when everybody goes into work and opens their inboxes. I didn't have an inbox. I didn't have a website, I didn't have a business card; all I had was a name and a logo and an idea about publishing Black writers.

Being an outsider can be an advantage

I'm dark-skinned, I've grown up in Hackney under certain circumstances, and in a lot of ways the world kind of disregards you – you don't count, you're not interesting, nobody wants to know you – so as result you are kind of left to your own devices, and in that world you get to create whatever you want to create. I learned really early on to bet on myself, from when I was eighteen years old without a clue in life I would always just rely on me, and it came from no-one wanting to put themselves out for me in any way at all. My approach was, *I'm on my own, if I sink I sink, if I swim I swim*.

That contributed a lot to my taking chances, which were always more like *Hmmm, I'm going to try that*, never *Oh my God I must!* because, I realised, I always gave myself the opportunity to fail. I would go into things with the idea, *If this doesn't work out it's not the end of you, you'll find something else to do*. Only once have I made something a be-all or end-all, which, again, I think comes from a place of Black people so seldom being given anything or having anything to start with in the society we live in. It would never be that I wouldn't try anything because I was scared I might not get it – if I don't get it I know what that feels like. I know what that world is to inhabit, so if what I'm trying doesn't work I'll just go back to it and I'll be myself.

Create a clear identity and stick with it

When I started Jacaranda I knew exactly the kind of books I wanted to see published. That was never in doubt. Ever. What I've learned since then was the enormity of what I did not know and I had no idea how hard it was going to be to start this publishing house, I didn't know what kind of a money pit publishing is, especially when you're small and independent.

I didn't know that we wouldn't have access to any kind of sales channels needed to get our books into shops, so what we ended up doing, which is what the bulk of the independents do, is go to an aggregated sales and distribution outlet which will take on the wholesale responsibilities for a number of small publishers. This came with its own set of problems: they will focus most of their effort on the titles that would pretty much sell themselves and they don't necessarily care about your list or about your key authors, especially if your authors are non-white or non-British. Or they can be very lazy and only take an interest in titles they feel an instant connection with, for instance if you get a small press from Cornwall that is publishing stories set in Cornwall the wholesaler can relate to that because they've probably been to Cornwall on holiday and the people in Cornwall all look like them – their idea of British that they are sure so many other British people can relate to.

It's a natural ecosystem, then here I come: 'I'm British, hello! I'm part of the scene!' but my author's name is Masande Ntshanga and he's from South Africa, or Obinna Udenwe and he's from Nigeria. These guys have written amazing novels but the distributors' response is, 'Well I don't know how to pronounce his name, I've never been to Nigeria and don't know who this Black woman is in front of me . . .' It means the energy they were putting in to getting that book in front of booksellers and really supporting your business was next to nothing.

It's the nature of the beast for all small independent publishers, and us being a dedicated Black publisher added to it, but I knew what I wanted to publish. At a brilliant event called Black Book Swap I met Jacqueline Shaw who had published her dissertation, *Fashion Africa: A Visual Overview of Contemporary African Fashion* . I looked at it and thought, *This is going to be the first Jacaranda book.* I formed a plan to publish one non-fiction and one fiction, or one illustrated and one fiction. I got Jaqueline's book, and I now realise we could have done it better, but we did it and over the years it's sold really well for us.

Then we published *Glass* by Patrick Wilmot, which we'll be republishing next year when we'll be celebrating ten years of Jacaranda. So those are the first two books, then I was invited to the Caine Prize for African Writing and met a few of the African writers, and we started making these connections in publishing outside the UK. We published Pede Hollist's *So The Path Does Not Die*; Pede was published by a Cameroonian publisher and we bought the UK rights and that was the most exciting day! Me and my business partner Jazzmine, working together at the kitchen table at my house, and that was the first deal that we made! It was so cool: an African publisher, an African author, and we're Black women publishers here in the UK. We were literally shrieking, 'We're doing it! We're doing it!'

We felt like that because we had stuck to our original idea and not compromised just to sell a few more books. We still have exactly the same ethos as we had back then and now we've done a distribution deal with Hachette, a major international publisher, and I think we've shown that you can have both success and integrity.

Go big or go home

There was always a level of resistance to us being in business. In 2017 we bought the UK rights to *Rest In Power*, the Trayvon Martin story – the Black Lives Matter movement came out of the murder of Trayvon Martin. We were first with that, people were talking about it and Waterstones – the whole of Waterstones – took one copy from us. It didn't make any sense; people were caught up in the heat of the moment, and in the US it had sold thirty thousand copies in hardback. So it was always a struggle, almost untenable, all of the time I'm scrambling, trying to rob Peter to pay Paul because when you sign an author you have to have all the money up front *for them*, when you've got no idea how the book's going to sell. Then compound that with the fact that you don't have the sales and the distribution behind you, it's just nonsense!

It was just ridiculous, but the importance of Jacaranda as a company within what I see as the culture was the thing that was driving us along all the way. We're getting emails and letters of support all the time, there's one church lady who sends me prayers: 'I'm praying for you today, that you will succeed, and bring on the young people,' she always tells me. I am in no doubt about the place that we occupy within the culture and therefore we *have* to exist, Jacaranda *has* to exist. That has been the driving force throughout and when we were coming from a really dark moment, 2017–2018, when we were thinking *It's not going to work if this is how we have to do it*, we were thinking 2020 was going to be a make-or-break year – either we're going to end it all or it's going to be miraculous for us.

What could I do for 2020? I thought, it's got be big, so I said, 'OK, we're going to publish twenty Black British authors in 2020 – it will be Twentyin2020 Black Writers, British Voices. That's the marketing banner that's going to take it forward.' Like everything else, I hadn't really thought it through yet and the team at the time, all three of them, were looking at me like, 'That's stupid! Nobody's going to go for that.' But it was just one of those situations where what did we have to lose? If it doesn't work we're right back where we started, so I might as well go for it. And if it does work then we'll see what comes out of it.

The industry reaction was something else: there was almost affront that an operation as small as us should want to publish twenty books in year. They didn't hold back: 'Who do you think you are . . . Why are you doing this? . . . You just want it for publicity.' I was telling senior figures about Twentyin2020 and they were telling me they didn't want me to draw attention to putting *Blackness* in writing. But the real kicker was when somebody said, 'Well who are you going to publish anyway? You going to publish your brother?' That actually made me question everything and I was ready to be just, *I'm done! That's it. Stop!* Then I stopped and thought about it: *No! I'm going to take this punt. It was a good idea when I came up with it, what's changed?*

We put out a call for authors and by the end of 2018 we had about seventy manuscripts. We sifted through, sifted through, sifted through and I was thinking these are bloody good. Whatever happens in the end there's some brilliant books in here. We got our twenty, ten fiction, five non-fiction, five poets. Now we had something to put out into the wider world, the *Guardian* made it a half-page story in the print edition and the digital version was retweeted five thousand times the day it was announced. That really was *the* moment for Jacaranda because it got us such an enormous amount of attention; we got all of these people coming up and when I say people I mean other publishing houses, other organisations, all the news outlets wanted stories – it just seemed to snowball.

We started the year with Njambi McGrath's *Through The Leopard's Gaze* which is a fantastic memoir, then the novel *Under Solomon Skies*, then the pandemic hit. Then lockdown, total disaster. For all the reasons I talked about earlier we pushed through and we published Twentyin2020. By the time the end of the year happened we were on our knees, just completely depleted as a team, financially, emotionally; we've still not really fully recovered. I know I'm still reeling from all of it. But we were so right to push on because the best part of it is at least a quarter of that list, maybe even more, have been either long-listed or short-listed or won major prizes. I think that the importance of that, culturally, is really significant because that's where if anybody's got any insecurity about 'Oh it's Black people' so they're putting you under this Black banner, well here's the mainstream culture telling you that these books are worthy. While I hate to have to feel this way about it, that's what other people need, they need to know that elsewhere in society people value these books. Which is what's happened over a huge chunk of the list.

Often with these ideas I have no idea how hard it's going to be to make them work, not thinking through the finances of how we are going to fund this, because it's always the case for us in the position that we occupy, that we have to think first about the culture and then how we make this work. Rather than, 'Well on paper this is not a very good idea, so we won't do it.' If we think that way, we'd not exist and neither would so many of these books.

For Jacaranda it's been amazing, we've got an amazing partnership with The London Library – two-year free memberships for our authors so they're able to find a place to write. That was a really important factor for me, that many debut Black writers will not have any experience of the publishing process so need all the help they can get. We got Audible partnerships for them, so their books are now in audio as well as print and ebook. We're constantly trying to overdeliver, and asking 'What more can we do for them?' These are new authors that probably wouldn't exist anywhere else so I feel Jacaranda has a responsibility to deliver them into the world.

Lessons

Look beyond your immediate circumstances for inspiration to fuel your ambition. For young Valerie that meant identifying passions that had the potential to fill her cup so that it was constantly flowing over with opportunity.

If at first you don't succeed, get up and try, try, try again.

Place the biggest bets you make on yourself.

Understand the power of vision setting and the discipline of sticking with it.

Affirmation: Today there are no limits to what I can do.

' The Negotiator '

DOMINIC CARTER

◆

The News UK group includes *The Times*, *Sunday Times*, *Sun*, talkSPORT, Times Radio and Virgin Radio – Dominic is EVP, Publisher of the *Sun*. In addition, he sits on the corporation's Executive Board and is Chair of the Diversity Board, meaning he is tasked with bringing about a positive cultural shift within an organisation not historically known for its efforts towards diversity and inclusion.

Dominic was born in Redcar in the north-east of England and but lived in Nigeria until the age of ten. His first job out of college was selling life assurance, something he saw as the purest form of selling. 'You're asking somebody to give you money *now* and in ten years' time you'll give them some back, but you can't say how much' is how he puts it. After two lucrative years in this sector, Dominic moved into advertising sales at Sales Direction, a business magazine. Six months later, he was the title's advertising manager. A move into newspapers seemed like a natural progression and Dominic became the first person of colour to become a display advertising executive within the British national newspaper industry.

Today, alongside his commercial duties, he has instigated several initiatives to help the company reach its target of 50:50:20 – equal numbers of male and female employees at all levels, and 20 per cent ethnic minorities.

Navigation is key to moving forward

My school life was interesting to say the least. In my early years, I spent most of it in Nigeria because my dad was contracted to work ten months there, then two months back home in the UK. When here, I'd spend four or five weeks at a local comprehensive school in Redcar. Then, at the age of nine, I was sent to boarding school in Durham.

I got through my O levels (GCSEs) but I if I'm honest, I probably didn't try as hard as I could have. What I did learn quite early on, though, was how to navigate my way with people. Travelling back and forth between the UK and Nigeria, then being the only Black kid in an all-boys' boarding school in the north-east of England meant I had to learn how to get on with different types. Durham School for boys is one of the oldest boarding schools in the UK. Most pupils were the sons of farmers; some came from slightly shadier backgrounds, but what they all had in common was that they were tough people. There were a few academic types, but not that many as it was a very sporty school.

I learned pretty quickly that as I was so different, I had to be good at something. My thing was sport. The only thing you got an accolade for at a school like mine was being funny or good at sport. Happily, I was good at most sports, in particular, squash. I learned to play in Nigeria then played at county and England junior levels.

What I learned at school was if you're good at sport then you're going to engage with people because if you're successful, they're going to want to know you. From there, it is easier to influence people and that definitely allows you to navigate through life much more easily.

Once I'd learned to do that, I had what I needed to get people to do things that they maybe didn't know they wanted to do. In my view, that is what sales is – getting people to do something that they don't necessarily know they want to.

Even the tedious experiences can prove useful

My first job was selling life assurance, and for the first hour of my day I'd go through the telephone directory and write out two hundred and fifty numbers that I was going to phone that day. My aim was, to make appointments and sell life assurance to as many people as I could. Not the most interesting of tasks you might think, but I credit that first job as being hugely instructive because it taught me so much about the principles of what I was doing.

Selling life assurance is probably the purest form of selling because no-one gets up in the morning thinking, *I'm going to buy some life assurance or a savings plan today*. It was my job to convince some twenty-two-year-old to give me some of their money with no guarantee of exactly how much of it they'd get back in ten years' time.

From those two hundred and fifty numbers, I'd aim to get twenty appointments a day. Effectively, trying to get twenty people to come in and buy one of the financial products I was selling. We quickly worked out that if you failed to get those twenty appointments, is was because they didn't like you on the telephone. If they came in but still didn't buy from you, it was because they didn't like you in person. The challenge was to get someone to like you and trust you very, very quickly. Once you've done that, everything else is incredibly easy.

I stayed in that sector for about two years, thinking it was the right thing to do because I wanted to make a lot of money. I did make money, but I realised it wasn't satisfying me on any other level. Around that time, I saw a job ad in the *Guardian* for a sales executive on a business magazine where a friend of mine worked as a journalist. I went in, met the owner, got the job and straight away realised what advantages my previous job had given me. In this new environment – selling advertising space in a magazine – I was selling to people *who are paid* to buy advertising. All I had to do was convince them to spend their money with me. I felt like I had a head start.

Answering every call I made would be somebody I know was going to listen. If they then liked and trusted me, they would buy from me. That is exactly what happened, very quickly. Within six months I was the ad manager.

'Easy' still takes hard work

When I got into sales on a bigger national platform, I realised the scope of what such a career had to offer. I learned about such a wide range of industry sectors, just by being in advertising. I came to understand so much about so many different companies. I honestly believe that within about five years, I knew more people and had more in-depth knowledge of business than most of the people I'd been at school with.

Of course, I had to work at this too, it didn't just land in my lap. I used to read all the time, consuming information about the different businesses I might have to deal with. I would research each company exhaustively before I so much as picked up the phone: Bear in mind this was pre-internet so it wasn't as easy as just going on Google and typing in a company name; I'd have to hunt down information and it took time and effort. It worked for me, though, as I remember one contact saying, 'No-one has come in here knowing so much about my client.' It was just standard practice for me to make myself informed.

At that time, I was the only Black person working in display newspapers and my main thought was that I needed to be impressive from the first moment they spoke to me. I needed to know my stuff and I needed to be really good, otherwise I would never get a second chance in the future. I knew very early on: I had to do the work and I had to be better.

Make the most of being different

When I was in business magazines, I didn't notice the lack of people of colour in my industry because most of what I was doing was selling direct to clients, via the telephone. It was when I first entered the newspapers sector in 1991 that it became really apparent to me.

Did it put me off what was by then my chosen career? Not at all; I think I saw an opportunity. I stood out, I could celebrate my difference and make it work to my advantage.

When I got into newspapers, all of a *sudden,* I had to go into the ad agency and media agency offices, When you're on the phone, no-one can tell your colour. I'd walk into agencies for appointments and be met by quizzical looks when they came to get me in reception. That was when I'd think, *OK! I've got you on the back foot because you didn't expect me to be Black. Now I'm going to impress you and I'm going to get you to do business with me.*

The only time I didn't upset anyone's expectations was when I had a meeting with a guy from an agency who I'd never met but turned out to be Black too. He came out to reception, looked right at me and went 'Dom Carter?' We both burst out laughing, because we knew straight away what game we'd been playing. We became very good mates.

Change comes from the top, so do your best to get there

Once at an industry function, a Black TV director at J Walter Thompson. explained the lack of people of colour in the industry to me, 'You know Dom, there's not one account director of colour in an agency. And the reason why is because no-one feels they can put a Black person in front of their clients.'

This didn't put me off; though. On the contrary, it galvanised me to be really good at what I did and to prove it didn"t matter what colour you were. I wanted to show that if you're good at what you do, you're good at what you do. Full stop. Your job is to make sure you succeed, and if you do that then you survive in this industry, and I'm proud to say, I've done that.

I feel a huge part of success for me, is that *I've survived* in this industry when so many people haven't — I'm fifty-six and I can honestly say, there are not many people who started with me and are still here. For me, it goes to the early lesson I learnt about how to navigate your way around different people with different personalities. Believe it or not, I've had six or seven different CEOs in my career in the news industry. The other thing is, you've got to continue to want to excel and to be better than everybody else. That will allow you to survive and move up.

But you can't take anything for granted. You need to be patient, then recognise opportunity when it presents itself. When I started at *The Times*, the difference between selling classified and display advertising was clear cut: in those days, classified deals were all done over the phone. You never went to see clients. On the other hand, selling display advertising was all external, going out to visit clients and agencies in their offices.

I was the first Black newspaper display exec in the industry. It's shocking to say, but I heard that a Black guy had once tried to get job in the same display advertising department, and the then MD had basically said he would not put a Black person in front of clients. But by the time I came along, that MD was gone and the incumbent that hired me put their faith in me, so I thought, *I'm going to be great at this*. Once I got the job, I can honestly say, I never had an issue with any client or agency, because I could do my job.

Be prepared to challenge your own preconceptions

After the England versus Germany football game at the Euros in 2021, the *Sun* was the only red-top (British tabloid newspaper) to put Raheem Sterling on the front page. Every other paper put Harry Kane on the front. But Stirling was man of the match, he scored the goal, he was all over the pitch, he had a fantastic game, so we put him on the front page. That other papers decided to put Harry Kane on the front page, despite the fact that he didn't score and obviously wasn't the best player on the day. Why? To me it suggests there is still bias in our industry.

Our editor was brave to have swum against the tide with that Stirling front page. We knew we were going to get criticism, mainly because of our critical coverage of Stirling's gun tattoo a few years ago. But I think the point is that happened then. Since that time, we've got a different editor and a different approach. I would say that the paper and the company, have become much more inclusive, but people still seem to remember the negative stuff.

There have been lots of little things, that cumulatively add up to momentous things – that *Sun* front page, for example. Many people have the perception that the paper is non-inclusive All I can say is, look at at the product, *today*, not the product it was ten years ago. Look at what we're doing *today*. Look at the makeup of the people that we're bringing in now, but more interestingly look at the *attitude* of the product, and what it stands for.

Businesses are allowed to change. Businesses take on different leaders and the strong ones will drive change. Newspapers can do the same. My view is that the *Sun* is driving change. It will take time for perceptions to catch up, but the paper needs to keep pushing. The easy thing would be to go back to the old formula of how things were. But we don't want easy. In five years' time, I want people to acknowledge how much the *Sun* has changed.

Changing the culture of a huge organisation is a huge task

I chair the company's Diversity Board and we've opened up a lot of opportunities to enable LGBTQ+ or people of colour or from different cultures to get into the organisation. We've got the Cultural Diversity Network (which would have been the BAME Network in the past). We've set up lots of network groups and I worked with some external companies to develop a strategy that we've now introduced in the business. We've got a Kickstart Scheme to get young people in from different backgrounds, we have an apprentice scheme so we specifically attract people from different social backgrounds and ethnicity who might not have gone to university. All this is an attempt to make sure our products are increasingly staffed by people who reflect society – not just Oxbridge or Russell Group graduate where, historically, a lot of our journalists have come from.

We have always said we want a meritocracy, but my argument has been: how can you have a meritocracy when you only ever fish in the same small pond? In this country the profile of journalism is 95 per cent Caucasian. The way to change this is to be more open and to look at a wider cross-section of candidates to interview. Historically, we've always used CVs to whittle down candidates for *The Times* graduate journalist training scheme, and I think that is where a lot of bias comes in (i.e. names and backgrounds). This year we have actually gone blank on the CVs and we're asking candiates to submit a piece of work. We did the same thing with the apprenticeship scheme and we've seen a huge uptick in diversity hires.

We know that diverse talent is out here and if you're going to call yourself a meritocracy, you have to have represent that. As Chair of the Diversity Board my role is to make sure we're continuing to drive the organisation in the right direction in terms of its makeup, its culture, and its training.

Our business targets are 50:50:20: we want 50 per cent male/female employees and we want 20 per cent ethnicity, across all levels. Every executive in the business has it as part of their bonus scheme. We've worked with a lot of external partners to educate people in the company at all levels, and this includes editorial around race and ethnicity and sexual orientation and gender. By such endeavours, we can become a better and much more inclusive business.

Lessons

Find your superpower early on by understanding what gets you positive attention and what gives you power. For young Dominic that meant applying his understanding of sporting competition to all aspects of his life. The attention and power, in turn, gave him real agency and social currency.

Get people to like you and trust you as quickly as possible.

Own your authentic difference because in doing so you get to own your true power.

Being the very best you can be is the most effective survival strategy in an industry that is constantly changing.

> Affirmation: Today I will achieve greatness by being my true self.

'The Curator'

GUS CASELY-HAYFORD OBE

◆

With not one but two Casely-Hayfords in this list, it is a surname that carries considerable weight. As founding director of the V&A East, a magnificent, very twenty-first-century museum and collection centre, at the time of writing under construction on the old Olympic Park in Stratford, east London, Gus has more than earned the right to be here. For good measure, prior to that, he was Director of the Smithsonian National Museum of African Art in Washington, DC.

As a curator, cultural and art historian, lecturer and broadcaster, Dr Gus Casely-Hayford is one of the world's foremost experts on African art and culture – he has spent periods at the School of Oriental and African Studies in London and organised Africa 2005, the biggest celebration of African culture ever hosted in Britain. He has been Executive Director of Arts Strategy, Arts Council England; Director of the Institute of International Contemporary Art; lectured and worked at Sothebys Institute, Goldsmiths, Birkbeck, City University and the University of Westminster and advised the United Nations on heritage and culture.

It's not lost on Gus the importance and, to a degree, the irony of an expert in African history, of African descent, curating a major British museum and lecturing on the nation on its relationships with its own history.

Dr Gus Casely-Hayford was awarded the OBE for his services to art and culture in 2018.

Familial success need not create a high-pressure environment

If asked, I couldn't really tell you that growing up a Casely-Hayford was something extraordinary because I don't know – how I grew up was how I grew up, as you do, and it all felt perfectly natural. However, I certainly knew that my siblings were special, particularly watching my sister Margaret who is one of the most profoundly hard-working and deeply talented people I've ever met. As I'm the youngest, at times it felt like being in a relay and watching the person go off with the baton and thinking, *Wow! That is incredible. How am I ever going to be able to replicate that when it's my turn?*

My brother Joe who was a fashion designer, was, in terms of just innate, discreet talent, unlike anyone I've ever met – he was born with it, then worked so hard to hone it. I watched my sister go off to Oxford and then my brother went off to St Martins (University of Arts) and did amazing collections. After that my other brother, Peter, went to the BBC and worked as Managing Editor of Panorama, in a period when if you were a person of colour that was nigh on impossible. And then I had to try and place these individuals who seemed almost magical into that bigger context of my own career. It was all both astounding and exhilarating.

Very early in my career I travelled through Africa and looked at previous chapters of our family history; at my grandfather who was a politician and who worked to try and fight against colonialism through legal means. At my great-grandfather, who was a minister and was part of one of the first confederations to attempt to fight back against colonialism. At his father who was an incredible merchant who tried to find ways of building the intellectual infrastructure to create a platform for pushing back against colonial encroachment. I discovered this long trajectory of people going back over decades or centuries who have all been invested in the same thing really, of trying to think about how you'd bring dignity and pleasure and perspective to where it might have been under threat. That's a tradition that I am enormously proud to have been a part of and that I put my immediate family in the context of, so what they were achieving felt very natural.

I didn't feel any pressures though. What I felt was the sense of privilege, of being in a position to be able to see my siblings do incredibly well and thinking, *Look, if you've had exposure to all of that, you can't waste it as a platform.* Then feeling as well that one needs to give back and one needs to try and offer the transformational opportunities and benefits to another generation, which is what I try to invest in.

My present job is trying to build the museum (the forthcoming V&A East) and trying to make it as inclusive and as open as it possibly can be, while in my previous role (the Smithsonian) I was working in an institution that was trying to rewrite those histories for the better. Across the course of my career those are the things that I've invested in, in an area that is ultimately about pleasure and enlightenment but also to try and force that area of the arts to rigorously address issues of equity. I've seen that as being something that has been a real pleasure and a privilege to be a part of, to begin to push back against the ambient conditions and make some real progress.

The great reward is actually seeing the progress we have made, and I think it's been far more a case of inspiration from my family than any sort of pressure.

You're never too young to embrace what's going on around you

One of my earliest memories is watching my older brother Joe drawing and making things. Watching somebody with that level of skill create things which were exquisite using very ordinary tools felt to me like a form of magic – it seemed beyond the bounds of what was logically possible. Even back then I used to think it was something that was a privilege to watch.

It was a kind of magic from which the connection can be made between great art, great creativity, and people, and I immediately fell under its spell. I believe it is a result of those early experiences that I've spent my career not just dedicated to and trying to tell the story of art, but trying to unlock something of that *magic*. It's a kind of intriguing blessing that we have as a species, being able to communicate through exquisite beauty, and I knew I wanted to be part of that process.

As a small child, watching my brother was a kind of transformative moment. I am delighted to be able to continue to see that in one of the great aims of my life, which is to try to unravel what I have found, to further inspire others with the beauty and the possibilities of great art and creativity.

I came to see art as far more than something beautiful you could put on a shelf or hang on the wall; it was an expression of culture and therefore of even greater importance. From my late teenage years I began travelling, in part to find something out about my own Ghanaian heritage, and as I travelled through Africa I discovered these histories that one generally isn't taught in the schools of Britain. I was seeing that the most sophisticated and lasting legacies of these incredible cultures were their creativity, their art, and I wanted to celebrate that. I wanted to put it on a pedestal as both a marker of these lost histories but also a defiant stand that we *must* begin to connect the wider global art history with these areas that seem to have been systematically cut from the sort of curricula that I was brought up on.

History belongs to those who write it down

Discovering, examining and presenting this great art gave us the basis upon which we could write different kinds of histories. The nineteenth-century German philosopher Georg Hegel very famously said 'Africa is this place without history and without culture', and that comes from a conscious ignorance of the material evidence that pointed in a completely contrary direction. By offering up that material evidence, that material *culture*, one can begin to construct a very different picture of not just our past but also of the future, because from studying what has gone before we get the basis of what our potential – all of our potentials – might actually be.

That for me is utterly thrilling, because while one can feel corralled by appalling racial constraints this was something that can break those kinds of barriers down and allow us to think about the periods in the past when we weren't contained by those very constrictive, limiting and discriminatory narratives. When there was much greater porosity and mutual respect between intellectual cultures. I find it absolutely fascinating that the past can be an example of that kind for the future, which is one of the great things about history and why it's so important we understand ours.

The African cultural trajectory is longer than any other – it's the place where humankind begins its story – so therefore it has greater variability. Within that longer trajectory, the ways in which it works across media are enormously diverse and complex. Yet we seem to know so little about it. Investing time and energy and focus trying to reveal some of that is not only doing the art and the people who can now access it a service, but has been *hugely* rewarding for me because it feels like I've had the privilege of discovering new areas of deeply rich inspiration on an ongoing basis.

Of course there's the deep frustration of feeling this isn't part of our wider understanding – the fact that these are histories and bodies of thinking that underpin so much of what we take for granted, but somehow that contribution has been subtracted from the wider global intellectual narrative. This means it's something that requires a *project*, it requires energy, it requires concerted effort to reinsert that narrative, that cultural contribution, back into the broader history and I'm delighted to be part of that continuing effort.

The rewriting and recalibration of history that is required is, obviously, an endless job but I think there's never been a time at which it felt more necessary, more immediate, or more critical that we address this. The events of the last eighteen months have reminded us that by not including, with a degree of equity, the stories and the narratives of the peoples of the southern hemisphere, there is a huge, deep, critical omission in our understanding of or in our comprehension of world cultures. I believe this is not just about writing good histories, it has a kind of moral imperative linked to it as well.

I think that almost anyone who's suffered racism from someone in a position of authority will then question the systems and traditions that are in place, and as soon as you begin to do that you then look to the whole kind of edifice of our learning and understanding and you think about how that might be shifted. It will be long and difficult, but we have to invest in new histories and we have to invest in questioning old histories. We have to be forensic in our quest to unravel the alternate and the true stories so we are able to point to different sets of examples of heroes and people in whose footsteps we can try and follow.

Also, we need to think again about the counter-narratives of people that, in the past, we have put on pedestals, that we have captured in stone and made heroic. We need to be much more forensic and forceful if we are now thinking about the moral structures within which our histories actually sit. This isn't about political correctness or something to do with being woke, this is just about good history, to end up giving our children what they absolutely need and deserve, which is really good history.

That is what I have been invested in across the course of my career. Not just providing the history but giving people access to it so *they* can transform their own understanding and their understanding of others by crafting history themselves.

It's really down to all of us

So much of what I do is about putting history in front of people so they can absorb it into their lives, as we all have a responsibility to it. If we have children or if we just care about future generations, I believe we have a responsibility to invest in thinking about how we engage with the truth. There are a lot of things about our history that don't reflect the complexity of the past, but also don't represent the fullness of it either, so there is a huge opportunity for addressing areas of imbalance in areas that have been purposely tainted by perspectives that today look very, very outmoded.

I believe we can all invest in that, as we inform our young and try and talk about particular areas of global history, as that may offer a kind of transformative opportunity to create, allowing someone a way of rethinking their relationship to the world around them. *That* I think is exciting. That's thrilling. That's history not being a dormant thing that is read in libraries but becoming an active thing that not only changes the way in which people think about the world they see around them but also the future that they might want to be engaging with.

Sometimes you need to step out of your situation to better appreciate it

I was director of the Smithsonian National Museum of African Art, in Washington, DC, for two years, which for me was a huge privilege as it is probably *the* great African art museum. It has absolutely superb collections, and colleagues of incredible expertise who have dedicated their lives to trying to not just fashion new histories but also to display them as well. That was amazing, and to do it in that particular period in which there was a kind of burgeoning of consciousness shifting politics, it felt incredibly important that we tell those stories and we addressed some of those sorts of old stories with real rigour. I adored that period, and it will continue to inform the way I think about everything I do for a very long period of time.

Growing up and being educated in Britain when you have a very particular understanding of race and one's position on it in relation to our history, then living in America for a while, you begin to realise that being a Black Brit and being an African American are two similar but *distinctively* different ways of experiencing the world. The ways in which you are treated, but also the sets of expectation placed upon you, the ways in which people relate to you and the ways in which you interrelate – they are very, very different. Then in looking back at Britain from that distance you begin to see things that previously were invisible to you, and see them with a degree of clarity. This is *so* important because one can see the way in which empire and colonialism and our peculiar kind of class structure still impose a very powerful set of cultural conditions across people's consciousness. Which is something that when you're aware of it you can then push against it in a conscious way.

For many Black Brits, because we are numerically fewer than African Americans and also proportionately fewer, we probably have less cultural influence on our condition than African Americans and it can be difficult to struggle against what can feel like an overwhelming ambient condition of opposition. It feels like from school all the way through every stage of one's professional opportunities there are barriers and locked gates, invisible and otherwise, and that becomes more complex because of class. How one navigates that is extremely tough, but what I do think of as a kind of note of optimism is what this last eighteen months has done to force so many institutions to sit up and ask very, very profound questions about how they are dealing with these issues. About how they might make the change that they have talked about for a generation but haven't actually delivered, and how they make those changes tell.

It has offered the kind of cultural opportunity that does hopefully mean that there will be shifts, and I think one of the fascinating areas to look at is sport. You have that appalling residual racism you see being expressed on terraces and in the chat rooms, but then simultaneously you have the sort of atmosphere that was created around Gareth Southgate's England and the diversity of that team. In a way that is setting the tone for what I think is ambient Britain as it sits in diametric opposition to some of the sorts of things that are being propagated by the worst bits of the media.

So I believe there is something to feel very optimistic about, it's almost a wave of consciousness and the acceptance that things must change. You see that manifesting itself in a variety of different ways – you see it in adverts, you saw it in the things that happened on the streets of Bristol . . . It's a fundamental shift in consciousness, that amongst the young seems to be deeply profound. I think that stuff all points to a kind of a shift in the wider culture. Of course there may be points of inertia and blockage, but where it needs to happen in the young, where it needs to happen in our cities, where it needs to happen in areas like the creative industries, I think there are real seeds that one can feel optimistic about.

Our museums are a lens through which to look at ourselves

At the moment I feel enormously privileged to be in the position to be the founding director of a new national museum in the twenty-first century, the V&A East. It's a completely new museum and storehouse being built to sit on the old Olympic Park in Stratford. The storehouse will house a collection of around 280,000 objects that tell the story of the very best of human creativity across five thousand years, and a thousand archives will also be housed in this space. We don't want it to be like other collection centres; it will be open and accessible – glass floors, glass balustrades, you could stand in the very centre of the space and see the greater part of the collection if you were to pirouette around. We want to then create a level of accessibility which will be unlike any other collection centre, so anyone can go into it and feel, 'This is a national collection, these are my objects', and they can interact with them and have hands-on time with a substantive part of the collection. We want that collection to then transcend the walls. We will take those collections out, we want to visit schools and I've made a commitment to visit all the secondary schools within the four boroughs that abut our institution.

Additionally, alongside that, we are building a museum that will be in a gorgeous four-storey building that is very unconventional in design, and it will house gallery spaces and also the kind of spaces in which you can just come and be there. There will be restaurants and shops, it will be a space in which we can show our collection and offer people the curatorial narrative links to make those connections across time and geography that really make sense of *this*, one of the great collections of material culture.

On the top two floors we will have some exhibitions dedicated to amazing themes, to telling great stories through focusing on the greatest creative practitioners of our time, then above that a space which we want to see as being a lantern on the top of a lighthouse. It's a space with stunning views, but also with stunning opportunities for creating new kinds of programmes that will be interactive and engaged and connected to all the sorts of amazing things that are happening across the globe at the moment. We are living through a period when it's probably going to be more difficult to travel and thinking of such issues as sustainability we probably won't be wanting to travel as much, so we want to bring the world to this bit of east London.

We want to make it an institution that can reflect our changing nation, its new sense of opportunity beyond Brexit as we find a new place within the world. But also to reflect back on those inordinately complex chapters of our history, in which we have navigated some really difficult and some dark issues. Museums need to be there at places where we can deal with those complex issues, but also one hopes with a degree of potential catharsis. They become spaces in which we can come together both to agree and disagree, but, I would hope, to work through things. If you feel the way the world feels at the moment about things – enormously polarised, in which opposition seems to be the tenor of most political discourse – one of the spaces in which we might be able to counter that is through the celebration of beauty, through consideration of contentious areas of history captured through material culture, through the historical consideration of what is important. These are things which museums in my mind do better than any other institution; in fact which national museums actually have a duty to deliver.

The past is the future

If you think Britain as an entity comes into its modern shape in the 1750s, it's not a coincidence that the 1750s are also the period in which we also crafted our very first national museum. I think it's because as a nation we needed a crucible in which our identity could be considered and ruminated upon, and museums are very, very good for that. They're good for looking back and defining the things that root us, for looking laterally at the things that connect us, but also for looking toward the future at the sort of direction of travel that we would like to deploy. Again in the 1850s, that's when the Victoria and Albert Museum, the Science Museum, all of those large national museums that sit in South Kensington came into being, and it was another moment of Britain thinking about its place in the world. Both for good and for ill, museums were the integral manifestation of that.

The V&A and the museums on Exhibition Road were established at a time in the nineteenth century when it was both a moment of colonial expansion and a moment of Britain re-engaging with its own population and thinking about how it might offer transformative opportunity. The V&A, from its inception, had gas lights so that people could come and study in the evening; it had an open access library so that anyone could come and use it; it was the first institution to have a café so you didn't have to come, visit in a studious way and then leave — you could come recreationally and stay all day. It was built and driven around this idea of opening up these spaces to a wider constituency, and part of that was about seeing the institution as a tool for the population. It was a public institution which should be a transformative tool for the population, for people's skills, providing points of inspiration and opening up people's perspectives and vistas on new ways of thinking.

If you think of this as being in the Victorian period which in a lot of ways was seen as being very constraining — if one says the word 'Victorian' you think about things being quite stiff — this is a very radical tool. This was about giving people the tools to change their lives and the world around them, what might be called social mobility, and that part of the museum DNA is something that we should be reinvesting in.

This is why it's only right for the twenty-first century that we give people the tools to transform our institutions too, which is in the digital space where people can not just learn from the curators who will offer layers of interpretation, but they can leave something of their own thoughts, feelings and understandings,. Over a period of time the museum will of course grow in terms of its collection, but it will also grow in terms of being an accumulative conversation that the nation is having around its own collection.

I think that is a thrilling thing. If you have a photo album that contains the pictures of your family across generations it captures those critical moments that tell the story of the lives of your loved ones. There is something hugely powerful about that, but what would make it become magical is when you sit down and you say, 'Do you remember that? That was when X or Y happened.' Then someone else sits down and says, 'No it wasn't, I don't remember it like that, it was something completely different, it was actually . . .' And then *someone else* might come and say, 'No. you're both wrong!' All of those layers of understanding and reconsideration, that beautiful network, that gossamer of understanding and connections with rethinking and reframing. That is an additional thing that is so often lost, but today we are blessed with the digital infrastructure to capture and offer a different kind of framing upon the museum experience, one which will make sure the new museum space remains absolutely inclusive and representative.

Get involved

I am on, and have been on, many different committees and boards. This is about more than just giving back or a sense of public duty – that would be the same for anybody – it's about being there to be the voice that, potentially, would have helped my young self create the platform that opened the door that would have meant I had a chance. So if I can be in the room, even if I'm the sole voice and I can make that happen, then that is a victory, and the one person that you might give the chance to may well be the person that becomes the transformative force.

For this reason it's absolutely vital for people of colour or minority backgrounds to get themselves on mainstream committees and boards, and in times like this it's become all the more important that we do. I'm a great believer that where we *can* contribute we *should* contribute, and we do so without any sort of moral compromises.

Most trustee roles are advertised, so I tell people: 'Apply, apply, apply!' You've got to apply and while it might be difficult in the beginning, there is a point at which things tip in your favour and because you have been on a few boards, you've demonstrated the value you can give and will be accepted on to others. I'm in the position now when I am asked – constantly. I believe what that offers is a sense of how, over the course of my career, the sector has changed enormously and now it would seem fundamentally wrong for a major body to have a senior team or to have a committee or to have a board in which diversity wasn't demonstrated.

We need to be in there and forcing the doors open wider to allow others through, and to be thinking laterally about people who may not have had the advantages that we have because of other areas of prejudice. We have to think, *How do we actually change hearts and minds to make sure that in this ever-evolving fight for equity we do not ever let up and that we keep pushing on?* There will always be a hinterland, a promised land, that means we will always have further things to fight for, so I just think it's important that we keep our eyes on the bigger prize.

Lessons

If you are lucky enough to have super talented or gifted siblings, don't look at them as rivals, look to them as inspiration. For young Gus that meant looking to his family for 'sibling inspiration' rather than 'sibling rivalry'.

In order for us to truly understand our fullest potential we have to spend time studying what has gone before us. Understanding the history and heritage of most things can help us lean into the future with confidence and purpose.

In order to fully appreciate THE world you have to be prepared to step outside YOUR world.

If you study hard, work hard and have a little bit of luck, your passion might actually become your professional purpose.

Affirmation: Today my purpose is to consciously study my passion.

'The Trailblazer'

MARGARET CASELY-HAYFORD CBE

◆

As the oldest sibling in a household once named 'the most influential Black family in the UK' it was never really an option for Margaret Casely-Hayford to coast through life, but her level of achievement and contribution is nevertheless astonishing. After graduating in law from Somerville College, Oxford, she progressed through the profession to become the first Black woman to become a partner at a City of London law firm, Dentons, following which she was Director of Legal Services for the John Lewis Partnership and their representative on the board of the British Retail Consortium. In her spare time Margaret has been a non-executive director of the NHS England, trustee of the Museum of the Home, and special trustee of Great Ormond Street Children's Hospital Charity. She has advised the Foreign Office on strategic reform of the British Council, Oriel College on Cecil Rhodes and chaired a review on diversity for CILIP (the Libraries' Association) in relation to the Carnegie and Kate Greenaway Book awards.

Since retirement Margaret is hardly taking things easy – she calls herself a Portfolio Woman, for a very straightforward reason: 'I have a portfolio of activities.' Margaret is on the board of the Co-op Group, is Chancellor of Coventry University and Chair of Shakespeare's Globe; she advises on board structures and corporate governance, with the Institute of Directors Centre for Governance, DeLoitte and KPMG and lectures on board diversity opportunity courses.

She is a trustee of the Radcliffe Trust, co-founder and Chief Executive of the Gallery of Living History, and is an advisor to Ultra Education, an enterprise teaching entrepreneurial skills. Margaret has been made an Honorary Fellow of CILIP; an Honorary Fellow of Somerville College; received an honorary doctorate from Middlesex University and was made a Bencher of the Honorable Society of Gray's Inn; and has contributed articles as a freelancer to *Country Life* magazine.

Margaret Casely-Hayford was awarded a CBE in 2018 for services to charity and for promoting diversity.

The privileges of growing up in a high-achieving family

I should start from the fact that my father loved language and books and read a lot, so we absorbed that – for me a golden moment would be when I could just sit with a book. While I was quite happy with my own company, reading, we had wonderful discussions at the dining table about everything from politics to art to music. What is interesting is that as my brothers and our respective spouses have grown older our children are very good friends, so we all regularly get together and there's nothing lovelier than us all sitting round the table. It really takes me back. My brother's son Charlie, a fashion designer, gave an interview to a magazine not too long ago and talked about it as sitting at a boardroom table with the intellectual sparring about all manner of things – the commercial realities of running a business, the politics of life, the politics of the world, arts and culture and so on. So clearly the environment we grew up in has created the way we are establishing an environment for our children.

What is also really interesting is they say the family that plays together stays together; we not only played sport together and board games like Monopoly, snakes and ladders and all that sort of thing, but we also engaged on an intellectual basis. I think that's been incredibly bonding because we have similar values, and I believe it's values that keep people together. So, we are very strong as a family and we're friends which I think is really important because it has meant we've always been mutually supportive.

94

It wasn't a pressure at all, or it never felt such to me. We were *encouraged*, which is why I believe there was such a disparate range of professions between us siblings. As I was bookish I went into law because law was quite a tradition in the family: my grandfather was a barrister; my father's older brother Archie was a barrister; my father trained as a barrister but didn't practice, kind of breaking the mould. The other lawyers trained in the UK and went back to Cape Coast to the family chambers to practice law from there, and as my father became an accountant, he remained in the UK.

I think he realised that you can't force anybody to do something they don't feel inclined to do because they won't lead a good life, they won't lead a fulfilling life. So, in spite of the family traditions, in our branch, for us it was much more encouragement than coercion. For example, Joe was a fashion designer and I remember when he said that was what he was really interested in, rather than my father saying 'Oh that's ridiculous, go and be a lawyer or a doctor or something in the more traditional professions', he simply said, 'Well if you're going to do that do it properly.' He sent Joe to pattern cutting school, so before he went to St Martins to study design he had this incredible tailoring knowledge.

There was a sort of pressure, but it was a silent pressure because everybody worked to succeed for themselves and to do the best for society. That's how we operated within our family: that you also give back to society. So there was a sort of silent requirement that we should all do that and no-one wanted to be the one to let the family down. This was something else about being a Casely-Hayford: it's such an incredibly distinctive family surname that if I walk into a room and I've got a name badge on somebody is bound to say 'Oh I know your . . .' and they're going to say brother, father, uncle or whatever, so you definitely don't want to be the one who is letting the group down!

The pressures of success can be difficult to cope with too

One of the most important aspects of being 'the first' anything is there's no-one there to teach you what to do. As a

Black woman in that situation you feel everybody's looking at you and they're expecting you to fail. But you can't fail, because if you fail you take everybody with you, everybody who looks like you, because, one suspects, the unimaginative would be thinking 'We've had one . . . we've had somebody like this and they couldn't cope, so we ought to think twice about another one.' Perhaps my mistake at times has therefore been being afraid to ask and having to learn the hard way.

It's fascinating that because of the pseudo-science that went into underpinning the relationships that people established during slavery and during colonialism, in particular during the nineteenth century, we are not seen as being capable of being in management or having superior roles, yet no-one comes out of the womb being a manager. No person has that right. There are the artificial constructs in monarchy and so on, but outside of that we're all exactly the same: there is no reason why, when two people walk into a room, one of them is seen as managerial material and the other one isn't. *Yet* because I have a Black face, I'm less likely to be seen as that. Because I am a woman I'm less likely to be seen as that. So you do have to strive to demonstrate not just that you can do it but also that you can cope with the pressures of being in that role, and that you can do it well without any form of corruption. Any failure will then be seen as a reason for not allowing the others through, so maintaining a level of success is really tough.

Not being allowed to fail also means that you are ultra-critiqued. If you do something wrong it's a terrible tragedy and it's all got to be scrutinised, whereas if somebody else does something wrong, it's a mistake and the response is all about how they are going to rectify it and let's see what they can do. There's that sort of dual-handed level of pressure.

So being a success can carry with it an enormous burden; it's very lonely, and I think people undervalue the notion of a network in keeping one buoyed up. What I've found as I've got older is life has got easier because there are more of us and there is a network – even just being recognised as one of many lightens the load. So suddenly, someone can fail and it doesn't matter because there are others who are not failing and it shows that it isn't a 'Black person' thing to fail, it's just that particular individual did so.

Coaching for high-level roles is as vital as for entry-level positions

I'm an Ambassador for a not-for-profit organisation called Board Apprentice, which was set up by Charlotte Valeur, an amazing woman, who is neuro-diverse, has had a long career in finance and was appointed Chair of the Institute of Directors. She is Danish and married to a Ghanaian, and she wanted her sons to have the same opportunities as other boys so she set up Board Apprentice. It's a formal way to give people the opportunity to shadow board directors and make sure they understand the structure, so when they go into it, it's not foreign to them. It allows them to ask questions in an environment that's supposed to be no risk and no challenge – just an understandable learning environment.

It is absolutely the right thing to do and I've been a really keen champion of hers. It once again goes back to the point I made that there were artificial constructs established as long ago as the eighteenth and nineteenth centuries that have kept people where they are, and one of the aspects I have really striven to change is to create greater opportunities at the top levels. When you have decision makers that are from differing backgrounds, of differing ethnicities, classes and genders, those people will be able to welcome others into the structure and to give them opportunity, build them a network and give them support. So, Board Apprentice is really, really important to me as it's fighting to change the structure.

Elsewhere the financial services giant Deloitte and the really good search agents like Fidelio run courses specifically to enable a wider diversity of opportunity to high level and I've given talks and lectures on those courses. People also ask me on a one-to-one basis through LinkedIn and other networks whether I would give them support and guidance for getting on to boards, or just tell them how to get on to boards, what to do and where to look, how to structure their CV and so on.

I think the coaching to be on a board is absolutely critical. First of all, if somebody is the only new board member they could be sitting there thinking *I don't get this, I don't feel comfortable with this*, or *I'd like to say this but no-one else seems to have this view, is it only me?* That's not unusual, but what is really annoying is so few people are helped to *realise* that's not unusual. So, one of the things we did when I was Chair of ActionAid, an international development organisation working against poverty and injustice, was to decide positively that we would think differently about equality. We looked at ourselves very, very carefully to see how we could change from board down, and one of the things we realised was that boards are meant to look to the future, but everybody around the table was middle aged or more! What we decided was that at any one time we'd have *two* people under twenty-five on the board. We decided on two at a time because inviting one on their own is less effectual for all the reasons discussed above. There would be a danger of them thinking *I just feel like a fish out of water ... I don't get this ... Who should I speak to? ... Do I know whether I'm thinking in the right way?* Hence the first thing we decided was that we'd have two people so that they could compare notes, talk to each other and be each other's support.

We decided that we would not use jargon, also that every board paper would be written from the perspective that whoever was reading it might never have seen one of these things before, so it was about not making assumptions regarding knowledge and concepts and so on. The thing is, if you do allow inexperienced but talented people to come forward, then you need to make sure there is a mentor on the board for each of the two new appointees.

This was what needed to be done in order to make genuine, structural changes to those organisations and that sort of consideration and effort is still the only way it's going to work.

Experience can be overrated

One of the things that was really fascinating when we first decided we'd have people under the age of twenty-five was that concerns were expressed that appointing very young trustees was not very wise because they don't have enough experience to understand their duty. My response was, 'People aren't born with experience.' If you only select on experience then you'll never get any new people. You'd exclude all women, you'd exclude all the people from the sorts of backgrounds where people just don't discuss that sort of thing, but they may be incredibly talented. You're actually preventing yourself from appointing talent.

Age isn't necessarily what gives people experience either – you could have people who are really elderly but really talented, who have never been on a board before and you're excluding them as well. So if you just say you're looking for people with a capability, regardless of experience, then you're asking yourself the right questions when it comes to appointing people. Then if this person has the capability but doesn't have the experience, what can you do to make sure they have a comfortable ride and they are coming into an environment in which they can thrive? And that means that *any* new person can similarly flourish regardless of age.

Suddenly we had an exciting range of talent through creating the opportunity: women who had never been on boards before; working-class people who had never been on boards before; elderly people who had retired but were incredibly capable, just worried about going on a board . . . All we had to do was change the way we operated, which we did from the board down, and it created a very different and welcoming environment. So, I think we just need to understand that it's to do with capability not experience.

Real change has to be structural change

Unless you make the broader changes to an organisation's decision-making structure you're not going to change things radically. Just to have one chairman who happens to have a view that diversity is a good thing is actually structurally ineffectual, because although that might attract outside attention, the moment that individual's gone everything ricochets back to where it was. What you need is structural

99

change and you're not going to get that until you offer a wider range of opportunities and structured support. That's why I enter at that boardroom level to try and bring about change.

I always will do my best to try and change structures; that is something that I'm not scared to do. I'm lucky enough to have that ability because once you understand a structure you can see where its strengths are, but importantly you can also see where its failings are, where the gaps are, so you can go in and try to fill the gaps or make change where necessary. Or suggest changes to others, and it's great when they do accept suggestions and move things forward.

Make sure you bring your best self

Part of the inner strength needed to get through is trying to see yourself outside the constructs society has imposed, and that is quite a tough ask, because it goes back to the earlier point I made about artificial constructs, and it can get to a point that becomes actually quite dangerous. I learned from the founder of Chineke Orchestra that if you do blind auditions for orchestras, ethnic minorities do very well, and the point at which they stop doing well is the point at which the audition ceases to be blind. In other words the trust that this musician will be a good musician is actually wrapped up in the colour of their skin, rather than their talent.

That is a completely outrageous and ludicrous notion but it tells you an enormous amount about how people essentially look for people like themselves to put into positions of responsibility because that is who they trust. I've met chief executives that have been mediocre in terms of decision-making and other leadership capabilities, but because they were white and male they were trusted by the others on the recruiting panel. That taught me such a salutary lesson because I realised there was too much trust reposed in this external wrapping of white maleness. What we have to do is get people to recognise that talent comes in so many different packages, and to do that talent has to keep presenting itself as unequivocally as possible.

Another construct that is inculcated in us from a very young age is that women tend to focus on what they *can't* do rather than what they can. Too often a woman will go into an interview where she will have 80 per cent of the requirements for the role, but when you come to interview her, she will say 'I can't do this and I can't do that'. Immediately you think to yourself, *You're focusing on the 20 per cent of the stuff, when a man would tell you about the 80 per cent that he can do.* On two occasions I've actually stopped interviews and asked the woman to leave the room, telling her: 'Please go outside, then come back in and tell me about what you *can* do because you wouldn't be here if we hadn't already been convinced of your capability, so don't emphasise the elements you can't do. Focus on your capabilities and come back in and tell us about them.'

While the world is still as it is, in order to facilitate necessary change, what we have to do is bolster ourselves up to give ourselves the resilience we need.

Education should be a rounded experience

I'm a patron of the Sir John Staples Society, which is a splendid enterprise as it fills a gap in so many children's and young people's lives by providing cultural experiences they might not be able to take advantage of because of their backgrounds. The aim is to help foster a wider interest in the arts. To be part of this, for me, is a privilege because I think that giving music, arts and a wider cultural knowledge to children is absolutely critical for their growth as people, their strength, their inner strength. Developing through school isn't about pure academic learning because we're not robots.

This roundedness is so important; it goes beyond school and plays a part in the success of people going out into the world. One of the things I tell young lawyers when they qualify is to make sure they indulge themselves in the arts, sport, whatever it is that is their passion outside of work because every year *thousands* of lawyers qualify. What the client is buying is not only your professional qualification, because there are thousands of other people who have exactly that same qualification – some might even be better – what they're buying is you as an individual. What is it you bring that makes you different, special, interesting, engaging? It may be that you can talk to them about their favourite sport or you can share with them a passion for music, so it's that facet of you that makes you an engaging individual. It will make you understand and analyse their business in a way that's different from the way another lawyer might understand and analyse their business.

In other words, book learning alone isn't going to enable you to build a relationship with your clients and it's that rounded aspect that will set you apart. All the way through, whether it is to get to college, whether it is to get into a good university, whether it is to get you whatever qualification it is you're going to get, then to retaining clients, all of that is predicated on a wider growth and an establishment of a rounded personality.

I've invited a group from one of the schools represented by the Staples Foundation to a concert by the Kanneh Mason family. I'm also a director of the Co-op and the Co-op Academy schools similarly try to give the students a more rounded education. I took the Russian ballet school up to Manchester to do performances for some of the Academy schools in Manchester. There's a heart-rendingly wonderful video of a performance in Manchester with parents and students filmed coming out and being interviewed about how they found it. Some of the parents say things like 'I never expected to see this in Manchester', 'It's wonderful to see this in Manchester'. It made me think, *Oh my goodness, that is incredible!* Manchester's not that far from London so why is it they feel so denuded of an opportunity to see a Russian ballet, a classical ballet? It's almost heartbreaking that it's so difficult for that sort of enjoyment to be more widely seen.

I'm very pleased to be a champion of the arts. I'm chair of Shakespeare's Globe, the theatre established in Southwark, which still has tickets for five pounds, and we have on our board the fantastic headmaster of the Globe Ark Academy. That's another academy that seeks to give a rounded opportunity for the students who might not otherwise have the chance, in the same way as the Staples Foundation. It's really, really important to me that students are given this rounded opportunity.

The Foundation also works with Russell Group universities, connecting them with the schools and academies we work with. This is another reason why the rounding out as part of education is so important, because the Russell Group universities take all of that into consideration and it's so often the applicants from the better schools that have that advantage. People often question whether it is right to work with just the Russell Group universities, but as part of the culture says only people from a certain background go to certain universities it is helpful for these schools to work with those universities so we can widen the opportunities for the young people.

I am also chancellor of a non-Russell Group university, Coventry University, which is a fantastic university doing exactly what these schools are doing in widening opportunity, widening access, and giving rounded support to the students in every way possible. We endeavour to make them work-ready by giving them a hands-on relationship with very many of the university's business partners. The courses are very well integrated with work opportunities, meaning something like 80 per cent of our students come out with a practical knowledge and practical experience of the workplace, so they are job-ready because they've had a year working in a hands-on environment.

One of our partnerships was with Jaguar/Land Rover, where Jaguar/Land Rover supports the university in order to avail itself of the research into workforce capability that the university offers. So it's a fully integrated partnership that gives mutual benefits, and within it, along with other partnerships the university has, we give the students structured support in conjunction to that experience and help them build their networks early.

Hidden histories should be investigated and celebrated

At Coventry we take very seriously the cultural rounding out of our students' life and at the moment we're establishing something called the Gallery of Living History, which will provide curatorial arts, digital research and historic research experience. I, the actor Andy Serkis – who played Gollum in *The Lord of the Rings* – and film producer Jonathan Cavendish who produced films like *Bridget Jones* and *Breath*, have set this up with Coventry University, Coventry City Council and the City of Culture Trust because Coventry was designated the City of Culture 2021. The aim is to give rounded opportunity for students to take part in many arts areas, particularly in digital arts and arts tech, by taking part in the project because it's right across arts curation and historic research.

It came about as a response to George Floyd's death and Andy working with Chadwick Boseman on *Black Panther* and being blown away by him, then going to the première of the film as one of the only two white people (the other was Martin Freeman) and realising that something really special was happening in the film world. Then when the Colston statue was toppled that summer, he felt inspired to do something.

We spoke about what we could do and what we set up is almost like a response. Rather than just saying pull the statues down, we were thinking about how to respond to those statues, so the Gallery of Living History is actually an enterprise that seeks to redress the balance of what is celebrated, by looking at people whose history has been unsung and untold. For example, who is it that actually built the wealth of the industrialist colonizer or owner of enslaved peoples i.e. the philanthropist individual commemorated there? How did they get to where they are? Who else was involved? Everybody knows Coventry Cathedral was bombed and a new cathedral was built, but who built that new cathedral? Before that, who were the firemen who tried really hard to extinguish the flames? Coventry is well known for taking in people and communities: Frederick Douglass, the African American social reformer and abolitionist, came to

Coventry in 1847 as part of his fund-raising campaign to end slavery. Ira Aldridge established his theatre in Coventry, from which he was the first well-known African American exponent of Shakespeare – why was it in Coventry?

We are researching all of this untold, unsung history at the university and establishing the stories. Then we're telling them through digital means and engagement, by talking to people whose forebears might have been involved, enabling multidisciplinary opportunity for the students, which not only brings the stories and characters to life but allows the young people opportunity for wider cultural growth as well as experiencing the tech aspects of the arts. After he'd played Gollum Andy set up a very hi-tech studio called Imaginarium and the Gallery of Living History is in conjunction with that, so we give the young people an opportunity of work experience, research experience, support, masterclasses, mentoring . . . It's potentially really, really exciting.

It's never too soon to learn entrepreneurial skills

In 2014 I met a young man called Julian Hall, who founded Ultra Education, which takes the teaching of entrepreneurial skills into schools. I've been working as a periodic advisor to him and helping him to grow this as an enterprise. We see this teaching as vital because one of the things we realised is that in any school classroom there is a spectrum of capability and neuro-diversity – people are just mentally *different* – but everyone can benefit from learning entrepreneurial skills. Yet the schools system focuses only on those who are purely academic, those who can learn in a specific way. The other young people can only hope to somehow get through, to come out at the other end without having been excluded because they see things differently and they struggle in that environment because the method of teaching doesn't tell them how they can make it work for the subject they might be passionate about.

Julian is from an ordinary background, brought up in Brent, and was a tech entrepreneur. He made his money and then thought, *Well I've become an entrepreneur, I don't see why young people can't similarly become entrepreneurs if the schools system would help them*. He set about facilitating that, began Ultra Education as a business, and when I came across him at a Black business awards event I spoke with him and thought this was such an amazing idea. What we realised was if you actually teach entrepreneurial skills *all* children benefit, the academics as well as the non-academics, because entrepreneurial skills include marketing, communication, business planning, team working, leadership . . . the skills needed, basically, to succeed in the world, as well as English and maths.

We realised that this allowed us to engage with the young people in areas that *they* were interested in. You go into a school and ask, 'What is it you're really passionate about? What do you really enjoy doing?' Then when they tell you, you can see the sparkle, they want to discuss that further, and they're astonished because usually the school would tell them to leave that at the door.

On one occasion Julian was asked to talk to some boys who had been excluded, basically to lecture them on being better people to try and get them back into the school process. It was a sunny Saturday morning and he thought, *These guys are going to lynch me!* He went in with a little pile of yellow cards and a little pile of red cards, gave them out and told them, 'I'm going to talk to you and if you think I'm being patronising or boring, I want you to hold up a yellow card, then I will ask you some questions and I will give answers to some questions you might have, and if you still think I'm being patronising or boring then I will have failed, so hold up a red card and you can leave. I know you don't want to be here.'

Within five minutes two boys had put up their yellow cards. Julian said, 'OK, first of all let me ask you a few questions – what would you like to be doing?' They replied, 'Parkour.' He asked, 'Are you any good? Could you teach me? Could you teach me so I could jump from building to building and not kill myself?' They said, 'Yes we're really, really good and it's easy so of course we could teach you.' That's when Julian started to explain to them if they could do that they could make money out of it, which, of course, they hadn't considered.

He began to explain that first of all they'd need clients, so to be able to communicate with the clients they'd need a decent standard of English. He told them he'd made his money out of tech: if they reached people through digital technology they could get a wide audience, but they'd need some basic maths. His next question was, 'Where do you teach your parkour? Anywhere? In the countryside?' 'No, no, in the town.' 'Any town or any city? 'Yeah.' 'Eastbourne?' 'Yeah. Why not?' 'Have you ever been to Eastbourne? It has a population probably 80 per cent over the age of sixty.' 'Oh! We'd rather be somewhere with younger people.' Julian explained to them they'd need to understand the demographic make-up of the cities in which they'd would best get their clients, which meant basic geography. He let the boys know if they worked at school they'd have a much better chance of establishing a successful business because they'd know what to do.

Those boys sat and listened to him for the rest of the morning. They'd been given six months by the school to turn themselves around and went back perfectly happy because now they understood how the school system would help them with what they wanted to do. Six months later they were great students because they could see the point of what was being offered to them.

I was educated at one of the Girls' Public Day School Trust schools, and put Julian in contact with them. One of the schools, which is quite mixed but predominantly white asked Julian to talk there and they liked him so much they made him resident entrepreneur. It was fantastic to see a young Black guy teaching slighty more privileged female students, because his scheme works so well it works right across the board. When we were in Brent in some schools we were giving hope to young people who might not otherwise have hope, and here a member of the Girls' Day School Trust was recognising his skills and how they could be of benefit to their girls.

Something else that is impressive about Ultra Education is that people who go into the arts seldom learn entrepreneurial skills – one of the sad things about this country is we don't actually support our artists in the right way. We saw it through the pandemic: when the furlough systems were set up it was the accountants, the HR people, the people who were working within the system who were supported – the freelancers, who are the creatives, had no structured support. If they had structured support through schemes like Ultra Education and they had actually learned early on how to set up their own business structures they might well have had a much better chance of making the case for structured support, because they would have had the network to collaborate and organise themselves to survive the downtimes better.

There's an awful lot to be said for teaching these skills from an early age – (Ultra Education begins at age seven) – particularly for that 50 per cent of young people who merely survive school, or who get excluded and could end up in prison because they're the entrepreneurial types who don't recognise structures as well. Something like 80 per cent of our prison population has a neurodiversity like autism or dyslexia and if we focused in the right way on supporting them in school, we could reduce the prison population dramatically. The expenditure that's lost in incarceration or in victim support could actually be at the front end, identifying how to look after these young people properly within the school structure.

Ultra Education is a really important scheme and I wish we could roll it out more, I wish we could get governments to listen better.

Lessons

Being the first to do something is incredibly hard because there is no-one to teach you. For young Margaret that meant understanding the pressure to succeed, knowing that if she failed she would have taken down others who were following in her footsteps.

Build your network so that in times of doubt you have a community that will help keep you buoyed up.

Recruit based on capability not experience, as seeing someone's future potential not past experience will help create a more balanced talent pool. In turn, candidates must focus on their

strengths and what it is they can do, not what they can't do or have been schooled to believe they can't do.

Spend as much time building your character, passions, thought leadership, and community as you do on your professional qualifications. It's the former traits that help people cut through in today's business world.

Affirmation: Today I can and today I will.

'The Visionary'

SOPHIE CHANDAUKA MBE

◆

Corporate finance and technology executive Sophie Chandauka went to school and college on three different continents: Africa, North America, and Europe. Sophie was born and raised in Zimbabwe. She earned a Rotary International scholarship to attend high school in Ontario, Canada. Whilst completing her undergraduate studies in politics and international relations in Michigan, USA, she enjoyed a year at the University of Birmingham in the UK learning about the laws governing the European Union. She completed her education with post-graduate studies in law at Oxford. Until early 2022, Sophie worked in New York as Global COO of Shared Services and Banking Operations for Morgan Stanley, a leading Wall Street investment bank. Before this, she worked for the Virgin Group as Head of Treasury for the legal function of Virgin Money where she played a key role in the flotation/IPO of the company. This followed several years as a Senior Associate working in London at Baker McKenzie where she played a major part in such high-profile acquisitions such as L'Oréal's takeover of The Body Shop and Nike's acquisition of Umbro. In January 2022, Sophie started a new role as Head of America's Risk Management and Intelligence at Meta, the parent company of Facebook, Instagram and WhatsApp amongst others. She is a fully remote working employee, mostly splitting her time between New York, London and South Africa.

This incredible journey was inspired by the powerful images of aspirational and affluent Black working families and professionals that Sophie saw on TV shows such as *The Fresh Prince of Bel Air*, *Desmond's*, *The Cosby Show* and the *Oprah Winfrey Show*. Sophie was determined to achieve the same level of success and to contribute to the narrative of Black excellence through her own work and by amplifying the achievement of others. In 2014, she co-founded the Black British Business Awards – the BBBAwards. This organisation is devoted to highlighting the business excellence and talent among the UK's Black population – an aspect too often overlooked by mainstream media. Sophie remains the organisation's Chair and chief strategist, and since 2014, the BBBAwards has become more than a ceremony – it is a catalyst for change working closely with policymakers, academia and corporations around the world on issues of diversity, equity and inclusion in the workplace and the opportunities to improve the attraction, retention and promotion of Black and other racial and ethnic minorities into senior roles.

As a campaigner for diversity, equity and inclusion, Sophie is Chair and Chief Strategist of The Network of Networks (TNON). TNON works with over 130 companies to create inclusive environments that support the attraction, retention and advancement of racial and ethnic minority professionals. She is also the Head of Race Equity Strategy for the 30% Club, a member of The Executive Leadership Council (ELC) and a member of the Advisory Board for the Kellogg Institute for international Studies at the University of Notre Dame.

Sophie was awarded the MBE in 2021 for services to diversity in business.

Sheer persistence can pay off

I was born and raised in Zimbabwe, in southern Africa, two years before the country gained independence. My father still lives in Zimbabwe, while my mother lives in South Africa. During my childhood, a lot of African countries were becoming independent, so I had the wonderful privilege of being able to live in a place where the words '*your voice matters*' were not loosely held concepts – they were a reality and critical to the liberation of Black people. We were living next door to South Africa during apartheid and Nelson Mandela was a powerful figure, even though he was in prison. The visuals around us reinforced this message – people taking to the streets and singing about the right to vote and making sure democracy prevails – these scenes were very real to us. From an early age, I was inspired by the idea of having "*agency*" to define my own destiny. In Nelson Mandela I saw firsthand the changes that a single person could inspire in others, and I learned those individual actions, when combined with the actions of others, can transform the world.

I wanted to see the world. I was inspired to do so because of the TV shows I watched whilst I was a teenager in Zimbabwe. I watched *The Fresh Prince of Bel Air*, *Desmond's*, *The Cosby Show* and the *Oprah Winfrey Show* and MTV. These were amazing portrayals of Black families and Black success across the globe – and I wanted to be in all those places too! Not because Black people on the African continent were not amazing and phenomenal – because they *were* – but I also wanted to see other parts of the world. I knew the only way I could convince my parents to allow me to move was if I could connect it to the pursuit of education. When all my peers were at the mall or going out to parties, I used to go to the US Information Services or the British Council on Friday afternoons to grab books, brochures and apply for scholarships.

I was so motivated by the idea that education could change my life, and I could see that, for all these amazing families on TV, education was a big part of their lives. I even went as far as writing to Michael Jackson because I thought that maybe, just maybe, he could lend me some money so I could get a good education abroad and travel the world at the same time. I would pay him back of course!

I kept applying and soon enough I got my first scholarship to complete a year abroad at a Canadian school! I was sixteen and lived in a small town called Sault Ste Marie. After the year was done, I returned to Zimbabwe where the political environment was slowly deteriorating. There was conflict because of President Robert Mugabe's divisive land redistribution policy which sought to return farming land to Black people from white farmers without due process. President Mugabe's government made some decisions that were disastrous for the future of the country. We started to see fractures among various

113

stakeholders and the economy plummeted because of social unrest and chaos in the governance of the country. This made international news headlines. Before long, one of my Canadian host families took it upon themselves to go to the local high school in Ontario, where they obtained my transcript and took it across the river to the university in Michigan in the US. There, they had a conversation with the board of governors at Lake Superior State University (LSSU) about me; they explained I was now back in Zimbabwe where things were not working. They asked if the organisation would consider awarding me a scholarship to study at LSSU.

As a result, I received another scholarship and studied at LSSU in America. All this time, however, I felt a strong affinity to the Commonwealth. I realised that I didn't want to qualify as an American lawyer – I wanted to qualify in and practice English law. Fortunately, I received *another* scholarship that took me to the UK for the very first time, studying at the University of Birmingham for one year during my undergraduate studies. I received one more scholarship for my post-graduate studies in law, during which I spent some time in Oxford, before starting my career in the city of London in September 2003 as a trainee corporate lawyer at Baker McKenzie.

It was all about having big dreams, tenacity and, importantly, the audacity to believe that anything was possible with the help of others!

Encourage other people's big dreams

My parents played a big part in allowing me to follow my dreams; they never stopped me from having ambitious pursuits. The never told me, 'that's unreal, it's never going to happen.' I sometimes tell people that 'Mama made me a pair of wings'. My parents encouraged me to be bold and to keep trying. Even now, I still live by that philosophy or daring greatly and, when I get bored, I feel comfortable to change my mind and do other things in life. That comes from my parents never stopping me from having big dreams and experimenting.

I believe in the power of visualisation – if you can imagine it, and have the willpower to go for it, then you can do it! The important thing is getting started in the first place and never giving up.

There can be goodness in perfect strangers

None of my journey would have been possible without the generosity of perfect strangers. In addition to my three Canadian adopted families, other everyday people have supported me in various ways. That's been the story of my life: perfect strangers believing in what I was dreaming about and committing to supporting me in ways that they could.

Looking at my own story, where it all began and where I am now, I have every reason to believe that most people are good: if it wasn't for good people, I wouldn't be where I am today. As a result of this good fortune, I am also acutely aware that there are small decisions that we make every single day about whether to intervene, contribute, believe, support, sponsor or invest in people, and these small decisions can fundamentally impact the trajectory of their lives. All in all, having loving parents, siblings, relatives, friends and thoughtful perfect strangers – has allowed me to have what I think is a really *blessed* life.

Be the change you wish to see

As a young Black girl who came from Africa, I wanted to be able to create a world where Black people could be relevant and respected in every single situation and place of influence. That is why I mentor others – so I can see my people represented in all the places where decisions are made and power resides. I realise that I have ways and means of contributing to the effort of ensuring that Black people are represented in *every* room that matters. There are many rooms that were not, and are not, open to us. I get up in the morning because I want to defy the odds and mobilise changemakers that will work together to ensure better prospects for my people in the future.

Sometimes practicality should be allowed to trump idealism

My original plan was to be a human rights lawyer, like Nelson Mandela. But while I was doing my post-grad, I realised that I loved business related subjects and I also had an entrepreneurial flair. I felt like a natural, and when I got my training contract to work in a city law firm, I found I could do corporate and commercial law; I loved the transactional aspects of the work and clients also enjoyed working with me. Being the pragmatist that I am, I made a decision on the basis that I could make more money being a corporate finance lawyer, and therefore better support my family. I was very well aware that Zimbabwe was on the verge of collapse – so I pursued a career that gave me enough financial freedom to contribute to raising my cousins. The responsibility to my family was a very big motivator for my choice of specialism in commercial law.

Work shouldn't be a popularity contest

When I was in London, I was motivated by working with lawyers who were wired to succeed. However, it soon became obvious that something odd was happening because I couldn't see Black senior lawyers in my organisation, in fact, there were no partners who were Black, or at least not visibly so. Law firms tend to recruit some years in advance, so I could see they hadn't recruited a single Black person into the future cohorts I had met. The insider/outsider dynamics were apparent from the get-go. After work on my first day, I called my mum in tears and I said, '*You know Mama, it kind of feels like day one at nursery school when nobody wants to play with you and you literally have no friends.*' She gave me some simple advice. She said: '*You're there to do a job. Do that well, and if you make friends at the same time, then that's the icing on the cake.*' Acting on the advice my mum gave me, I made a decision: I was going to keep my eye on the prize and work hard, regardless of the external factors – I was diligent, effective and efficient.

I was always the outsider; when people invited each other out for weekend plans, I never got the invitations. Even when people went for lunch I didn't get invited. But it didn't matter – I felt like I was doing something that was bigger than me. I focused on the work and did the basics brilliantly – and it paid off. Clients would ask for *me* to be on their accounts repeatedly. One thing for sure is this – when clients speak, the senior managers listen. I garnered the support of influential people in the firm because of this – they couldn't ignore a talented person who the clients liked.

As I began work working on relatively high-profile projects at an early stage in my career, the legal industry noticed. I was not the one who won the popularity contest in the firm, but my good work was recognised – I received various prestigious industry awards in the early years, and this made me a valuable asset for the firm and its franchise.

I always tell people – young people – that there will be times when insider/outsider dynamics may make you feel like you're not good enough. It may feel quite lonely at work, but there are other ways that credibility and credentials will come. In my case, it was the clients and the industry awards that made the senior managers pay attention. I was not always invited to colleagues' birthday parties at the weekend, but in terms of what the firm was there to do – delivering value to clients – I was solid at that and received sponsorship from key people in the firm because of that. That gave me the ability and confidence to become an insider – on different terms from the others. I was an insider because I had a good reputation and the partners believed that I had the potential for a successful long career at the firm. There are different ways of getting validated and it's not always going to be through popularity!

However, let's not kid ourselves –how you feel at work matters, and if you can't quite figure out how you're going to have a sense of belonging, fulfilment and validation at work, it's a *big* issue and should be addressed. Maybe that firm or profession is not where you should be. You do not have to contort yourself to fit in. If you are emotionally taxed in ways that deplete you, then it's almost impossible to put your energy into doing the work you were hired to do, as you're caught up in playing a game and pretending to be someone else. That can be depressing and exhausting, and it will prevent you from finding any joy in the work. People will notice when you are not being your best self, and you will not be given the most interesting assignments. This will result in you being both unhappy and unable to engage with the work that allows you to reach your full potential. Go somewhere else that will make you happy!

It's not surprising diversity action has taken so long, but it is changing

It doesn't surprise me that action on racial diversity, equity and inclusion is slow, because it's a challenging issue. Commercially speaking, the extent to which an organisation is prepared to invest in resolving an issue is tightly connected to how much the issue impacts the bottom line. The sad truth is that, for many years, businesses could not see the 'business case' for focusing on race equity as part of their key investment strategies – they could not see the correlation with business growth or profitability.

Businesses are here to deliver long-term value to shareholders whilst taking into account their impact to the communities they serve. However, up until the summer of 2020 – shareholders had not taken strong action for race equity at a systemic level. As a business person, I'm not surprised at this. But, as a citizen of the world, I would have expected more prior to 2020. However, I believe that where there's a will, there's a way, and we are starting to see a different climate now.

I've been working for strategically important institutions in the City of London, on Wall Street and now Silicon Valley since 2003, and I've seen tremendous change since the summer of the tragic death of George Floyd. There has been an intense focus on race equity from investors and regulators which will, I believe, continue. For example, in 2021, the UK's Financial Conduct Authority started saying they are looking at culture, values, conduct and board representation, and will start asking for disclosure regarding these matters for publicly traded companies on the London Stock Exchange. Similar action has been seen by regulators in the US. When regulators begin to change their policies, key stakeholders in the economy focus on the relevant issues differently – they have to.

We have seen shareholders begin to introduce new policies and vote against companies that are doing poorly on race equity and representation. This has been significantly impactful in terms of converting what was perceived largely as a moral concern, into a moral concern that has *commercial implications*. Shareholders are requiring companies to adopt effective strategies, plans and metrics in their annual reports.

A lot of corporations are thinking more deeply, and in a more exacting way, about what is it they have to do to improve their cultures for inclusion and to recalibrate their processes, practices and procedures to promote race equity and to ensure more positive outcomes when it comes to attracting, retaining and promoting talent for racial and ethnic minority groups. I don't think there's a public company that's not thinking about this.

The game changer is going to be when companies decide to set ambitious targets and begin to embrace public accountability for progress on sensitive subjects such as representation in senior roles and on ethnicity pay gaps. Investors, policymakers and regulators are requiring more, and so the future looks hopeful in the corporate world, but that is only one small domain. There are other structures in broader society that need to be reconsidered – education and healthcare, for example – that impact the wider population in significant ways on a day-to-day basis. Society is on a journey that's more inspiring than ever, and that's fantastic – but we have some deep and difficult work to do to advocate for and ensure change at an accelerated pace.

If it's not there and it's needed, build it

I co-founded the Black British Business Awards for the same reason I'm involved in mentoring. When London hosted the Olympic Games in 2012, we were immersed in these amazing visuals, showing the city at its best. But in the months leading up to the Olympics, there had been serious riots. The media portrayed these riots as largely instigated by Black people. I thought ... *here we are, all eyes on us, and this is how they depict Black people.* I watched a BBC interview where there was a young girl called Mercy who attended a primary school in Hackney, and she'd been one of the torch bearers. The morning after she was asked, 'How did it feel?' and she replied that she was just so grateful to be there because she 'didn't think they would allow people like us!'. That really struck me. It was as if she was already convinced that she was going to be disqualified on the basis of how her community was depicted months before. I thought ... *we've got to find a different way of depicting our relevance to London and to the narrative of Great Britain.*

Hence, I co-founded the Black British Business Awards – BBBAwards – in 2014, which is firstly intended to be a beacon to young people who have aspirations, a message that they belong and they can do it; secondly, to respond to the common refrain that says Black talent in business doesn't exist. We exist, and we exist in meaningful numbers. The BBBAwards have been growing from strength to strength, and I would love to find a way of making it a global campaign that elevates the global Black brand across continents.

While the heart of the BBBAwards is ceremonial, we also kickstarted a lot of systems and culture change work. We help multinational companies to recalibrate the way they operate in order to promote greater inclusion through systemic change. We advise companies regarding what they need to do to attract, retain and promote talented Black and other ethnic minority professionals. The BBBAwards is not just a series of amazing red-carpet events – it's a community of excellent companies that are focused on driving inclusion and supporting future leaders from the Black community. If we can be a catalyst for systemic change, then I think that that will be a phenomenal legacy.

I have a tremendous respect for the art form of storytelling. That's one of the elements that I love so much about the BBBAwards – we tell stories about the experiences of being Black professionals or entrepreneurs in the context of Great Britain. There is a need for us to understand each other and to be honest about the difficulty of the journey, figuring out whether we can make it any easier one for future generations. The conversation we're having with business leaders is about how their employees experience life in these unfamiliar workplaces – the 'employee life cycle' is the technical expression. We discuss at what points in that cycle we see peaks and troughs in terms of participation, engagement and retention of Black people and other minorities. We look at hiring, onboarding, induction, promotion, mobility and more. How do you do structure and run these activities? What outcomes are they producing? Are the processes effective? Do they produce differentiated outcomes for Black people? Then there are those tough decisions to be made around reduction of workforce – also known as redundancies and retrenchments: how are those decisions made and does the methodology have a disproportionate impact to some demographics in your workforce?

These are not simple discussions, as they are with organisations that have had various systems and processes which have existed for decades. But this is about shifting hearts, minds and decision making. It's also about creating safe spaces where we can have honest conversations. We see ourselves as the outside third party that can referee or broker new ways of working, suggesting how to perhaps experiment in one department, and if it's effective, scale up.

I'm pleased to say that the business world is taking us seriously. We have incredible sponsors and a wonderful list of companies that partner with us. The BBBAwards have had the privilege of working with excellent international brands including Baker McKenzie, Barclays, Bloomberg, Credit Suisse, Goldman Sachs, J.P. Morgan, Meta, Ralph Lauren, Virgin and Visa. From a sector and systems-change perspective, we're *driving* change at significant levels through cross company collaboration. There's no other way it could work; we need this level of collective action in order to see impactful change at scale and on the wider community.

Our aim is to challenge the status quo and lead from the front through strategic partnerships for years to come.

Lessons

Understand from a very early age that education can transform lives. For young Sophie, that meant hustling hard for scholarships and financial aid.

Share your wildest gravity-defying dreams with everybody. Sometimes even a perfect stranger can help you realise your biggest dream.

Do all the basics of your job brilliantly, it sets you up for success and to be on the short list when the big deals come.

Understand that you deserve to find work in a place that gives you a sense of belonging, fulfilment and validation in return for the work you do.

Affirmation: Today I will help others to see how they can make their dreams come true!

'The Changemaker'

PROFESSOR FRANK CHINEGWUNDOH MBE

◆

It took Frank Chinegwundoh seventeen years of training to reach his position as one of the most respected urologists in Britain – he is a Consultant Urological Surgeon at Barts Health NHS Trust; he also works within the private medical sector and is an Honorary Senior Lecturer at the University of London. He is a Fellow of the Royal College of Surgeons and a Fellow of the European Board of Urology. Prior to that he was Clinical Director of Surgery and Anaesthesia at Newham University Hospital NHS Trust, Visiting Professor in Urology to the University Teaching Hospital of Enugu, Nigeria and Visiting Professor in the School of Health Sciences, City, University of London and was Vice President, Europe, of the African Organisation for Research and Training in Cancer (2017-2021).

Determined to redress some of the inequalities that exist within the British healthcare system, for the last twenty-six years Frank has been part of the voluntary organisation Cancer Black Care (and Chairman since 1998), devoted to raising awareness of cancer and providing support for patients within Britain's Black population. He is a trustee of the National Federation of Prostate Cancer Support Groups; for over ten years he was a trustee of Prostate Action, funding research into the fight against prostate cancer; and he is on the management committee of Reach Society, a social enterprise dedicated to encouraging and motivating Black boys and young Black men to fully realise their potential.

Frank Chinegwundoh was awarded the MBE in 2013 for services to the NHS. In 2022, he became a founding trustee of the British Association of Black Surgeons.

It's never too early to take responsibility

I was the eldest of four children, growing up in south London, and it was very much the expectation, whether said or unsaid, that I would lead the way and set the example for my siblings. So, from quite a young age I was always aware of that responsibility on my shoulders – if the parents were out then you had to look after the younger ones.

It wasn't a case of having to work at assuming this responsibility; I knew nothing different so whether it was easy or hard never occurred to me, that's just how it was. My parents are Nigerians who came across at the end of the fifties and I'm assuming this is something they brought with them.

If it's worthwhile it's worth working for

I wanted to do something surgery-wise rather than medical-wise, because I found surgery more interesting; I just liked the idea of being able to do something physical and to directly intervene using manual skills as opposed to intervening via tablets or medicines. On that path, for me to become a Consultant Urological Surgeon took twelve years, and that was after five years at medical school. Once you qualify from med school, depending on what you want to do – general practice or surgery or medicine – there's another period of study which could be of varying lengths. I qualified at twenty-three and became a consultant at thirty-five, and that was young! It wasn't unusual for doctors to be pushing forty before they reached the top of the tree, so to speak; in fact I was one of the youngest consultants in urology at the time and in 1996 the first Black–British urological surgeon.

You're working while you're doing this so you're gaining more and more experience as you go through the grades. There are lots of very difficult exams to be done along the way, with low pass rates, but while you're studying you're gaining the experience: how to deal with patients; how to recognise certain conditions; whether you need to operate and so on. You have to do research as well: I took two years out to do a research degree which was genetics-based in a laboratory, to write a thesis for a Master of Surgery degree. On the way to becoming a consultant you have to write papers, present research at international meetings . . . there are a lot of things you have to do to make yourself competitive.

You have to go through the various grades of increasing seniority, and each grade level is achieved by competitive entry. You start off applying for a Senior House Officer, as it was then, by competition, so you go to several interviews. You then apply for a registrar's job, the next level up; again, that's by competitive interview and I went to several interviews before, eventually, I was successful. And even then I had to leave London because I couldn't get a registrar's job in the capital, so I went to Birmingham. Once you've become a registrar, there's another competitive interview to become a *senior* registrar. Then you get a crack at being a consultant. You've got be extremely motivated to get through it all.

It never occurred to me to give up, or even not to carry on up the levels. What kept me going was I felt I was good at it, and I saw no reason why I shouldn't be able to achieve the same levels as all my peers. There were quite a few situations where I didn't get the job that I should have got for no very good reason I could determine other than the colour of my skin, but I was determined that I was going to make it. It's the old adage about working twice as hard . . . so I did!

Another motivation was an Egyptian consultant urologist who was maybe ten or fifteen years ahead of me, who had had it even harder than I did. He came from Egypt, with English not his first language and with a heavy accent, then through sheer hard work and no small degree of persistence he made it to become a consultant at a teaching hospital. I thought, *Well if he can make it and I've got the advantage of being born here and understand the system here, I should be able to make it too.*

Sometimes it takes more than just hard work

One of the things I learned from the Egyptian surgeon was how you have to *reduce* the things that people can hold against you, which would therefore prevent them from giving you a job. For example, they could say, 'You've not written as many papers' or 'You've not presented at enough meetings' or 'You're not able to do this particular operation' or 'You've not done enough teaching at medical schools', and so on. What you had to do was to cover all the bases as that reduced the grounds on which they could deny you a job – make sure you write the papers, present at the meetings, do the teaching . . . Which is what I did; I made sure I covered all the bases and that there weren't any weak areas. Whether it was academic or clinical or operative, there wasn't anything about it which would cause someone to say, 'Well, you're not quite up to the mark.' And eventually, when you do that, sooner or later you're going to get the job, you're going to get the break. And that's what happened to me, at each level.

The other very important lesson that I learned very early on was that I had to get myself in front of the consultant who I was applying for a job with. Back in the eighties it was common practice, and I saw this myself, for the applications for a junior post to come in and as the consultant hadn't got time to go through all of them the first cull was of any name that wasn't obviously English. The thinking was, in the 1980s, that anybody whose name didn't seem English wasn't English and doctors from overseas weren't regarded as highly as somebody who was trained here. Also, it was a commonly held 'wisdom' that there would be a language problem.

My surname is Chinegwundoh, so they wouldn't even have looked at my CV – it would just get tossed straight in the bin. I was advised that what I had to do was get face time with the consultant I was applying for a job with, to put myself in front of them, physically, as much as possible, before the shortlist was done. This was so they could see that I was born and bred in the UK, and my language skills were as good as anyone else's, that I am British. Black British. It meant that others could just put the application in and wait, but I had to not only apply but then badger the consultant's secretary to get some face time in front of them. Essentially, I would have to impress the consultant with my credentials and personality and I was able to do that because I get on with people, I always have, so it worked pretty well.

It was just what you had to do in those days; it's changed now for the better and the reason it's become fairer is partly because people like me led the way, although there's more to it than that. The whole selection process has changed and now you have national interviews. If you want to become a registrar, which is halfway along the road to becoming a consultant, you go for national selection. It's no longer dependent on the local consultant either liking you or not liking you, so personalities and prejudices come into it much less. You go for *national* interviews that are held once a year and you're interviewed by several different people from all over the country, then you're scored according to your portfolio. It's a pretty fair system now.

If you build it they will come

I'm Chair of Cancer Black Care, a registered charity that's been going since 1996. It was started by a gentleman of Ghanaian origin called Isaac Dweben, after the death of his older brother from prostate cancer. Isaac found very little information about prostate cancer for people like him or specifically for Black people, so he set up the organisation. I think he came across me through a friend of a friend and he asked me to give talks in the community about prostate cancer to raise awareness of it and the importance of testing for it before any symptoms – the PSA blood test. I was involved with the charity pretty much from the outset, became a trustee once it was registered, then from 1998 have been the Chairman.

Cancer Black Care has been through thick and thin, we've expanded and we've contracted over the years, but it's still going and our unique selling point is it's still supporting the BAME community, although anyone that wants to can access its services. We offer counselling, we offer support with the welfare benefits system for cancer sufferers and their carers, we provide a monthly meeting group where people get together and talk about things of interest, we might bring in an external speaker to talk about nutrition or whatever it is. We work quite closely with Macmillan Cancer Trust and we've worked with another charity called Orchid to deliver a big Lottery-funded project.

Cancer Black Care does various things: primarily it's there to support individual patients on a one-to-one basis, but it has a collaborative role and also a policy role in terms of lobbying and advising. A very good example of what we've achieved is that many years ago if you'd had breast cancer, you'd had a mastectomy and wanted a prosthesis, all that was available were pink prostheses and if you're brown or Black or whatever, that's really not great, especially given the inherent trauma of the situation. Why can't Black women have Black prostheses? It was simply something those in charge hadn't considered because it hadn't occurred to them. So it was me, through Cancer Black Care and one or two other charities, who lobbied the powers that be to let them know we needed Black and brown prostheses. Now they are available, and it came about because people and groups have lobbied and said, 'This isn't right! You should be doing better for my community!'

Cancer Black Care and other specifically Black cancer and medical organisations have proved remarkably successful, and made the point that because not everybody is the same not everybody can be approached in the same manner when it comes to offering potentially life-saving care. Breast cancer provides another example. Every year at meetings I was going to, people from the Department of Health were saying 'Black women don't go for breast cancer screenings' and after the third year of hearing the same statistic I asked, 'Well, what are you doing about it? If Black women aren't going for their breast cancer screenings, what are you doing about it?' I told them if they gave me the funding I would do something about it, I would show them how you can up their numbers for breast cancer screening. Which I did.

I worked with another breast cancer charity, a Black organisation called Better Days, and what we decided to do was recruit what we called 'patient navigators' – they introduce the patients to whatever the process is – but ones that would appear understanding and welcoming to the women we wanted to reach. Better Days and I got a list from Kings College Breast Cancer Screening of six hunded Black women who had been invited for screening but didn't turn up, then we raised funding from Public Health England (as it was then) to employ two middle-aged Black women who contacted the names on that list, usually by phone, to find out why they hadn't attended. They were able to book those who wanted screening directly onto a screening programme and we converted a lot of those absentees into attenders.

It worked, because by employing the women we did we offered a welcoming, familiar-sounding approach to something that otherwise might seem cold and clinical – then Public Health England told us it was too expensive. So although we proved it could be done if you had the political will to do it and the money to do it, the funding wasn't continued after the first year.

There are various projects that I have been involved in that take a community-specific view on how to reach people where conventional methods might not. For example, many years ago, I set up a men's prostate clinic in Newham, and showed that if you set up a service that men could just drop into, men will come and will have their PSA blood test done – that's a blood test specifically for screening for prostate cancer – and will have the rectal examination. There is something about setting up services in the community that is very different from setting up services in the GP surgery, or in the hospital: it removes the *officialness* that in certain areas causes mistrust and the informality of not needing an appointment made it very convenient.

Of course it worked; we showed – and this was actually published – that we found all these prostate cancers that wouldn't otherwise have been detected. But again, the same issue – 'Great, you've shown that this works, but we're not going to fund it any more.' It was so disappointing, so I approached the charity Prostate Cancer UK to see if they wanted to take over the funding of it and they said, basically, 'No.' However, it did inspire a similar project in Nottingham where the local health authority have funded a very similar thing to what I did in Newham – a drop-in service for men to find out about their prostates and get themselves tested, if they wish – and that's still going. Which means some good came out of what I did in Newham.

My big frustrations, which lead me to doubt how serious the authorities are about improving the health of Black people, is that you demonstrate how to do it, and you show results, yet they don't want to continue the funding.

Just because a thing is hard, there's no excuse not to try

Frustrating as it can be, I'll still get out of bed in the morning and push for something else because you live in hope! For example, what if I was able to get a national screening programme for prostate cancer where men would be invited, rather than men having to know about prostate cancer and go to their GPs? If there was a national screening programme then all these men would be encompassed in that. That's my big ambition, and so if the funders choose not to fund community initiatives, then I'll try something different. I'm still dreaming of coming across a philanthropist with some money – a Black 'Bill Gates', who's willing to back me to set up what I think we need to do for our community's health.

Get involved

I sit on the Department of Health group the Bowel Screening Advisory Committee and the United Kingdom Lung Cancer Coalition, plus I've been Chair of the Prostate Cancer Advisory Group and advised the Department of Health on what they should be doing in terms of prostate cancer. I still work closely with Prostate Cancer UK, where currently we're trying to get prostate cancer screening as a national thing, I work with organisations such as the men's health charity

CHAPS and Tackle Prostate Cancer, also known as the National Federation of Prostate Cancer Support Groups, that are all trying to lobby and say, 'Why don't you screen for prostate cancer in the UK?'

I believe it's really important that we have representation at these policy-making bodies, that Black people get involved on committees on a national level as well as a local level, so take part in discussions on issues that aren't simply Black issues but that affect the population. It's vital we show ourselves as being part of the wider conversations.

It's when you get on to these boards that you're in with a chance of influencing things, because the people on these bodies are, mostly, very reasonable people but they have a different background, and tend to be coming at things all from the same perspective. This is why you need diversity of thoughts, so when you point certain things out to them then they listen and if they are able to they can make changes. It's important to be there; even though it can be time consuming I try really hard to keep up with what's going on and go to these meetings.

But therein lies a big difficulty – how do you get on to these bodies? You've essentially got to be invited, so someone has to know about you, so too often it becomes a matter of who you know. Because, and this is going back to the 1990s, I've done research and I had shown that Black men had a twofold risk of getting prostate cancer, that got me known in the prostate cancer world, which led to getting invited on to, for example, the prostate cancer advisory group, which is a national Department of Health body.

So you have to get known before you get invited on to these national committees, but that shouldn't put people off as it's much like I had to do when I was up and coming and I had to put myself about and get in front of the consultants. The more of us that sit on the national bodies, the better, so people should use every means at their disposal to try and do this. If you can't get there one way then try another.

If you can, you should

Making myself available, especially to the community, is very important. I don't want to say I came from the streets, because I didn't come from the streets in that sense; I was born and bred in inner London and went to a tough primary school, then I managed to get into a grammar school. It was state schools all the way, I didn't go to a top private school and have a silver spoon in my mouth, so I was very much grounded in the community. As I was growing up a lot of people took a lot of interest in me and took pride in what I was doing so I always felt supported by my community. Now I believe if you've had that level of support and you have the opportunity to give back, then you should. That's always been my ethos.

I've always felt a man of the people, therefore it's important that I don't distance myself from the community. Whether that's with Cancer Black Care or it's with Reach Society, an organisation of Black professionals that helps Black youth fulfil its potential, or with various other organisations that I'm part of, I try to be visible and available. I give lots of talks to various community groups that ask me to talk about whatever it is – prostate cancer – or go into schools and try and talk to the kids, take assembly, Yes, I think being visible is important.

Also, in the 1980s and 1990s there were relatively few Black consultants or Black *British* consultants, – I was the first Black British urologist, not the first Black urologist because there were are a handful who had come from overseas and become consultants, but in terms of being born and bred in the UK I was the first one to go through the system like that. Although it's better now, even in 2021 there are still not very many of us. I think it helps when somebody has visibly made it because I'm a great believer in 'You can be what you can see', therefore if I'm visible others will see that it is possible and hopefully this will inspire them to get to where they want to be.

The NHS still has a way to go as regards equality and diversity

I set up and ran, for about ten years, the Black and Ethnic Minority Section within the Royal Society of Medicine (RSM), then much against our wishes the RSM decided it wasn't well enough supported, as they put it, and it wasn't bringing in the money and therefore closed us down. However, it did a lot of good things in those ten years. We shone a light on various conditions that affect Black and ethnic minority patients, so we had a lot of meetings on maternity, pediatrics, skin conditions that affect Black people, sickle cell, HIV, cancer and so on. A lot of things just don't get the focus and the attention that they should.

It was incredibly useful, but they shut us down and now, interestingly, since the whole Black Lives Matter movement blew up in 2020, various bodies like British Medical Association have set up a BAME section, the Independent Doctors Federation have a BAME section, and the Royal College of Surgeons of England have published a study looking at diversity and inclusion and highlighted that they are a long way short of where they should be. So although they shut us down, this seems to show there is a need still to set up groups to focus on our needs and our wants and to inform the mainstream. The mainstream does listen to groups like this, even if it isn't always obvious.

However, in terms of how both patients and staff are treated, change is happening very slowly. There is a publication every year called the National Cancer Patients Experience Survey, a huge survey of cancer sufferers that asks upwards of sixty-four very detailed questions as to respondents' cancer experiences. Every year Black cancer sufferers say they have a less good experience in terms of their cancer journey; this has been consistent for several years, so there's clearly still some work to be done until their experience mirrors that of white patients. Baroness Helena Kennedy published a study in 2021 with the Royal College of Surgeons of England and if you look at that publication it is very clear there is a long way to go for Black surgeons in terms of their career aspirations, in terms of getting into top positions, in terms of being represented at the decision-making bodies of the surgical associations. We've set up the British Association of Black Surgeons to address this, and I now think that the pace of change is too slow, that something more needs to be done.

Change won't happen unless you're proactive about it

I remember in 1996 going to Barts in London and when I looked at their organisational pictogram, a who's who of the Chief Executive, the Chairman, the Finance Director, the HR team and so on, it was completely white. When I gave a talk there in 2020 for Black History Month, nearly twenty-five years later and as one of the senior staff, the leadership pictogram was exactly the same in the lack of diversity. It was all white, not a single Black face. I think there may have been one Asian face, but basically the only difference in nearly a quarter of a century was you had more women there in executive positions. In terms of people that look like me, there had been no shift.

The decision-making bodies in the health service need to take a look at what has been done in politics: thirty or forty years ago, there were relatively very few female MPs and I know that both the Tories and Labour made it their mission to get more women into politics. And how did they do that? They had women-only shortlists, for example, and they took positive measures to get women into politics, and now you don't bat an eyelid at women MPs – I don't think it's 50:50, but it's a whole heap better than it was.

It strikes me that that is what you've got to do. *You have to*, because there's more than enough qualified Black people for any position you can think of, but they're not given the nod. We need positive discrimination if we're going to move the dial to see a difference in the next five years as opposed to the next fifty years.

The other thing I think we should be doing is what American sports and the English football league have done which is a Rooney Rule, so for these senior positions you *have* to interview someone of colour. If we don't do that, it will be another fifty years before Boards are reflective of the population and the staff.

That's the next thing that's occupying my thinking – how do you make a step change? Rather than *leave it to evolution*.

Lessons

Reduce the barriers that people will put in front of you so as to not give you the job. For young Frank that meant covering all the bases so that they couldn't deny him the job. He did the extra work and put in the extra hours.

Get yourself in front of the people that may have an influence on your success. Network in person and use social media to power your industry voice.

You can be what you can see, therefore being visible is very important as it might inspire others to get to where they want to be.

> Affirmation: Today I will be the change I want to see in the world.

' The Pioneer '

CHRISTIANAH HODDING

◆

Christianah Hodding's sunglasses have been seen on some of the world's best-known faces – Beyoncé, Billie Eilish, Millie Bobby Brown , Lizzo and Bella Hadid – as her eyewear collection makes inroads into such prestigious stores as Selfridges and Kith. And this is all within five years of her first setting up shop. In 2020, she was listed on Forbes 30 Under 30.

After graduate jobs in recruitment and research, Christianah realised she was devoting more energy to her side hustle of reselling pre-loved clothes than she was to her day job. Her top-selling line was sunglasses, vintage one-off designer pieces sourced from her solo travels around the flea markets of the Far East. Korea was a particularly rich seam, and when her collection completely sold out at a pop-up shop she ran, she decided to design her own rather than rely on the diminishing second-hand market. Using promotional skills learned from her days online and following some very street-level market research around London's Shoreditch – 'I'd stop random people and ask them "Hey! I've got these sunglasses, what do you think?"' – CHRISTIANAHJONES Eyewear was born.

With the business going well, Christianah, who is profoundly deaf, set up #earmeout @emobycj, a deaf resources Instagram account, where deaf people from all backgrounds share their stories and experiences and deafness is celebrated rather than seen solely as an impairment. It also serves to educate the ableist about what it really means to be deaf and how best they can engage with it.

Christianah is now a mother of two girls and settling in her newly bought home in Cornwall while taking a break from the city. She is currently working on a fun project as an actor

represented by Deaf Talent Collective as she explores a new area of interest; part of her quest to find her place in the world. Nominated for best actress at the British Short Film Awards, Christianah adds acting onto her list of life experiences.

Even bad news became normal

As a child I went through a lot of phases. In one of them I was obsessed with telling stories, but like a journalist. I was obsessed with world news, sharing information and narrating everything that anyone did. My parents used to have a VHS camcorder at home, so I'd put that on a tripod, get a little curtain behind me and film myself reporting news. At that age I'd watch the news with my mum, and as we lived in Milton Keynes which is just outside London it seemed to me that everything on the news happened in London or in the US. Only those two places. And the stuff they'd talk about was always dark. It's more politics now, which I understand. But every time I watched the news as a child it was something bad or sad. I didn't really think anything of it, though, and I would just copy it when I did my 'broadcasts': 'Oh, two people died yesterday ... *devastating* ... and next we have the weather.' It wasn't long after that bad news became normal for me.

School should be about more than just the book learning

I'm the youngest of four so I was always surrounded by older siblings which meant I was, naturally, pushed out because I 'didn't get it'; I became very independent. My siblings went to school together growing up, so I had to quickly grow up and fend for myself.

I went to quite a few different schools, mainly because of my deafness which meant I really needed support. It was always the same situation, with either a lack of resources or staff who weren't trained to assist me, so I'd be moved to a different place. I think because I was being moved to different schools I became quite reserved and even more independent. I was once sent to a village school in the countryside an hour away from home. It was much smaller and more self-contained, with the idea that I'd be able to get the assistance I needed, but it doesn't really work like that. I'd also be the only Black girl at the school and, at the time, I felt like nobody really considered what impact a child going to school without the right help would have.

The thinking was, 'She just needs to do extra homework, she can sit in front, I can raise my voice for her to hear.' Nobody thought about the consequences of leaving one Black girl in a school full of white people or leaving me in a school with no deaf units or no-one qualified to support or assist a deaf student. In that respect the schools used to say, 'She's doing just fine in the bottom class,' without really seeing my potential to do better.

As for being the only Black girl in school thinking back, it was quite sad because I actually started to question it and I wanted to be fairer. I would want to adopt the culture that was around me all day as well as on TV. So much of that would be about the lifestyle, how we look, talk and English food too. At home I would eat rice and stew every single day, but at school I would have lasagna, sausage and mash, spaghetti bolognaise, *roast dinner* . . . and I started to really want that when I got home by cooking it myself and I'd be laughed at in a nice way. It was as if I was starting to resent being home because it was such a culture shift. I couldn't share my experience with my white friends as we lived such different lives and telling my family sounded like a joke. I think then I started to move away from my culture and why we do certain things.

This was a really confusing time because I couldn't really understand why I stood out so much . I never saw my skin colour as any different until I had questions from other kids like, 'Oh, you're from Africa are you? You must be poor.' I can't swim, which was quite an issue. I didn't get bullied for it, but because of the whole cliché that Black people can't swim, as soon as they knew I couldn't swim it put me straight in that bracket along with every other stereotype. I was eleven years old and always made excuses not to do swimming at school. On top of being unable to, it escalated to it being about my hair and hearing aids that I never actually got to learn. Which would always leave me out, and everybody used to talk about it being because I was Black. I didn't really see it like that. The other stereotypes include 'Black people don't ski', 'Black people can dance', 'Black people like spicy food' . . . the list goes on.

It's those kinds of intersectional things that constantly kept me out of activities, and people were so naïve in their reactions. But I get it, because they take what little they know from TV or other things. They're not properly educated. We don't have Black history in our lessons at school. We learned about the war, which my family never participated in. It was things like that, which at that age you don't really process, so I didn't really understand. I was just like, *Oh, OK . . . Moving on.*

And this is all on top of me being deaf. I'm the only Black girl in the school, I'm the only deaf girl in the school, so it was a weird time for me as a child figuring life out. I couldn't really process my identity and how I could fit into the world, I was in denial of my disability for a long time.

A very big moment in my education came when my mum was still trying to find a good school for me and she took me and my sister to Nigeria for the summer. My sister is deaf and my brothers are hearing and nobody is sure why. We found a school out there that my cousin was going to and mum decided I could stay there for a year while they worked out what school I could go to back in the UK. I stayed behind, with my cousin, attending a private school in Nigeria, and it was *so* difficult, because although everyone was Black – brilliant – I was the only deaf person there so that was another barrier I constantly had to go through. The culture out there means people don't actually see your disability. It's dismissed. If I told somebody I'm deaf and I've got a hearing aid they would say, 'Well that shouldn't stop you from doing anything anybody can do!' I get that, I get the energy behind that, but I genuinely needed some help with my disability.

Then I found that I got accepted to a deaf private school back in the UK, so Mum picked me back up, brought me back and sent me there. That was OK because everyone was deaf in that school and it was slightly diverse, but after the journey through several different English schools, then having gone to Nigeria and from there back to the UK, it was like, *OK, this is it.* My mum always made sure I knew my worth and value, as well as the journey it took to get from where we were (my mother migrated to the UK in the 80s). I believed I deserved adequate education. I had a shaky start but I held my head high to ensure it went right this time. I couldn't disappoint my family.

I joined this school when I was about fourteen and I was there up until sixth form, but before then it had been year seven and do my exam and go to another school, then after year eight go to another school, and year nine go to another country . . . All because I needed to find a unit to support my disability. It was exhausting and lonely.

I wouldn't say I *enjoyed* the specialised school, but I don't regret being there because it was a place where I could finally relax, knowing I would have the support I needed as they knew exactly what that should be. They even helped me with things I didn't realise I needed help with, like speech therapy because I had a speech impediment. I had grammar classes and literature classes, which I would have been excluded from previously. So if I hadn't gone there I would have been quite behind in certain areas.

Then I left and I went straight to university which is where I had to grow up quite quickly, because I'd spent all these years just trying to pass and survive.

Be bold

As soon as I finished my A levels, just before my first year at university, I joined one of my high school friends to go to Thailand for about two months because I thought it was my only chance to travel before I got stuck into what we call 'life'. In truth, I didn't even want to go to university and I only went there because that's the journey you're *supposed* to go on – you go to school, you do your exams, you go to university and you get a job . . . That was the path I thought I had to follow, so this was truly my rebel era.

I knew I had to be more cautious or more careful than most people, but I approached it almost like I was proving a point. I believed I was quite grown up and had become independent fairly quickly; however, I was still getting a lot of, 'Oh you know you can't do this'. To which I'd always think, *Well why not?* So I've always kind of gone my own way. I just told my mum I was going to Thailand and it did surprise her because it's not like I was just going to Paris for the weekend. The funny thing is, my mum is very encouraging but also, obviously because I'm deaf, quite protective at the same time, but she knew I had to do it and I would have to manage. She always supported me in my decisions.

Once I got to university while I was studying I got sponsorship to go to China. I was the only person that went from my university and when I was there I met a bunch of other people who are now my best friends. I got an internship with the British Council in Beijing. Then the next year I went travelling by myself for about three months: I went to Japan, I went to Korea, to Malaysia, to Singapore . . . and that was great. Since then, every year I went away alone then eventually dragged my partner with me.

I do know there is a very fine line between brave and foolhardy, but sometimes you don't actually realise you're taking that big a step because it's your passion. I could be going to Ibiza and taking just as big a risk, so it doesn't really register. Other people may call it brave, but I always think *You will never know*: after all everybody knows that flying on a plane is risky, but they fly anyway. Would you call that brave?

A lot of times, the decisions I've made have barely been thought about, and I tend to take things one day at a time – if it's meant to be it's meant to be. There have been some absolutely shocking times from when I've been travelling, on a few occasions I don't know how or why I made it back in one piece, but I always think the important thing is to have taken that risk. I am incredibly lucky and blessed to be alive.

Solo travelling gives you the chance to learn about yourself

If you go away alone, you can really discover who you are because you have that time to think and care about yourself. You can be selfish for once. I believe people really underrate that. From going away by myself I learned about my strengths, my passion, my goals. It wasn't until I'd put myself outside my comfort zone that I saw it. I had been constantly relying on what I was *supposed* to be good at and worrying about why I'm not good at it or thinking about why I should be good at it. I was never thinking about what I *can* do, or what I am *actually* good at. I was never thinking about what I was doing in terms of what am I most confident in.

I became much stronger in terms of my confidence and being more headstrong about where I wanted to be in my life and why. I was also able to bring my faith up a bit more. I was able to put it back together again, which was great because I'd grown up in a strong Christian home and once I went to school I had lost that a little bit, even more so when I went to university. So, leaving university, after I'd been away by myself a few times, I had the confidence to say, *Right, clean slate, who are you?* Knowing that is especially useful when you have these graduate interviews in which they ask you questions like, 'What do you like about yourself?' or 'Why should we hire you?' and all you can think is *I just want to get paid!*

Travelling like that I believe contributed to the drive that I have now, later in life, as I just constantly wanted to explore outside of the environment I grew up in. My brothers and sister were very settled but I was always thinking, *There's a whole world out there and we're on the planet for a reason. There must be something that I can do, that I can be good at.* It was that drive that was making me really want to find myself, to get out there. It sounds corny but, being a young girl, I really wanted to figure things out and do it myself. Find out what the world is.

Your first job sets you up for the rest of your life

My first graduate job was as a recruitment consultant, recruiting nurses into hospitals that needed them, and a lot of it was about building relationships with the people you are placing. That bit was fine, but it was very competitive, very scary, because you got given targets, which if you beat you got some sort of award. There was a whiteboard at the end of the office, where they coloured your name in every time you reached a target. Imagine the pressure.

That was in Milton Keynes but I wanted to move to London, so I took a new job there, a junior role as a data analyst. That was quite sad because, after telling them 'I'm deaf so there are certain things I'll need help with', they didn't seem to make those allowances. For example, if you are talking to me with your back to a window then because of the brightness of the window you are suddenly a shadow and I can't see your face, meaning I won't be able to lipread you. This feedback was given to people quite high up in the company, the people that actually carried these meetings. I'd go to these meetings and they'd have completely disregarded that and were continuing to take meetings in front of the windows. I was even brave enough to put my hand up and say, 'Sorry, but I can't lipread you which means I can't follow the meeting. Would you be able to move? You know, to stand by the wall?' The reactions used to shock me — they would be disgusted as if I'd done something completely outrageous: 'Well, the meeting is almost over.' But my distress would remain. Make it make sense.

This is when I knew the corporate lifestyle didn't work for me. And it was quite early on I knew it *wouldn't* work. I don't mean to put myself down, but the corporate world at the time just didn't have time for what they might call little changes, and the things that I needed were worthless because I was junior. My thoughts were that in this industry it was so fierce and so corporate they just didn't want to have to help you, like that was weakness or something. I couldn't really see myself in that industry because you have to fight for everything, and all respect to people who did that, who really put themselves on the table constantly, pushing themselves, that's great, but I genuinely didn't have that energy. It was all about not being inconvenient and doing my job right.

I gave them my feedback because it just didn't work out. I was too afraid to speak up. It was unfair on them because I couldn't do my job properly and they had to keep things moving. A part of me wishes I had stayed and fought for it a bit more – 'This is my right and you should be able to accommodate me!' – but the reality was, *How long am I going to be in this job for? Do I really love this job? Am I passionate about it?* Those were the questions that were far more relevant at the time. Little did I know, the next deaf person would suffer simply because I didn't want to fight. Makes me sad whenever I think about it.

Also, as such a young member of staff, changing corporate culture like that seemed like a big deal. It felt like a huge responsibility for me to suggest changes to make it easy for just me. Like I was a borderline intern trying to get a head of department to adapt. At the same time they need to be educated, *someone* has to say it. HR probably don't know about it which means *you* probably have to go and tell them, and because they've got no experience in this area HR will probably tell you that on a Tuesday afternoon can you do a big pep talk about deaf awareness? So suddenly it's down to me, a junior person earning maybe ten grand a year, to deliver this educational class to a whole company. I had to think, *Am I willing to do that?* My thoughts then go to the role I play as part of the deaf community and how I can contribute to making our lives easier than it is, simply because we're part of a bigger society. We've got to be willing to put the work in for ableists to actually understand why we need these changes. I massively regret not doing that then, but at the same time it takes drive – you really needed to have enough energy and confidence in that world and I was still very young and new to it. Lesson learnt.

Look after the side hustle because it may look after you

While I was working at the job in data analysis I was also selling second hand clothes, online and in markets. This was back when it wasn't too frowned upon to go into a charity shop, find an amazing piece for, say, one pound fifty, and actually be quite naughty by flipping it on the app for ten pounds. It was really that simple. Now that so many people do it, the competition has gotten so big. You can DIY an old shirt, YouTube how to sew, make it look new and earn two hundred pounds a day.

It was brilliant, and then it became a personal shopping experience because people would message me telling me they're looking for a denim jacket, so I would go out of my way to find a denim jacket from a charity shop and let them have it for at least double the price I paid. Service charge and that.

This was all my own money too, so in my head I was thinking, *I'm making loads here, by myself, and I didn't have to work for somebody to do that.* I thought I didn't actually need the job, that I would work for myself full time, then go freelance so I didn't have long gaps on my CV, which is never good. I didn't mind having to take jobs because you can always learn from experiences.

Selling was something that came quite easily to me because I can remember as a small child having these little businesses. When I was about ten I would do cupcake sales. I would bake cupcakes and sell them to my neighbours for twenty pence each. Thinking about that now, that is insane – *twenty pence for a cupcake!* I'd knock on their doors, smile sweetly and say, 'Hello, I've made these cupcakes, would you like one?' They'd put their twenty pence in my cup, and when I went home, I counted up and I always had about five pounds. That was *so* great, it used to make me *so* excited, *so* happy, then I'd go and spend it all in McDonalds and I'd had a great weekend! I also used to braid hair quite a lot as well, not extensions, just cornrows and babysit babies up to three years old. I used to do that for the neighbours as well which was a quick ten to fifty pounds, and to a fourteen-year-old, that was amazing money. That was my childhood, earning my own money, supporting Mum and picking up new skills especially as a deaf person.

While the competition was growing as more and more

people started pulling stuff from warehouses overseas, I started to collect quite a lot of used pieces while I was travelling. In the Far East there are a lot of flea markets, and especially in Korea there would be a lot of postwar stuff. I'd go to them and there would be so many pieces from the forties, from the fifties, but these markets would be a wonderful mess. They were literally chaotic, but if I really dug in I'd find a gold chain, vintage Chanel sunglasses, I'd find a gas mask . . . a whole range of desirable, glamorous pieces.

Through my travels, especially in some parts of Europe where they have these flea markets, I started gathering a lot of sunglasses – they were easy to bring back and could be very profitable – and what I then did was a pop-up in London for one day only and the majority of my stock was sunglasses. I called it a Summer Sale; I said 'I've got all these sunglasses from all around the world, vintage pieces, designer pieces, all one-offs, you literally cannot find them anywhere else,' and I sold all of it.

Know when to shift your business focus

The money I made there was really great, but this is when social media really started coming big and people started sharing their purchases on their feeds. They would show a pair of my sunglasses – because they were all one-offs I knew what my pieces were – and they would say things like, 'I bought these amazing vintage Chanel sunglasses from this shop.' I'd look at these posts and think: *I went all the way to Japan, got those glasses, smuggled them in my suitcase, came back in the country, for you to say you got it from 'somewhere online'?* I was like, *Right, something needs to change!*

Also, as successful as that was, it was so time consuming and I was thinking I was going to have to do it all again because a lot of people were asking me, 'When are you getting some more?" I knew that would be a lot of work, because sunglasses were my top-selling pieces and to keep them so special, so different, I'd have to source all these different pairs from these different places. Also, the supply of vintage sunglasses wasn't going to last forever.

I had a conversation with a friend of mine from the Facebook Marketplace app and we were just talking about working and long-term plans, and it was a case of, 'OK, I've just done this pop-up, I've just sold out of all of these sunglasses, what's next? How can I keep that up?' Plus I knew I had to be constantly thinking about how I could do better than I did before. The conversation just came round to, 'I'm going to make my own! I'm going to design my own.' It just made so much sense.

The thing was, I knew *nothing*. Nothing about production, nothing about design, nothing about fashion at that point, but I was determined and did all of my research to do my best to try and make it work. I stopped selling second-hand pieces and started to form a brand. I went to France, I went to a big exhibition where they do bits and pieces – they sell lenses, they sell materials, you go there and network, take some emails, take some business cards, go back home, make some contacts. From there I was able to make a prototype and test it out in the market, see what people thought. At that time I lived on Old Street. That community was wild, it was great, lively and bubbly and I was able to go up to somebody quite random and say, 'Hey, I've got these glasses, what do you think?' The chances were they'd talk to me about it so I'd immediately get that feedback. Because it was so positive, I thought, *Great! That's it! I'm going to make some more!*

Next I went to the Afropunk festival in London in 2017, and sampled the glasses there. Again, I got such good feedback, the tax year after that I thought, *OK, let's set up the business properly and really give it a go*. I had no idea about setting up a business, but I knew I was ready to take that leap.

Now I've been working with some big retailers and stores such as Selfridges and Kith, and Barneys in New York, with the idea being that when you look for the brand you seek the stores for it rather than a website. With a website it's a lot of labour, you have to do admin, customer services, the coding . . . it's quite intense. At first I was quite niche and fashionable, but now I want to go more of a functional route, more in the luxury goods market, where in order to be a really established brand I've had to kind of rebrand. I've had to change the image and am currently looking to get in the major stores and hopefully have a CHRISTIANAHJONES Eyewear store in places like Mykonos, Dubai, London, New York, LA.

Sometimes this can be a bit daunting because I'm one person – corporate-wise – and when you approach Selfridges they say things like, 'Oh can we speak to the marketing point person?' That's me! 'Can we speak to press?' That's me! 'Can we speak to the invoices financing?' That's me! 'So who's in charge of stock?' Err, that's me as well . . .

That's when you really have to step up and come across as a team. Don't let them think you're just some girl from London and that you don't even know what you are doing, don't really know how to do business. You have to ask for what you want, and you have to network in a really particular way so that you're able to get what you want and they can get what they want too then everyone is happy.

All experience is valuable experience

I wanted to do pathology at university, I wanted to get into the crime side of it, but at my school the options in my A levels were quite limited and I ended up doing psychology. So I started working in that direction, then in my second year an actual psychologist came in to talk about what it involved and how it took them nine years to become one. At that time I had very little patience and thought, *I cannot or will not wait ten years until I can get into an institute and earn my own money* – I don't come from a wealthy background, so I couldn't afford to do that. I was thinking I would have to switch courses and find something else, but I didn't and luckily, I have been able to pool the different skills I had learned to get my degree and use them in my journey from there.

Most importantly, studying psychology helped when I was selling online and had to work out people's buying habits or how they wanted to have things presented to them, as well as when it got to the personal shopper aspect of what I was doing. Psychology helped when I was a recruitment consultant too, because that was all about building relationships with people, but as a sales person, first on a marketplace platform and later building the CHRISTIANAHJONES Eyewear brand, it was really fabulous to be able to go into the networking situations I described earlier having studied human behaviour.

So even if I didn't want to be a psychologist, a psychology degree wasn't a waste of time at all. As I said earlier, all experiences can be valuable, even the ones that might not appear that way at the time. You don't know when something you learned could be useful because you just don't know what you are going to be doing later.

Don't let success catch you unprepared

If there was one thing that was almost a negative it was that the business took off too quickly. If I could change anything, I would have done a business course – although the psychology helped massively on one side of what I was doing, if I'd done a business degree instead I would have known a lot more about what I needed to do and made less mistakes. Maybe I should have taken a crash course on things like how to do your taxes, PR, how to market, what to expect if you want to build a brand, but it's no good thinking *Coulda, woulda, shoulda*. I just wanted to jump straight in and I was taking one day at a time.

It took off so quickly that I didn't have the resources to manage it all. I kind of lost my place a bit in terms of the correct PR and how to deal with the legal things, loss of copyright or infringement or trademarks. Even now I'm dealing with a guy in China who trademarked my brand name in China and now he's asking for money! I've always said to myself it's good to work independently, but to seek support because there are things you are not trained to know and things that need to be done.

If you can't do something at a particular time, its time will come

Before I got into the sunglasses, right after I left the data analyst job I started to set up an employment agency where we hired deaf professionals into workplaces. Again, I was so inexperienced – that was me taking a brave leap – but I managed to get through the first round of funding and assemble a small team, although really my heart was already set on something else. I was already selling all these clothes, I was selling sunglasses, I had that pop-up, and that was where the thrill was and I couldn't give my best to the employment agency

I have more time and I'm older now so I have set up #earmeout, a deaf resources Instagram account where we share stories about deaf awareness and deaf experiences and my long-term plan is for it to be somewhere where we can constantly educate the public. We want to talk about deaf awareness in a way where we have panels, we have big talks, TED Talks and things like that. So it's almost like I'm wearing two different hats with this and the eyewear brand, but this is my personal side, because as a deaf person having gone through so many different experiences, people need to know about this!

It's so crazy seeing the willingness of people of colour within the deaf community to talk about their journeys on this account, because a lot of people of colour talk about their race first then their deafness, and obviously for other people they would tend to talk about their deafness first. So there's a lot of communication around that. It also a shame because it was sometimes so hard to get information and stories out of people of colour, especially in the deaf community. Because of people like me and the things that I go through, being deaf, on top of that being a woman and then on top of that being a Black woman, I feel like there's a lot of hurt in that area.

I am very proud of it, because in our society we've been conditioned to talk down something like deafness, and I think I was like that too. Take a brand like Specsavers: they would constantly promote that they made hearing aids very, very small, so you can't see them. Obviously I've grown up in denial thinking my hearing aids need to be as small as that so I can hide them and therefore hide the fact that I'm deaf. It doesn't allow us to celebrate it, to celebrate why we have these things in the first place! They're life-changing! I put my hearing aids on in the morning and I'm ready to go. It's not like I can hear the birds singing but there's nothing like a car horn or dog barking aggressively to kick off your day.

I feel like it comes from the people around you; I could tell someone I'm deaf and I'll probably say 'Sorry, I'm deaf', and straight away it's as if I'm apologising for being deaf and immediately I'm uncomfortable, they're uncomfortable. Then they're not really sure what to do and I'm apologising for something that I can't really control. Because of that you get to a place where you don't really want to talk about it. It makes me feel like I'm inferior, as if I'm not on their level and that's what makes them start to believe that deaf people are not really part of society.

But *now* I'm proud. This is me! I'm like, 'Yes, this is me and I'm unapologetic. I'm through apologising for the fact that I can't hear you. If I can't hear you, I'm going to tell you!' People don't complain on #earmeout, it's all about sharing our experience, we're present, we exist, and this is the situation, this is why we struggle. We just need to educate people – the sad questions presented to us about being deaf with speech; or being deaf and listening to music; or being deaf without speech, only signing; being deaf and lip reading. It all needs to be normalised and understood. I once got asked if I could read. Now imagine my reaction.

Lessons

The traditional career path is not for everyone. For young Christianah, that meant having the courage to walk away from her first corporate job because it was diminishing who she knew she was.

It's perfectly normal to want to be very different whilst at the same time desperately wanting to fit in.

Be aware of the negative, misconceived narratives imposed upon you by others but never accept them as truth.

Take your biggest vulnerability and turn it into your greatest strength. There is real power in being different.

Affirmation: Today I am going to be unapologetically me.

'The thought leader'

SHELINA JANMOHAMED

◆

When Shelina Janmohamed decided to write a book, she chose her subject and narrative for the best possible reason – it would be a book she had been waiting a long time to read. Her debut work, *Love in a Headscarf: Muslim Woman Seeks The One*, dragged the young-Muslim-women-coming-to-grips-with-life story out from the previously imposed shadows and into the UK in the twenty-first century. 'Of the stories that were out there,' Shelina maintains, 'none of them were mine or my friends'. I knew there were more stories and I wanted at least one of them out there.'

In stark contrast to its literary environment, *Love in a Headscarf* maintained the honesty, insight and humour of Shelina's media contributions and became an immediate best-seller. Her follow-up, *Generation M: Young Muslims Changing the World*, examined how a rising group of young Muslims have no issue with entwining their faith and modernity and are expected to have a disproportionate global influence in the future. Otherwise, Shelina has turned her attention to a considerably younger readership, telling the extraordinary story of tennis icon Serena Williams for children, while a new book called *BeYOUtiful* aimed at pre-teen girls asks, 'What does it mean to be beautiful?' She's also the host of the news podcast *The Shelina Show*.

As a 'day job', Shelina is Vice President of Ogilvy Islamic Marketing, part of media giant WPP and the world's first bespoke global Islamic branding practice for building brands with Muslim audiences. She is the author of the groundbreaking 'Consumer Equality Equation Report', the UK's most comprehensive study ever into the relationship of Ethnicity and consumer experience, and is Ogilvy's Director of Consumer Equality. AdAge named her one of Europe's Twenty Women to Watch. *Campaign* magazine said, 'Janmohamed, who radiates positivity and goodwill, is an articulate and fearless commentator', and Advertising Week described her as 'brave, bold and kind'.

If opportunities don't present themselves, make your own

I don't come from the advertising agency world, that wasn't my background. Since I graduated I had worked in various technology and communications roles: I started off at Mercury Communications, which those of us of a certain age will remember as the first competitor to BT, and I had worked on internet product services around cable TV and broadband. I went on to work for Vodafone on their content business, and for Motorola looking at technology and phones within the product proposition, but my career very much faced a turning point after 7 July 2005 and the terrorist attacks in London. My now husband, then fiancé, had missed the train that was probably the one that went through Russell Square; I remember he called me that morning grumbling about being late for work and how everything was at a standstill on the underground. Then he found out what happened directly after that.

As I watched the day's coverage unfold I began to feel quite angry and upset, but also unrepresented by the kinds of voices that were discussing what was happening and the way the community was or should be reacting, or ought to be treated. It felt to me there weren't people who identified as British Muslim who were anything like the British Muslim people I saw around me – in particular I cannot recall any women talking about it in the mainstream.

This was also the time that blogging was a thing; obviously we have social media now but at that time unless you were writing for a newspaper – which Muslims typically weren't – there wasn't really any other way to get your voice heard. So I set up a blog, just writing about my experiences of being a Muslim woman and of being British, literally just commenting on any relevant story that was coming out in the media. There was a lot, so I was quite busy.

I'd never written before so I was apprehensive about anything I published, but I knew that was the only way I was going to get my voice out there. I had to work at it. I thought more and more about what I was doing, so I became a more experienced writer and I started doing more public appearances – my first public appearance was on BBC *Newsnight* which was a pretty big way to go for your TV debut, right in at the deep end with a flagship news programme.

As I grew my voice and my stature and my view on things, I started writing more about what was happening in Muslim communities and Muslim trends rather than just commenting on things that had happened. I was very interested in the rise of products and services and how things were growing; for example, there was a really interesting trend around alternative colas like Mecca Cola and Ummah Cola, which were being launched by Muslim businesses as ways to boycott bigger cola brands which they thought, basically, needed to be challenged. That was how I started writing around issues of branding and values and Musiim audiences, which coincided with Ogilvy seeing similar conversations in a bigger sphere.

It was a very early intervention from Ogilvy, very prophetic, that meant I stepped into an industry which was totally unfamiliar to me, but I felt there were some important stories to be told there. Now I was being given these opportunities. It wasn't a career I set out to go into, it was my third career by that point which has now developed into a number of different things.

I ended up at a communications agency partly by fate but partly because I could see the power of creativity to change culture and representation. It was the same with the books. The reason I wrote *Love in a Headscarf* is because I walked into a big bookstore across the road from me when I was living in central London. They had grouped together similar books by different authors on tables just inside the door. I'm not sure what the subject was on this particular table, probably something like poor 'oppressed' Muslim women, as all the stories were these kinds of 'kidnapped' or 'sold into slavery' or 'escaped from Islam' narratives. And all the pictures were of camels and deserts and women with black veils on their faces and kohl-lined eyes. I just looked at them and I thought, *Where is my story? Where are the stories of people like me? And then I thought, If I'm not going to write it, then who is?*

That was the moment I decided that I was going to write a book – there is no story like mine out there, so the only way to change that is for me to write it. It was the moment that changed my life.

Don't be afraid to challenge the social attitudes of the day

It doesn't matter how sophisticated or well-researched an industry like advertising is, like the wider creative economy I don't believe it is exempt from the social attitudes of the day. I often talk within the industry about how all of us are people walking the streets and we see these different trends around us, but for some reason as soon as we walk in the door of the office, we forget everything we actually experienced and suddenly revert to the stereotypes that pervade the world we are in.

This is when we should be *leading* the conversation, because the entire job of the advertising, communications and branding sectors is to *properly* understand your audiences in order to persuade them to do X, Y or Z – buy your product, change their behaviour, advocate for your brand or whatever that might be. It's our creative superpower. So this seems a very puzzling paradox to me that the entire purpose of advertising and branding and communications is to know your audience and yet, somehow, the prevailing stereotypes are not challenged when we sit down and think about the kind of audiences that we are talking to.

The good news is that as soon as you get a brief in the door and you have to really, really think about your audience there is some progress towards trying to dissect the nuances and complexities of that audience. The challenge is that these industries simply don't have voices and representation from the wider world, so it's too easy to revert to type and start to think about stereotypes that are safe or known rather than what is actually out there. I call that lazy thinking. And that for me is a cardinal sin in creativity. One of the specific challenges is that there isn't much original research out there. But we have to start somewhere. That's what I tell people. We don't have to be perfect. We don't have to do it all at once. We'll make mistakes along the way. But we must *start somewhere*.

This challenge to me is particularly important to solve across *all* of the creative economy sectors. I started in technology and communications and then began blogging – digital story-telling – then started writing opinion for newspapers, then published a book, my memoir, *Love in a Headscarf*, and then moved into advertising. I've published several books since then, a huge industry changing report and more books to come. I've inserted myself into the story-telling industries because who owns our stories and who tells them and therefore how those stories are proliferated across society, is one of the most powerful things that we have. It's cultural capital.

Not everybody needs to be like me or has to agree with me – there are lots of Muslim women, lots of South Asian women who have had wildly different experiences to me, but at the moment there only seems to be one story. The more stories are out there the more likely you are to be able to live life on your own terms and have your own opportunities. For me, I've pivoted into the creative economy because I've realised one important fact: owning your own story and telling it on your own terms is one of the greatest powers you can have. But right now, on an individual level, there just aren't enough people owning and telling their own stories in the creative industries – representation and power are sadly woeful.

Also, systemically, how do you get your story told and progressed? Again, that's very challenging, particularly when you come into an industry and if you're quite junior, your story is dismissed, or your ideas are dismissed. For example, when you pitch a book or a story you have to go through a number of gatekeepers who can accept or pooh-pooh your idea, meaning it takes time to get to the point where you have power over commissioning. When I have pitched books, and I know a lot of other people have had similar experiences, an editor will come back and say, 'That's not the Muslim story I'd like you to tell. I'd like you to tell *this* Muslim story.' And my response is, 'But that's not my story! I have nothing to say about that story!' Or I simply didn't want to tell that story. Or I thought it was quite an old-fashioned story and I would have liked to have told a more contemporary story. I was giving my expert view on what that story should be.

The people who hold sway over which stories are selected are incredibly powerful and so my passion over the last twenty years has been about how we can tell our genuine stories either for commercial advancement, which I think is a very reasonable goal, or to change the cultural conversation. That's a long game, that's not something that happens in five minutes or even five years, it's a ten-, twenty-, fifty-year goal, but one that has to be given a strong start at some point. I would certainly hope I have played a small, perhaps an important part in it, but certainly a part.

Being an outsider can be your superpower

When I started in the advertising industry at Ogilvy, a confluence of three different things that happened at the same time made it very challenging. I had just become a mum for the first time, and somewhat gung-ho I thought it would be fine to start working when the baby was three months old. I was working at home, but I was nursing the child so she had to be with me pretty much constantly for at least several months. That was also at a time when working from home was not the norm it is now – it's hard to imagine now, but to ask someone to accommodate you not being in the office was a very strange thing to do. The third thing was I was entering an entirely different sector to the one in which I had been working.

Don't forget, all this is quite apart from being a Muslim woman going into an industry not known for its diversity (something that thankfully is changing, and Ogilvy has been a great place for it.). It wasn't easy – it still isn't – but I believe I brought a certain optimism and naïveté and obliviousness to the challenge and I think part of that was because I'd gone to a girls' school, one of those notable ones, and I'd then applied and gone to Oxford so I already felt like a misfit. However, I always feel I have a paradox which is feeling like a misfit or an outsider but also feeling entirely comfortable within the situation, thus having a misplaced sense of confidence – that it's all perfectly fine to be there. In hindsight, I think a lot of the discomfort I felt about not fitting in I internalised and thought very much that there was something wrong with me rather than the environment feeling exclusionary.

This has taken me a lot of reflection to get to: I'd gone to Oxford which is obviously very establishment, although I went into one of the more progressive colleges; then I joined a graduate scheme, where again I didn't know any Muslim women who were covering. So I feel on the one hand very fortunate that I had all of those opportunities; as I said I was perhaps oblivious to the fact that there were barriers and I was just feeling confident in my talents and my abilities, that I had every right to do all of those things. Then looking back, as I've become more experienced and I've grown in stature and seen a bit more of the world, I can see where the barriers have been and they still are. That's when I retain that sense of feeling I'm an outsider even though I'm also in what I describe as 'the bubble' – when I'm with people who do have influence and names that we might all recognise who do have decision-making power, and feeling like I don't quite fit in.

Some people might call it impostor syndrome, but for me it's more about feeling like a slight outsider than an impostor because I feel conscious that I *do* have a right to be there. I've made my peace with that, and think that feeling like being an outsider is a superpower if you believe that there is still change to be made; because as soon as you become very comfortable in a situation then you lose your drive to make it better or to see things that other people can't see. Retaining the ability to think like that is actually a strength needed in order to create some disruption in the system and to see where it needs to be changed.

Of course, being the source of that discomfort is in itself an uncomfortable feeling and none of us want to feel particularly uncomfortable; it's much lovelier to feel you fit in and people agree with your arguments, that you are part of the gang. I think of it as a superpower, to be aware of your difference, the impact it is having and where it can benefit the people that you are with.

161

Take time to hone your craft

Compared with when I started writing in 2005, the world is a very different place now in terms of having your voice heard. Nowadays anybody can say pretty much anything to anyone at any time – thanks in great part to social media and the ability for anyone to publish – so of course the parameters and dynamics of how your voice gets amplified are completely different, and what we might call the *mainstream* – newspapers, books, TV and so on – are, in our present conversation, not as omnipotent as they were at that time.

When I reflect back on that time when I was blogging I remember that I'd write a few hundred words and then I would just be terrified to publish it – nobody's going to read this and then they're going to say I'm wrong or I haven't written this properly, and I'm going to get criticism either from the Muslim community or from people more broadly ... So I'd show it to my husband, who was in an editorial role at that stage, and say, 'Is this OK for me to write?' He would just look over it and go 'That's fine'. When I reflect on that period, I think it was about not having the confidence to own my own opinion and stand by it.

What I also see in that period of blogging though is what today I would call a honing of my craft. There is a skill to writing an opinion piece and there is a skill in commenting on an event or situation in order to effect change. That is something I learned over time. Today I certainly hope my writing is much better than it would have been ten or fifteen years ago.

My worry for an upcoming generation of writers is that they have a platform available to them, but what still needs focus is the understanding that you have to craft your work and make it impactful and you need to learn the skills to do it. And that applies to whatever you do, you have to keep working at it. When I talk to people that have community-run publications or platforms online, they will say that people can write a really great paragraph but if you then ask them to elaborate on their opinion, they don't have the skills to do it. While it's really great to have as many different kinds of voices as possible, you also need to have really well-crafted, well-created stories or opinions that can deliver on their intentions.

To me that's where the gap is today – I think we're overcoming that challenge of getting your voice out there, although there are issues about who you get heard by and where your voice is amplified. I think we're struggling with how you have a public voice as well as honing your talent and making your voice as powerful as it can be.

Don't let people pigeonhole you to conform to their ideas

People ask me if I see myself as an author or an advertising executive, but I'm going to assert my right to be both, and to be many more things than that. The problem with those little bylines on your social media is they don't leave you much space – I think of myself as writer, author, columnist, public speaker, presenter, Vice President in Adland, working mother of two, primary carer to parents, wife of hopefully happy husband . . . I see myself as many things and I find it very difficult to pick just one that could be me.

Even if you asked my short description in what you might call my identity, I would still be a South Asian British Muslim Woman. There is no way you could give me one word. And I'm happy with that. That's exactly how I see myself and want to be seen. I want to be many things and I want to have the door open to be whatever I want to be because there's only one me and I need to be the best and most multi-faceted me I can be.

When I look back on my life and career the facts simply say that I am many things. I am the daughter of East African Asian immigrants, I grew up in north London, I went to Oxford, which was a big deal for both me and my community, also for my school I think. They didn't expect me to, even though I was in a high-achieving school. I was going to be a lawyer, I was going to be a psychologist, then I worked in marketing and then I worked on some of the most well-known technology we use on the internet – the Motorola V3, the first phone that had Apple iTunes on it – then I wrote a book, and after that I wrote newspaper columns. I work in the advertising industry and I can be on television commenting on just about anything from modest fashion to terrorist attacks, and then I've written a book about Serena Williams who I think is great because she's been a working mum campaigning for maternity rights. I'm an expert on 'consumer inequality'. I'm thinking about girls and women as the author of *BeYOUtiful* and how beauty ideals shape women's life experiences and chances.

The facts simply are there are lots of things that I am interested in and can have an opinion on; the disconnect is, who lets me be all those different things? I'm not going to wait for their permission! The structures we work within don't always permit you to be all you want to be or could be, so I'm very much holding out for whatever plot twists there are going to be in my career that I don't yet know about. You don't have to be the same thing you've always been, you can develop new skills and learn about things. Isn't that what is exciting about life? For me, writing and public speaking, telling stories and changing minds is something that it took me time to find but it's something that I feel quite excited and passionate about. I love it – to me it doesn't even feel like work.

Never underestimate your own creativity

It's quite hard work trying to write something that is creatively fulfilling, and as you progress that sense of creative fulfilment becomes itself part of the objective of writing. I came to a point at which my writing was not fuelled just by 'There's a terrible news story and I need to counter it'. Rather, it developed into 'I have something to say because it's not being said but I would like to do it in *my* way, my way that is true to my voice. A way that fulfils the creative need in me'. This led to one of the other big discoveries I made about myself which is that I am a creative. But nobody spotted it! Or maybe I was boxed in by the expectations of others, and they never bothered to look.

Now I look back at my childhood and I can see the seeds of that, but it was never spotted at school, I think because I was always into sciences. I did sciences for my A levels, physics and maths; I also did French and Spanish, but I really wanted to do history and economics and I was really put out that I couldn't do six A levels. I started at Oxford studying law, then went on to do psychology and philosophy and it was only really much later than that I started engaging with my creativity. That was when I started realising that I wasn't what my school teachers had told me I was. They thought I was a quiet unremarkable soul, not really a public rising star with something to say to the world.

I think that was one of the reasons that I was very quiet when I was at school. That, and never really feeling like I fitted in. Very, very quiet – my self-perception was that I suffered massively from lack of confidence. I'm not ashamed to say I was a nerd, that I studied hard. When I look back on my childhood I can see that I was writing the kind of essays in which I was trying to create new stories, but at school it didn't develop any further.

The writing I do now does seem to want to have a sense of creative fulfilment, but it's hard to know if you're having an impact or not, because it can feel quite lonely when you don't have people who are in a similar position to you.

Creativity evolves, so make sure you allow it to

My most recently published book in May 2022 is a total departure from all the books I've done so far. It's a children's book aimed at girls, eight-plus, answering the question 'What does it mean to be beautiful?' As I've grown in my experience, I've expanded my purview of the kinds of things that I find that I want to talk about around women's identity and women's representation. It's called *BeYOUtiful* – because the ultimate goal for me is for girls to grow up – for all of us – knowing that being YOU in all your wonder, is the most important thing. It's something that it's taken me a long time to figure out for myself. In fact, I think I'm still on that journey.

Studies show that girls as young as six think their looks are their most attractive feature and as many as a third at that age have even started dieting. Girls from eleven onwards will refuse to go out if they feel they don't look good – 50 per cent of girls will stay in. So there is a whole piece around how girls understand what being beautiful means, obviously against a bigger backdrop of women more generally. I have two daughters who are ten and six at the time of writing, but when I started thinking about this they were six and two. It occurred to me, thinking about the work I do in advertising, that if you tell *teenage* girls they should feel better about themselves and have self-esteem it's already too late. They've already formed their structures about the world and how they understand the information given to them. You need to get in there pre-teen, and I thought eight was about the right age because that's when they can start processing ideas and deciding for themselves.

So rather than writing about what might be classed as *representation* or a news story I wrote a fun, engaging playful book to create a toolkit for girls wrapped up in stories. My first book was a memoir about being a British Muslim woman, written as a humorous romcom, but it gets classed as a Muslim woman's story, and to be fair I wrote it like that because I wanted it to be a Muslim woman's story, and this was in 2009. Today, if I was to write a book I would write it as a woman who happens to be Muslim; that, I think, is a reflection of where the world is, but also a reflection of how I see myself. My second book was *Generation M*, which was a study of Muslim audiences and the rising young Muslim generation.

The third book, *The Extraordinary Life of Serena Williams*, was for children, so while you could categorise the previous books as stories about trying to change ideas about groups that don't have stories told about them, this book emerged when I got to that point and thought I didn't want to be writing that any more. I believe I have a lot more to say, and I would like to tell stories and change minds and make an impact by talking about important issues for everybody – stories which are never told by somebody like me, someone who is not given a right to tell them.

The topic of being beautiful is something very important to me because I'm a woman and because I have two daughters and they have lots of female friends.

That's exciting, because it's a huge creative challenge. You can't just say to children, 'The idea of beauty is manufactured and it changes, so don't worry if somebody tells you you're too curvy or you're too skinny. Wait fifty years and ideas will change.' That's not how it works; it's actually about crafting a creative approach to sharing an idea and information in a way that can be foundational but also fun and inspiring and uplifting and meaningful. That I have found to be one of the biggest creative challenges I have had.

If you're trying to create a totally new non-fiction perspective on something, that is like creating a new world. I've had to reimagine what our world looks like and how to introduce readers to this utopia and how they can transition from the feelings they have now to this new way of seeing the world. It was extremely challenging, very painful, but it felt very satisfying to produce it in the end.

I call that 'creative torture', the act of bringing an entirely new idea to fruition that re-imagines the world in a better way. That was the driving force behind the most comprehensive study ever in the UK to understand the role of ethnicity and the consumer experience. I led the project and the publication, with the resulting creation of coining new concepts to act as a framework for businesses and society to understand that consumer experience matters and that 'consumer inequality' affects lives and generations. But delivering more equal consumer experiences leads to growing business success and ultimately to a more equal thriving society. Having led the two-year project across multiple WPP agencies it is an initiative that brings together everything I am so far: a change-maker, a storyteller, someone who believes in the power of creativity, who believes business has a role to play and that cultural capital is crucial to change, and that, by having a simple powerful idea and taking people with you on your journey, you can make big, powerful impacts. As one person said to me, it's the kind of work that is not just career-defining but industry defining. That's huge. But I have my sights set even higher: society-changing.

This report was published in November 2022 and is one of my proudest moments. In the The Consumer Equality Equation Report, I coined a problem that we didn't even know existed: 'data inequality' that we simply don't even have information, data and insights about certain groups, which means inequality starts right there. And by centering consumer experience as something vital to improving lives, and linking it to business success, it gives businesses the chance to do something actionable and tangible in their control. To see that data, insight and framework given as a gift to society and rolled out across businesses has been a moment of immense personal as well as professional achievement.

Don't undersell yourself

I wrote *Love in a Headscarf* as a way to have a conversation with people who are not Muslim; I wanted an established publisher to do it. It was very early for self-publishing in those days, so I wanted it to be a *public* publisher; I wanted it to be read by people who wouldn't ordinarily know or meet a Muslim. That's also one of the reasons that I chose the subject of love because I didn't want it to be a textbook like 'Here is what Islam is' – even I wouldn't read that! Also I didn't want to write a book proclaiming that I wasn't a terrorist, which was kind of the prevailing narrative at the time.

Then finally, and I think this is a little twinkle of what was to come, I just wanted to write a book that I wanted to write – as a story – and I was very much thinking about the subject of love. I spent my twenties thinking about arranged marriages and thinking about community; divine love was also a very important part of my twenties. I just thought, *You know what? I'd just quite like to write a book about love.*

What was very satisfying was that a lot of Muslim women said, 'Oh my God, this is the story about me that has never been told.' Even today, twelve years later, I still get emails and messages from Muslim women around the world saying 'I've read your book and I finally felt heard . . . This has changed my life . . . I didn't realise I wasn't the only one that went through this . . . You helped me see the world through your writing.'

My journey as an author started from having a particular passion or political (with a small 'p') reason for writing book, then progressing to discover writing before thinking *Maybe I'm quite good at it* and continuing with it.

If I look back at the ten years since I wrote *Love in a Headscarf* and the writings by Muslim women during that time, I think what I did was very early, because I now see quite similar things coming and they have a much bigger reception and a much wider audience and much more push with their publishers. I'm only human, so it's natural that I feel disappointed that *Love in a Headscarf* didn't have that massive push, but I also wonder if the others are getting that attention because that book was already there. I talk to publishers today who say, 'Oh yes, I remember your book,' which is quite a surprise for a little book from ten or twelve years ago. I do hope my book was part of opening the way for other writers and other cultural commentary.

Shifting a cultural outlook is a lengthy, finely balanced process

When Ogilvy took me on they were just starting to learn about how to talk to businesses about underrepresented audiences, and because it was very early in the conversation even clients would feel quite challenged by the idea that they could or should talk to people in a way that wasn't reflected by, in quotation marks, 'the mainstream'. They didn't know what this was and how to do it. I have given many presentations and stood on stages in front of the world's biggest CEOs and CMOs and joked, 'Muslims buy stuff too!' There would be a ripple of laughter across the audience at this very banal statement that Muslims are consumers (people!) like everyone else and have money to spend; businesses ought to be thinking about how best to engage with that audience.

On the other hand, as somebody who might be described as a Muslim activist, as somebody who's thinking about Muslim community development, there's a fine line between making sure the advertising agency is as engaged with Muslims as we are with any other consumer and a sense of being exploited or commercialised or homogenised or flattened into simply a pound sign. This fine line has always been a challenge: how do you uphold certain values and principles that have put you in the position that you are in, while fulfilling your professional objectives for businesses which are, essentially, trying to make some money?

The answer is that a good commercial offer will not diminish the consumer, because it is respectful to the consumer. It does not elicit consumer cynicism. For a brand to do a good job and for me to do my job well means understanding that Muslim audiences and audiences more generally feel that it is mindful of all parts of their lifestyle. Muslim audiences, like any other, need to feel there's a legitimate connection.

What has been quite interesting is how certain businesses and brands, supermarkets for example, have started to engage with Muslims. Take Ramadan: if you go into some supermarkets in locations that have high Muslim populations, you'll find they'll have Happy Ramadan banner on display. While there's still a long way for the offer of those supermarkets to go, there is something that feels so inclusive, walking into a place and seeing yourself reflected. You *This supermarket knows it's an important time of the year for me*. This is meaningful to me, as I'm sure it is to a lot of other Muslims. This applies to any audience: to women who are treated in sexist and stereotypical ways for example, or people from minority ethnic groups who are ignored through data inequality and consumer inequality. And the consumer experience is simply a reflection of wider societal ideas, stories, cultures and equalities. That's why business, advertising and consumer experience are so exciting but also so powerful – they literally shape people's lives and stories.

Seeing yourself as part of the range of what everybody else does is powerful and satisfying and gives such a warm feeling. We shouldn't underestimate the power of this cultural capital. It needs to be developed across every part of our society. It needs people who can transition from outsider to cultural storyteller. In needs voices that aren't just 'diverse' or 'representative' that speak to specific audiences. It needs voices, people, stories, culture and individuals who can speak to all of us, and who shape culture and ideas in the most creative way possible.

Lessons

Sign up for doing more than you think you are capable of; you will be surprised about how much you can actually do. For young Shelina that meant writing the stories she wanted to read in the world.

Shelina's favourite mantra: 'Don't ask, don't get' (followed closely by: 'What's the worst that will happen if you ask? They'll say no. So what? Find your yes.')

Craft your voice and, over time, your industry stature will follow.

Your superpower can come from being an outsider. Use it to create change.

Don't wait for permission to be great, do it anyway!

Affirmation: Today I will use my voice, because my voice has power, and only *I* have my own unique voice.

'The Resilient'

VANIA LELES

If women in senior executive roles in the diamond industry are rare, Black women are pretty much shooting stars, yet Vania Leles, as founder and Creative Director of Vanleles Diamonds, has built her company into one of the foremost jewellery brands. Born in Guinea-Bissau and having completed her education there and in Lisbon, Portugal – as a former Portuguese colony, Guinea-Bissau is Portuguese-speaking – Vania relocated to London, where she trained as a diamond and precious stone specialist – a gemmologist – at the respected Gemological Institute of America. where she has been a resident for over twenty years as part of the British gemstone industry, establishing her own business after a decade working for such high-ranking diamond brands as Graff and DeBeers and Sotheby's. Although Vania has recently relocated her familial base to Lisbon, Vanleles Diamonds remains in the UK capital, meaning she commutes, spending every other week in London.

In 2022, Sotheby's held a solo exhibition of VANLELES in Monaco for over six weeks. Today Vania Leles's jewellery creations are regularly featured in the world's top magazines and dress some of the most powerful and fashionable women in the world, including Catherine, Princess of Wales, and Rihanna.

What might seem chaotic can be an advantage

I was born and raised in Guinea-Bissau, one of the world's poorest countries, and I come from a very humble family. When I say 'raised' I do so simply because my home was there, but as a child and a teenager I spent most of my schooling years in Portugal and studied in Porto and in Lisbon. My mother was a single mother and she worked very hard to provide an education for me; sometimes she would send me off to live with my aunt in Portugal so I could go to school there. I remember one year she lost her job and couldn't afford the fees for me to stay in that school so I had to be sent back to Guinea-Bissau; however, she worked hard and saved and sent me back to my aunt in Lisbon.

Talking about it now, from where I am today and the times we live in, it looks like it must have been chaotic and very unstable for a young child growing up, but that wasn't the case for me at all. While I was living it I felt it was very wonderful, like an adventure, and I felt I had the best of several worlds – *I can go to boarding school, if that doesn't work I can go and live with my aunt or then perhaps I can go back to Bissau.*

It was actually very nice and it leaves you with resilience and grit – if you go through that at that time in your life, when you get older it has taught you to cope with just about anything that comes your way. Nowadays I look at my children and if I take them out of their comfort zone there's panic! My seven-year-old son is like, 'OMG! What is happening! The world is ending!' My husband too, he grew up in a very loving, conventionally stable home; he's Danish, from Roskilde, and as a child he lived in the same house for ten years. I don't think I ever lived in the same place for anywhere near that long! When I take my son out of his comfort zone my husband starts panicking for him! He says, 'What's going on? What do you mean?' I tell him it's because of how his brain is wired, while I don't really have a comfort zone and will do my best to take on anything.

Recognise opportunity however you might come across it

I moved to New York in my early twenties, to see what there could be for me there, and I stumbled across fine jewellery. I worked as a model very briefly and I was in a photoshoot that involved all these pieces of magnificent jewellery, with diamonds and emeralds and sapphires; I was literally mesmerised. I'd never seen anything like this before. I think I must have been staring at the pieces when somebody said something that struck really struck a chord with me. They said, 'You seem so surprised with all of this when all of it, or certainly some of it, came from where you come from – Africa, the continent. It's where so many of the precious stones come from.'

That's when I started to do some research. I saw all of these brands that made this magnificent jewellery and had existed for decades – some for 160 years, and some for about seventy years – yet I could find nothing about Africa. I thought, *How come I grew up surrounded by this affluence in natural resources and never actually associated what it can generate in wealth in knowledge, wealth in skills, wealth in employment, generational wealth and generational skills?* Then I looked at the industry itself and I realised that perhaps 75 or 80 per cent of materials used in fine jewellery come from the continent of Africa, and yet there was no representation, or at least I didn't know or hear of any. This is in 2002, 2003, 2004.

Next, in my quest to find out more about the gemstone industry, I looked around and didn't see anyone who looked like me. You can find out so much about the companies through their brochures and through magazine pieces, which have photographs of those involved, and I searched companies and brands but I didn't see anyone. And I am not talking about ad campaigns where they use models. What I found out was it is a very generational business and firms were kept within families and within communities. I looked at a city like Antwerp that is built on African diamonds: a quarter of a million people in employment just from African natural resources, yet no Africans taking part in it. It took me quite a while to find all this out, and I'm sure that if there had been someone who looked like me in the industry, I would probably have had a little more information and found it out sooner.

That left me with two reasons to want to get into the gemstone business: I am fascinated by the pieces themselves; and I am a great believer in representation and I was sure being part of the industry would be the best way to set about changing how it looks.

Make sure you are properly prepared to take on an industry

Once I had made my mind up this was what I was going to do, my first question to myself was, *How, realistically, can I make a career out of this?* I didn't know anything about precious stones, I didn't know anybody in the industry. I had to find a place to start and during my research I'd read about the Gemological Institute of America. Enrolling in a course in gemmology there seemed my best option – I had saved enough money to pay for it which was all I needed.

There I studied gemmology. We focused on diamonds and what is called the Big Three which is rubies, sapphires and emeralds, although we learned about pearls and the other colour stones too. I came out of it as a gemmologist – a gemstone specialist. It taught me so much of what I needed to know in identifying and appreciating stones and how best they can be used, but it was more about the commercial side of things than the creative aspect of making beautiful jewellery. Because I wanted to make jewellery rather than just deal in gemstones, after I'd qualified at the GIA I did a design course, then I did a business course because I wanted to understand business in general rather than simply the precious stone business.

Now I had gained these qualifications and knowledge, I was absolutely sure I wanted to do this for myself, I *always* thought that some day I was going to have my own diamond business – the first African-owned fine jewellery brand. However, in spite of the courses I knew there was so much more I needed to know about how the industry operated. I needed to familiarise myself with all the nuances and the ins and outs and make contacts. So I went to work in it for about ten years.

I got a job with Graff Diamonds, a well-established family firm in Mayfair, which at that point that was my dream job – from my research I believed they worked with the best stones, and because they were a relatively small firm I knew I would be able to learn a lot more there than if I worked at a big corporate operation. And learn I did. I soaked it up, I was always asking questions and at times I felt it was like going back to school! I worked very hard too. I figured I had started at the top brand – to my mind Graff *was* the top brand – and it was an opportunity I wasn't going to waste. I was the first to arrive in the morning and the last to leave at night, I would work through weekends, week in week out, and it simply never occurred to me to take a holiday. I remember once HR called me up and told me, 'Vania, you need to take a holiday. In this country we have to; by law you have to take your holiday.' It worked for me because while I was learning the sort of things they could never teach you at a college, I was given responsibility, I got promoted and, most importantly, I was getting noticed within the industry.

After two years at Graff I got headhunted by DeBeers, the famous diamond company that had just become part of the French-owned LVMH luxury goods group (Louis Vuitton Moet Hennessey). I could have stayed at Graff, but now I wanted to be part of this huge luxury brand because I wanted to learn how to navigate the big corporate world. I stayed there for over two and a half years and it was as great a learning situation as Graff had been, simply in a different area of the business. My time at DeBeers came to an end when I was headhunted once again, this time by Sotheby's jewellery department.

Working in an auction house like that was one more learning experience for me because it really helped me to fully understand the selling side of the fine jewellery business. For me this was the final piece of the puzzle and was really a dream come true. Over the last ten years I had worked for a family-owned business, then a big corporation and then an auction house and I believed my education was complete. Together they had given me the overall view of how the industry operated and worked. I knew it was now time to strike out on my own.

Persistence pays off

When I told my mother I was going to start the first African-owned diamond business – this was before I'd worked anywhere – she was baffled! Her big question was, 'How will you be getting your start?' She had said to me, 'Why don't you give yourself ten years working for other people and then you will learn and realise why there's no diversity in that industry and why there are no Africans on these brands.' Which I did, but at the time we joked that if that was the case then who would give me a job to start off with? Which was so nearly the case with Graff.

I had made my mind up this is where I wanted to work, or at the very least it was going to be my first choice; I was going to try everything to get a job there before I went anywhere else. I sent my CV to them fifteen times and at one point I wasn't even getting an answer. I was getting bored with this and I needed a job to be able to keep myself in London. I printed out my CV and decided to hand deliver it, not to HR or anything like that, but to Mr Graff Senior or Junior in person; I knew what he looked like because I'd Googled his image. The company offices were on Bond Street, in London's Mayfair, and I was outside them at eight o'clock every morning for about two weeks hoping to get to Mr Graff as he came in, then I'd stay there until about half past ten, then go away to come back the next day.

It was the same every day: I'd get up, dress professionally as if I had a job to go to and wait outside Graff Diamonds. Even if I didn't get to talk to anybody they must have known I was there because there are cameras all over the place on Bond Street. In fact, when I got the job and started work there I used to joke with security, about it – they told me they had seen me on their screens, hanging around, and at first thought I was going to work somewhere, but then I'd still be there at ten o'clock and would come back the next day. They said they knew all the plain clothes security around Bond Street and I wasn't one of them; they'd laugh about how they'd say the only thing this very odd woman can be doing is . . .

Eventually Mr Graff came in to the office early one morning, for a board meeting I think. I approached him cold, gave him the envelope with my CV in it and in my broken English with my very strong African accent I said, 'Mr Graff, my name is Vania, you don't know me. This is my CV and I want to work for your company. I don't have experience but I will work very hard and I'm very smart.' If he was taken aback, he didn't show it, he took my CV and simply said 'OK' before disappearing into the building. A few days later I got a phone call, I was called in for an interview, then back for two more after that and they offered me a job. That was my break, which is why I was ultimately able to found Vanleles Diamonds.

You are your own best advertisement

When I approached Mr Graff, although it was out of the blue I was presenting myself professionally – I had dressed like somebody who could work at Graff Diamonds – and although I was polite and didn't come across as overbearing I was honest, eager and very enthusiastic about the diamond industry. I'm sure he must have known about me waiting outside the building, because it would have been impossible other employees hadn't noticed me and had talked about it, so he would have been aware of the effort I was prepared to put in. One day, after I had started work there, Mr Graff said to me that the people he worked with had been there twenty, thirty or even forty years and the only people he took on were his children and his nephew and his brother – as I said, the diamond business is almost completely familial. Then he said he took me on because he could see the fire in me, the passion for what I wanted to do, and as a self-made man himself could appreciate I was somebody who didn't have much but wanted to do something. He said he wanted to give me that opportunity.

Don't be shy about making use of your connections

When I started my own company, I did it with my own savings and you would be surprised at how quickly you can get through those when you're starting a business! When I set up I simply didn't have the funds – I had the savings of a regular working woman in London, and how much is that? I had enough to do my website, do my company stationery and create this nice branding, but that was it and to have the product – jewellery – was impossible. How do you manufacture your product? It's diamonds and gold and labour, so we are talking about a *lot* of money.

What I had, though, were contacts. I was known within the business for having a stellar reputation, being honest and reliable. Through the brands I'd worked for I knew gemstone suppliers, I knew the some of the best workshops in the world where the craftsmen could create fabulous pieces. Then working for the auction house had given me access to all the clients all over the world. I was able to tap into my contacts, to call them up: 'Hi, I'm now on my own, this is what I want to do, this is what I have.' I approached the ones that I figured would be most supportive. I had a gemstone supplier that I knew well from when I was working with brands; he showed he trusted me and believed in the business I was trying to start by lending me over a million pounds' worth of diamonds – which is actually only about eleven or twelve stones. I would design the settings, and he said to sell them and when I did I could pay him, but if after about six or eight months I hadn't, I could bring him the stones back.

He wanted to help me because he knew how hard I worked, but also if my business succeeded, he would have another customer for the stones he supplies. It was the same with the workshop I approached to make the jewellery for me. I knew them well, I told them I couldn't pay them until the pieces were sold and they gave me very good terms. Once again when my business took off, they would have another client.

It worked, because I sold those first pieces and while I've never looked back, I remain grateful to these people who helped me out when I had nothing.

It helps if your business has a greater purpose than simply making money

After the eleven years I did working in the industry I had built my skills, built my craft, I understood the industry, and when it came to my own business I knew *what* I wanted to do but, more than that, I completely understood *why*. I wanted to have my own jewellery brand to honour Africa where so many of the gemstones in the industry come from, and to honour and celebrate the continent both through my own business, Vanleles Diamonds, and across the industry as a whole.

On an immediate level I use only African-sourced stones and other materials, and they will always be ethically sourced, wherever possible from locally owned artisanal miners so the communities will benefit. We also visit mines to make sure working conditions are as good as they should be. We don't just purchase stones from the artisanal miners; we build relationships with each of them to ensure they are taking their 'corporate' social responsibility seriously. Our designs and collections are inspired by my memories of living, traveling around Africa and celebrate the continent, its art, its history, its culture and its architecture. We have designs based around African batiks and historic emblems and motifs while the colours we like to use are as intense as the colours you'll experience all around you on the continent.

On the general, industry-wide level I wanted the business to acknowledge African natural diamonds and stones. While I was working for the brands I was visiting all these big gemstone and diamond fairs across the world, and everybody would proudly mention non-African diamonds, but no-one was mentioning any of the African country diamonds. We don't have to mention other less politically stable diamond-producing countries – indeed the *only* time people seemed to mention African stones was in relation to conflict – but Botswana, Namibia, South Africa . . . we can honour those countries. The African continent would have supplied around 80 per cent of the diamonds that were in any of these fairs, yet they had big banners up proclaiming Russian and Canadian diamonds, but no mention of African diamonds or African gemstones.

This is very important in more than just commercial terms, as if you look at the history of African civilisation it was one of the very first civilisations to use gold and precious gems to adorn the body and the clothes – look at Cleopatra. Then we had this four- or five-hundred-year gap when, to be politically correct and very gentle, the skills and the natural resources got transferred to other parts of the world, like Europe. In Africa the gemstone-crafting skills got stopped and died and one of the things Vanleles aims to do is restart the skills we don't have any more – why isn't there a Gemological Institute anywhere on the African continent? Obviously, I don't have the financial means to do this by myself, but I have the knowledge and the will, I just need the support.

It's building towards a more sustainable future, because I think Africa has the youngest population on the planet, and creative arts is one of the most important industries because so many of the youth don't just want to be lawyers and doctors, the traditional career paths. I believe being creative, being an artist, creating – everything we consume comes from creativity – is the way forward and a domestic jewellery industry could contribute massively to that.

Things are changing. I speak at conferences and industry events now, saying we have to honour the African countries where these gemstones come from, honour the communities where the gemstones come from. Only by honouring them are we going to inform consumers, which is the only way we're going to see the status quo changing because the ultimate power is with the consumer. If the consumer doesn't know that change is needed how can they demand it?

From what I can tell, my key clients love what I do and support me very well; obviously some don't care but overall the reaction has been good from the consumers. Not so from the industry: my message and ethos has meant I am fighting some of the giants, as a lot of the big players don't appreciate my message. But that's not going to stop me because the consumer has the power and with the internet and social media the world is becoming much more transparent – everybody holds the questions and the answers in their hands on their phones.

Know when to give up some of your business

I had worked very hard to set up my company and get it going. It was very difficult, and I knew that the only person in the diamond business who could sustain a company like mine at the time was me, but after three years I gave up a percentage of it. One of my clients was impressed with my creations, he really liked what I was doing and wanted to help me out. He asked me, 'What do you need to grow?' and I replied 'Capital'. I didn't even have a proper office space, so I couldn't welcome clients and build a proper collection, so he invested for a percentage of the company.

Although Vanleles is my company and I am very proud of what I have achieved, the truth is if it wasn't for that investment I wouldn't have the brand I have today, so the way I see it is it's better to have 80 per cent of something than 100 per cent of nothing. If I still had total ownership of my company, I wouldn't have the presence I have today. It's a balance that has to be struck – what do you want? Do you want to *own* something, maybe just for the sake of owning it, or do you want to fulfil the potential of the thing you started? If you want to keep everything for you, how can you grow?

Entrepreneurs are usually very passionate about what they are doing and can be very protective of their baby, but every baby has to grow and if that involves doing a deal then it's what you have to do. I needed to be able to grow in order to move on with what I started.

Don't let outside influence distract you from your goal

Once I started to grow and could start to involve proper PR and marketing, so many of the industry-regular corporate companies I talked to would straight away tell me I had to be less passionate, less vocal about what I wanted Vanleles to achieve – some of the PR companies I was looking to hire even told me you need to tone down the *African bit* a little bit because no-one will be interested, no journalist's going to write about you because the consumer doesn't care!

That was the biggest reason why I wanted to start in this industry, so I wasn't going to give that up. I knew they *would* care, and while it took until Black Lives Matter in 2020 to give birth to this new movement that is talking about the minority segments, and being more inclusive and diverse, I started long before that. I was getting press about what I had to say and my work because there were a few journalists that had the courage to write about me and they'd do brilliant stories in publications like the *New York Times*, *Forbes* magazine, American and British editions, and all the fashion magazines.

I didn't drop or tone down what I believed in and I don't think it did me any harm, but one thing I always do when I send out my press cuttings is to send the press I have from before summer 2020, just to show we have been doing this for a while.

Define your identity for yourself rather than let others do it for you

On my company website I define myself as Afropolitan, because I am a Black African woman from Guinea-Bissau and I want to define myself within this industry for my broader client base with both a geographical association and the idea that I am also very much part of the wider world. Defining myself there is very important because in this industry I am not the norm so I needed to be able to describe myself from my perspective rather than anybody else's, but do it in a way that made sense to everybody.

On a wider issue of identity, I keep on correcting other people when they say, 'Oh, you're from Africa?' I say, 'No, I'm from Guinea-Bissau, which is in West Africa on the African continent. Please don't put fifty-four countries under one country!' Some people aren't happy with that as a statement but it's important – when I say I'm going to London I don't say I'm going to Europe! If somebody tells me they're going to South America I say, 'Oh, amazing. Where?' When it comes to talking about Africa it's almost as if people expect us to stay silent when they say things like 'I've just been to Africa', but there's no reason why we should.

Beware of social media

I'm very careful with the social media I create and put out there because I sponsor schoolgirls in Congo, and what I want them to see is content to inspire them to *become* something, not to inspire them to *acquire* something. This is why I would never show a handbag that I have or what I am eating or how I travel. No, I will show you me at my desk, I will show you me working, carrying my children my or dog, just to let you know if you work hard you can build something for yourself and change the course of one, two or more generations to come.

Lessons

You can create an opportunity for yourself in the present that your future self will thank you for.

Learning how to be the best is never a waste of time. Put yourself in places where you can learn expensive lessons without having to pay the cost.

Creating the change you want to see is a step-by-step process, sometimes a generational one. The best you can do is make it easier for whoever comes next.

Don't be afraid of persistence. It can feel humiliating or embarrassing trying the same thing over and over again but remember why you started. Most importantly though, think through your end goal – how else can you get there. Don't be afraid to innovate if it helps you get to the end goal.

Think about the wider implications of your work – are there opportunities to collaborate with other industries to strengthen your impact?

Affirmation: Today I will let my light and my passion shine.

' The Audacious '

RIC LEWIS

◆

Born just outside Boston in the US, Ric Lewis grew up as the son of the town's fire chief. He went to the Ivy League college Dartmouth, where, standing at six foot ten, he made the university's basketball team and played against Michael Jordan, which highlighted the gulf between 'college good' and NBA level. Ric opted for Harvard Business School and a career as a businessman and private equity investor and venture capitalist.

Settled in the UK for over twenty years, he is a founding partner and Executive Chairman of Tristan Capital Partners, a property investment company which in 2019 was named the largest Black-owned business in the UK, with around £14 billion of assets under management. He topped the Powerlist (a list of the hundred most influential people of African or African Caribbean heritage in the UK) in 2019 after being runner-up for the previous two years. As a philanthropist, Ric established the Black Heart Foundation in 2000 and its Black Heart Scholar's programme in 2013 to provide funding for young people who otherwise would not be able to access higher education. He is Chair of Impact X, a double bottom-line venture capital company, founded to support underrepresented entrepreneurs across Europe. He is a board director of Legal & General Group, and a trustee of the Royal National Children's Foundation, Imperial College London and his alma mater, Dartmouth College.

Get into it, get involved

I grew up in a predominantly white community just outside Boston – Salem, where the witches come from – where my father was the first Black firefighter and fire captain in that community. It wasn't that I didn't experience racism – I can look back and say I definitely did – but at the same time there was something cheeky and curious about me as a child that I just thought, *Why not me? Why shouldn't I?* Like I thought, *Why can't I try to win this art prize for the region?* and I just started drawing. That's how I am today, it's how I created my foundation and started my businesses – why not me?

It was essentially curiosity that had me settle in London after coming over for what was supposed to be a limited time; coming from outside I had more freedom to question things and ask, 'OK, this is the model of how you're doing it, but why?' As I grew in confidence over here, I had the cheekiness to say, 'I know you've been doing this a long time, but wouldn't it just be easier to go straight from A to B? I don't get it, couldn't we do it faster or better or more profitably than the old way? I'm sorry if that's the way that's worked for a hundred years but are we not in business to do it twice as fast?' If you do it with respect and kindness and thoughtfulness and explain yourself at every step, then few people will have a problem with it.

One of my least favourite sayings, and I talk about this a lot to young people or in my house with my two daughters, is 'I can't be bothered'. That's a mortal sin. You can't say that. You're saying you can't be bothered to care, to think, to strive, to grow . . . Can't say that, absolutely not. I think part of the reason I dislike this sentiment is that my curiosity has led me into things that I would have thought previously were *impossible* and became very, very possible and achievable. I'm not saying I didn't have talent, or skill, but a lot of it's in the doing, in the deciding '*I'm going to do this*' and let the objectors have a go at trying to impede you.

One of the things I say to the young people that I talk to is, 'Contrary to popular belief no-one wakes up playing man-to-man defence on you and your life. It's usually *you* that's in the way of you. No-one wakes up with somebody telling them, "I'm not going to let you get your toothbrush . . . you can't get in the shower . . . I'm not going to let you get on the bus." The truth is no-one cares enough to play man-to-man defence on you; usually you're in your own way.'

I think one of the single biggest things anybody can do in their personal human development is to pull themselves out of their comfort zone and learn something new or do something different. Even if it's just for you and your curiosity, because it forces you to do something you're not going to do from the comfort of the chair you like the best. It gives you more resilience, more grit, more freedom and more confidence to do the next thing because it lets you know it's OK to think, *I'm not sure how to do this, but I'm going to figure it out'*.

It all begins with imagination

I've just finished a ten-year stint on the board of an organisation called the Institute of Imagination, a charity in London with the fundamental belief that imagination is at the foundation of all human endeavour. If you can imagine something and give yourself the freedom to imagine it then maybe, eventually, you'll see yourself in the picture and believe that you want to do it and can do it. Otherwise nothing gets created – we don't go to the moon, we don't start a company, we don't start investment banking, we don't start a charity, we don't start a food bank. First, you have to imagine yourself in the role.

What's to 'like' about social media?

One of the things I struggle most with today is the duality of social media. On one hand you have this amazing tool to connect people and show you all the things you can be, or do, but it's also soul destroying. Instead of being the liberator it purports to be, it is in fact the oppressor – I saw something today that said, 'Unfollow every posting that makes you feel you should be somebody else'. So much social media doesn't inspire you to be better and bigger and have aspirations in life, it makes you feel like you're failing in life and leaves you thinking the game's so far away and there's so many people in front of you, why bother? Then you see the people who are posting and they're the *image* of success rather than *being* successful.

If you can move away from the unproductive, torturous hamster wheel of trying to get the appreciation of a third party who's going to stop clapping at some point, then you will be all the better for it. Too many young people think *I either have to be a billionaire or it's not worth doing*, or *If I can't write a bestseller why even try?* I'll tell you why. Because maybe that one book you write could be so joyful and joy-bringing to people that all you have to do is write one to spread your glow. But, thanks largely to social media, that's not how many people think any more.

Always have a Plan B

I'm six foot ten (208 cm) and played four years of National College Athletics Association Division One basketball when I was in college. Mine was a small Ivy League school, but we played against schools with big programmes like Notre Dame or North Carolina – I played against Michael Jordan. I was a pretty talented player, but the truth is there's always a ton of talent out there and as regards the NBA, think about the numbers: there were twenty-eight teams in the league and you take the star veterans, the people that have signed the long-term contracts and the people that have been there two or three years that they want to keep, which means in every year there's one to three spots in every team, or somewhere between thirty and ninety in the whole NBA against how many million people hoping to get one of them.

You must be extraordinary. I was good – I was very good – and of course I had that adolescent dream of making it in the NBA and I got invited to camps and stuff, but even in my friendship groups there were players that were better than me and I didn't have scouts coming down to start contracts with me. In spite of my aspirations of being big and a relative success, I had those dark moments when it was a case of '*Naaah, I'm not good enough*', so when Michael Jordan graduated the same year as me and you saw the gulf between him and everybody else, what the standards are becomes pretty evident, if you're realistic. Luckily my parents had been so focused on me being also very good at school, so I had a backup plan and I started concentrating on business school and a career in finance. My father was always very realistic – he was a firefighter, he had no choice – and his approach to that was, 'It ain't gonna happen. Go to Plan B because it's better for you than Plan A.' I was so glad I had a Plan B.

That's so true in so many things, especially in business. In addition to my business, I'm a pretty significant investor in different companies, as a private equity investor with my own money. I talk to founding partners all the time, always asking them 'But what's the Plan B?' If it's 90 per cent as good as the Plan A then if you get blocked off from Plan A and Plan B's ready, you're in a good place because it's still pretty lucrative. Look at the numbers: if you're going to sell shares of a stock to the public for a billion, but that becomes not possible, you can take Plan B, pivot and do a trade sale for 800 million. If Plan B and Plan C are significant improvements on your life, your net worth or your social or professional connections, don't overlook them.

Oppression can come from inside as well as outside

I believe the world has never been more open, so we're going to have to get used to the notion that we need to start helping ourselves, and get over that *internally* created oppression that goes along with the *externally* created oppression. Yes, the struggle's real, but what do we want to do with it? I have this game I play when I do TED Talks, I ask the audience, if I gave you the choice to be in the here and now, with all the struggles, post-George Floyd, Black Lives Matter, the legacy of Donald Trump as president and how the whole world sucks, would you choose now, or would you prefer to step back into your grandfather or grandmother's shoes, or even your father or mother's shoes? *Everyone* gives the same answer: they'd choose now.

This is the most open the world has been. It's going to get better, it *can* get better, at the moment it's not good enough, but nobody wants to go backwards. Let's just deal with it and strive for bigger, better and brighter.

What happens after the protests is just as important

It's easy to get complacent when things seem to be going OK – in America we had two terms of a Black President – and what happens is the majority sees what's going on and respond with, 'Hey, they're doing something. We'd better start disassembling that.' It's clandestine, you don't see it, but they're trying to limit promotions on the job, the opportunities, or the conglomerations. Then at the same time, your kids are becoming contented or having less drive, which makes things two times harder because the majority of the community that looked and initially said, 'Oh, those rusty-assed folk can do whatever they want,' suddenly it's, 'Oh, they're doing something! We'd better reclaim what was ours.'

We're going through that right now in the UK and the US. With Black Lives Matter the majority community are looking at it and thinking, *'They're well educated, they're organised, they're together and it looks like they're going to outnumber us ... Oh hell no! We need the Donald Trumps to make it our country again'*. But that story has gone. The key for us is to not let the hardships make us complacent and just be in the protest. The moving forward, the what happens after the protest, is even more important. Of course, the protests are important, but we have to make sure it's not our biggest art form.

Nobody left behind

I created the Black Heart Foundation in 2000 and at first we just backed a lot of community organisations, teaching underprivileged, under-resourced kids from Notting Hill, or introducing kids to culture they might not experience and taking them to the ballet – to a Black ballet company. Essentially, we'd just support people who were on the way to being bigger and better, and the groups that were enabling them such as the Eastside Young Leaders Academy in Newham or Amos Bursary Trust. Then in 2013, we created a scholarship programme to endow three students who wouldn't otherwise have the means or the opportunity to have one of the best educations. I wanted to give three hungry, gritty, growing young people scholarships. Now, not even ten years later, we have over 500 Black Heart scholars at more than 125 schools and universities taking part in the project. We used to get a hundred applications every quarter, but as the story has spread, we now get four to five hundred applications every couple of months. We have five hundred scholars now but it could be five thousand in a few years. So, at some level I've gone from a drop in the ocean to building an army, but it's an army of people that feel empowered by being helped on the path to realising their dreams.

The first cohort are now becoming junior to mid-level people in what they're doing, in law firms, in banks, in the Ministry of Education, so we don't have them at the top of organisations yet because they're five years out of school and they're just starting to get those jobs. We've just started working on an alumni organisation and I've hosted a young Black men's dinner and I'm trying to create the women's dinner now. I'd just started it before Covid but couldn't continue because of that. The idea behind this is that much as I love spending time with these young people I've told them, 'I can't mentor all of you, you need to spend time together and help each other – network.' Now, every time I talk to them, they're telling me how they talked to another Black Heart scholar, who knows all about whatever and can talk to other people about it.

They're starting to use the stuff that matters and take the same steps that have been second nature to the world's successful people for years. I've been collecting people that way through the foundation, and my aspiration is to continue to foster a powerful network that can say to each other, 'I was a Black Heart scholar, you were a Black Heart scholar too? How can I help you, Brother? Sister?' I don't think there will be a secret handshake, but you never know.

It's what I refer to as *geometric change*, where it's more than just starting with a few and building it up. When you help somebody in the way we do, you don't just help them because their brothers, their sisters, their cousins start to look at them and think, '*Wow! So that's possible!*' I'm seeing what's going on and I'm seeing breakout speed out there. You start helping whole communities as they realise there's a different way to do it.

All I ask of people is that they're focused, aspirational and willing to co-invest in their own success with the few pennies that they or their family have, I'll provide the rest. It isn't difficult, but corporate giving is just so different at the moment. It's: 'What's the cause of the day? I'm going to fake the Black Lives Matter thing'. So while there is money out there it's often being used just to be seen to be making a statement rather than thoughtfully invested.

We have good support though, from the sports and entertainment worlds where I have a lot of connections, and I make it fun for them, like with my Black Heart Foundation caps with just a simple black heart on them. On the one level you could think that it is just a cool cap, but the first thing is you couldn't buy it anywhere, so when you get cool people wearing it, other cool people don't want to feel left out and will be like, 'Where did you get that?' and the answer would always be, 'You can't buy it!' Which leaves them thinking, '*I got to get one of those caps*', and it brings them to the Foundation. Celebrities, musicians, sportspeople are so proud they've got one and they crop up all over – Stormzy, who has been helping and investing alongside the Foundation, was wearing one on the BBC, and on his concert tour recently, and so many people started talking about it. It's a simple black cap, but it's very well done, and it allows people to feel they're an insider – I'm with the cool, successful, meaningful kids who are focused on making change – and that brings them to the Foundation.

League tables can be a good thing

I won the Powerlist in 2019, that's an annual list of the most influential Black people in the UK, and of course I was very proud, but really I loved the fact that we were celebrating each other rather than looking for outside affirmation – you want your family to celebrate your birthday before your friends do. Another important aspect of it was we reached down and did a power futures list so we're capturing the young people too as us old heads go, 'These are the Black people we ought to be paying attention to.'

What people don't realise either is what an important resource something like the Powerlist can be, as it provides a list, endorsed by our community, of who the important and relevant people are, so the outside world can find out about them. So last year Channel Four devoted a whole day to Black issues, did a segment about the Powerlist and the twenty of us that have won it over the last twenty years. This is important. It's not because we need the acclaim, but so often our young people don't understand that we're out there, successful in areas that don't make us into celebrities. It becomes aspirational for them – 'Wow! The head of Credit Suisse . . . the head of this and the head of that'. My hope personally, is they see me out there and how I'm motivated to give back and help and that becomes part of their lexicon.

Some people think the competition element is not such a good thing, but you have to have a sense of humour about it. I was in the Top 10 for eight years and came second twice, and the second time I was like, 'What!?! Am I going to have to climb into the Thames and save a baby to win this?' When I won, Mo Farah was sixth and I said to Mo, 'You won two gold medals at the Olympics, what have you got to do to win?' The great part is after you've won it you become emeritus, they can't pick you over and over again, so it doesn't destroy the aspiration of the group. I still write a cheque, I still show up, but I'm not in it anymore. So I'm relevant but irrelevant.

Also, if I started to get too carried away with myself at having won it, I just remember that in the States I wouldn't even be in the Top 500: President Obama, Michelle Obama, the head of NASA, Oprah Winfrey, LeBron James, Maverick Carter . . . I could go on forever.

Be who you are

We all code switch, we have to, but code switching doesn't involve changing your ethics or your base personality. One of my favourite thoughts in the world is 'Integrity and authenticity are not optional and are non-negotiable.' You can't be somebody who code switches to something somebody might feel comfortable with if they can tell that's not who you are, because that won't last as a relationship. You have to convey who you really are no matter where you are. I learned it as a valuable commodity, to be myself whatever. In business, I felt it gave me an advantage because I could be in a meeting looking at somebody and thinking, 'You're trying to figure out who my big, six-ten Black self is, but at the same time we're building a relationship and realising commonalities.' Whoever it was would be laughing with me and thinking, *'He's just different looking or different sized but he's the same guy I am'*, because I was myself.

Being an imposing figure, that's a real skill and that has stood me in good stead well in international business. We operate in Europe, but we have clients all over the globe and I was speaking yesterday to a client in Korea, then next week I'll be talking to people in California or all across Europe. This is where code switching matters, it's about understanding how people build trust.

There are so many different models; for example, my clients in Italy say, 'How are you, my mother wants you to come to the house . . .' You know you're a part of something and it's because you've treated them with integrity, but you've gone at their pace. You've been really clear with them, but you didn't go faster so they ended up saying no to whatever you were proposing because it was too fast.

Being able to do that across cultures is a valuable personal commodity to anyone, but it has to be done genuinely; with a natural curiosity and coming from your authentic self. Sure, that might take you out of your comfort zone because it might feel like you are making too many compromises but it's not going to work if you're dragging yourself kicking and screaming to it.

It's cooler to be smart than to be cool

It's cool to be cool, but where are you going to go? You haven't got any money, you're cool on the back of the bus, but that doesn't get you anywhere. Then one day you're an adult and what's cool done for you? Somehow, between the social media, the edgy stuff and the proliferation of our art and our culture it has made looking cool sometimes more important than the basics which are to be smart and be successful by the old metrics, because that's power and influence, *then* you can do all the really cool stuff.

The single biggest thing I try to teach people about aspiration is you're not trying to buy a new house, a new car, a new vacation home, you're trying to secure freedom of choice, the freedom to choose and be whoever you want to be to get to a place where people have to negotiate with *you*. So when they're asking, 'Why are you doing that?' you can answer, 'Because I want to and you don't get to tell me I can or I can't.'

This is something I've made sure I've extended to my kids – to be smart first. They know if they make their grades then they'll have choices and they'll be able to decide what they do and where they go in life. There will be things open to them that they may not want to do but the really cool thing is they could if they wanted to.

Freedom of choice is the smart place to be. Somehow that pursuit of being cool without the end goal is pointless, and the irony is what we're really trying to pursue is freedom to choose whether to be cool or not! You can be the biggest nerd or weirdo, but so what? I'm doing my thing! You're at the beach wearing all the wrong clothes and people are thinking '*Wooo! Who dressed you?*' But you don't care. Your house! And being smart put you in it.

Lessons

Allow your curiosity to guide you out of your comfort zone. However, you should expect doubt to creep in. For young Ric, he asked himself 'Why not me?' and put the doubt to rest.

You control the role that doubt plays in your life. Doubt can come from many sources (including yourself) but only you have the final say in determining how much doubt influences your actions.

Social media shows you all the things you can be, but there's a danger of getting stuck on the hamster wheel of comparing yourself to others. Who can you follow whose posts will encourage you, uplift you and inspire you to dream?

Code switching is an essential part of personal and professional development but that doesn't change your ethics or base personality. Integrity and authenticity are not optional and are non-negotiable.

Affirmation: Today I know that freedom of choice is the smart place to be.

'The Globetrotter'

SRIN MADIPALLI

◆

Whatever you do, don't make the mistake of attempting to corral Srin Madipalli into one of life's more conventional pigeonholes. After doing A Levels, he studied genetics and biochemistry for his degree, winning prizes for Science, Technology and Engineering; he then switched to corporate law. After several years as a corporate lawyer, he found life a bit dull, so took six months off to travel round the world, returning to the UK to do an MBA at Oxford, after which he taught himself coding via YouTube tutorials and a very inexpensive online course. A little while after that, via a self-published newsletter/magazine devoted to disabled travel and how to have the most fun, Accomable was born with Srin as co-founder and CEO.

Unsurprisingly this venture – a platform dedicated to disabled travel and holidays, recommending experiences, places and accommodation, complete with booking facilities – was a massive success. And, just as unsurprisingly, it was only a matter of time before Airbnb bought it out.

Not that somebody as restless and curious as Srin was too bothered; as much as anything else this was a chance to do other stuff. He now describes himself as a builder, an advisor, an investor and a speaker, looking to build his own ideas, advise other budding entrepreneurs and invest in their ideas if he fancies it, and glad to have time to relate his remarkable life to those coming after him.

Most recently, Srin co-founded People & Robots with Luke Webster, a former Accomable team member. It's a very early stage startup focused on building products in the Generative AI space.

It'll get better

When I was a kid I was inquisitive, I liked finding stuff out and I was really curious about why things are the way they are. At the same time, though, it was a journey of acceptance and awareness of why I'm different to everybody else. *Why am I disabled? Why can I not do the things that other people can do?* So while I was inquisitive, in another way I was probably very frustrated and not very happy with the world as I felt very different from the people around me.

All that changed as I got older and I believe what changed it was starting to make friends and getting to know people; also, when you're older people are just more accommodating. If it's a group of teenage boys it's so often a case of 'Let's go play football . . . Oh, you can't play football . . . OK, then that's that, let's go and play football anyway.' Whereas as you get older, it's very much, 'Oh, you won't be able to play footie in the park, so let's go to the cinema or for a drink.'

As you get older people just get more understanding and generally aren't just as useless as most teenage boys can be.

It's OK to change your mind no matter how good you might be at something

At Kings College, London, I did a degree in genetics and while I was doing it I was the university's nominee for the UK's Best Undergraduate in Science, Technology and Engineering, plus I'd won some prizes in that field, then I switched to law! Quite a jump, but it wasn't the first time I'd changed my mind. Indeed if I'm honest I probably fell into biochemistry and genetics because I wasn't sure what to do.

The original plan when I did my A levels was that I wanted to do medicine, and I wrote off to a bunch of universities and at the time the thing was – and it is even to this day – if you wanted to qualify as a doctor you needed to be sufficiently physically able to undertake a bunch of physical and manual tasks, in order to get your doctor's registration. I had already started along the medicine path with my A levels, but was beginning to understand it was just not a realistic opportunity, I remember thinking, *Dammit! I've done all these maths and science A levels, now what am I going to do with my life?* I simply thought, *I've always liked the science subjects so I'll do a degree related to that area,* there was no real big-picture view of what I was going to do.

In my first year at university there was a guy who lived in my halls who was a first-year lawyer; we got chatting and he told me there was another way into law if ever I was interested, called a conversion course. At that time, while I found the genetic degree really interesting and I liked doing it, there were a lot of things I simply couldn't do. Genetics is a very hands-on subject, you are constantly expected to do physical work in the laboratory and I wasn't really able to do much. I'd already started thinking further ahead in my second year about what I could do where I wouldn't feel disadvantaged. What career would be more of a level playing field? But something in which I could still use my scientific knowledge.

Through this friend and speaking to lots of other people I went through a process of elimination and ended up at the idea of doing something like intellectual property law, where I would be a lawyer, but my technical background would be a huge help. Also, the idea that it was very intellectual particularly appealed to me because I wouldn't be at a disadvantage since there would be nothing physical involved – I wouldn't have to empty things in laboratories or whatnot!

That was the early thinking. I applied to lots of firms, then the funny thing is when I did the try-out for the firm I actually started working for, I did an intellectual property rotation and I really didn't enjoy it – I thought, *Wow! This is a little bit dull!*

That wasn't my last change: after a few years as a corporate lawyer I realised that wasn't for me either. I took six months off for a trip around the world, then went back to university and did an MBA at Oxford, with a focus on entrepreneurship, but what really fascinated me was the tech side of business and I began to move in that direction.

Your mum and dad usually have your best interests at heart

In many ways, in this respect I was lucky as a disabled person, because what so often puts people off changing careers is people saying to them 'Oh you can't do law, you're a geneticist' or 'What does a city lawyer know about coding?' I could just ignore that because having a disability means you get so much of that from a very young age that by the time you're at university and beyond it's already just noise.

A bigger potential issue was my mum and dad. I was very fortunate in that they've always taken the approach 'Do whatever you enjoy, do whatever you find interesting', but they did get a slight case of the heebie jeebies when I was leaving law. To them, it was a profession that they totally understood, and it was a safe career that very much ticks all the boxes. However, their approach was never flat-out objecting, it was more a case of asking me questions: 'Srin, are you sure you want to do this? Are you sure you want to give up a well-paid career that's highly respectable, has got this very established career path, to go and do these funky, wacky start-up things?'

Fortunately, I didn't have to do a lot of convincing to bring them round. I believe it would have been much harder if I didn't have the law background, because they took the stance, 'Who knows what's going to happen? It's great that you can always fall back on your career in the law should you find things don't work out.' I think if the conversation about me doing the start-up had happened six or seven years earlier, before going to university and getting those qualifications, then they would have taken some convincing. Because I already had that established foundation, I do believe they felt more comfortable about me going off and taking some risks.

It was only later when I looked back on it I realised what they were doing – they're my mum and dad after all, and they wanted to make sure I knew exactly what I was getting into. More than just telling me 'Don't do this' or 'Don't do that' they – especially my dad – asked me a lot of questions because they wanted to make sure I was asking *myself* all the right questions and going into it for the right reasons. Knowing what they know of me, they know there's quite an independent streak within me, that deep down I don't enjoy being in large organisations. They know from a young age I've always been my own person and a free spirit and that I'd always be happiest starting a path and going off and building my own thing. Deep down they knew that was what was in my heart of hearts.

There's a difference between doing what you like and liking what you do

In some of the dark days of Accomable, even when so many things weren't going right, I liked the problems we were solving and I liked the fact that we had done this fantastic thing, but I wasn't particularly enjoying the endeavour. Being in the grind of running a business actually meant I was just miserable! I had to push through it.

I liked what I was doing in Accomable but I didn't enjoy the day-to-day life of it. I wasn't doing as I liked – which goes back to the 'why' of what you're doing. If you're intertwined with the whole thing and you care about the end result enough then it's never a problem to work through the hard yards. It's about having a strong enough 'why' because that will get you through.

Without it, as I feel is the case in in most big corporate firms, so many people are just going through the motions – marking time. Often that feeling of resignation will be prevalent, people asking themselves, 'Do I love what I do? No, but it's a job, it pays the bills, it keeps me chugging along, I'm comfortable, there might be some interesting people I work with . . .' They *sort of* like it, or they don't actively dislike it, and I think they're doing what they're doing as a sort of least worst option rather than looking for what makes them feel alive.

With me and the law it was a case of both really and not in a good way – I didn't like what I was doing and I wasn't doing what I liked. I'm not even sure it would have been possible to get to where I could have learned to like it. I'm sceptical as to whether you can, deep down, force yourself to enjoy something if fundamentally you don't care why you are doing what you're doing; I don't think any real enjoyment can ever develop. I think what happens instead is you probably just cognitively dissociate any lack of joy in what you're doing in order to find a way to get on with it. That bit is the bit I've never been able to do.

I believe that when you feel alive in what you're doing you're willing to overlook the unpleasant tasks that come with everything. If there's too much focus on the individual aspects of what you do then you don't end up doing anything, because there will always be stuff that isn't *exactly* how you'd like it to be. It's naïve to think that everything's always going to be fun every day, every minute, but at the same time it's perfectly OK to think there must be other things you'd enjoy more. One of the things that was seeded in those years in the law was that I would follow my instincts – if I do not enjoy something or I find it boring, I will not carry on and I'll go and find something else which I do find interesting.

Then it's important not to see whatever you might be thinking about leaving as a true write-off, just because you think it's not right for you at that time. Pretty much everything will equip you with some skills you can then deploy in other areas, but maybe a little more indirectly.

Time away travelling can be much more than just a jolly

After two years in a law firm and finishing my initial training contract I decided to take six months off to go travelling, before rejoining again as a fully qualified solicitor. I had been feeling very bottled up and frustrated in the job that I was doing, and feeling very trapped within the big corporate offices of a London law firm. I needed to break free. I was at that time of my life when I was ready to embrace the adventure, and just really go for it. I went on safari in South Africa, I went adapted scuba diving in Bali, wheelchair trekking in California . . .

204

There were plenty of experiences like that, but for me the whole thing was really about being outside my comfort zone There are many branches of the history of my life where I could have been that 'Oh, we don't do that' sort of person. My decision to go away was born out of a sense of *Huh! I wanna do stuff! I wanna get out and see things!* Travelling to me was about seeing different things, seeing things that are new, exploring things that are new, experiencing new cultures, meeting new people. That was what drove my curiosity and I believe a lot of joy and cheer comes from newness.

Breaking those boundaries to see so many new things and have so many new experiences was like a massive educational experience – everywhere I went there was something different that I wouldn't have known before. I believe that discovering completely different ways of thinking and finding out about other cultures was a journey that was very stimulating as regards all the other things that would follow in my life.

A big part of the adventure was actually figuring out there were adapted safaris out there or there were diving centres where people can help you learn to scuba dive. It was amazing to realise there were some pretty cool things out there in the world and people willing to go the extra mile to help you experience them. However, while it was great to have those opportunities I also realised how time-consuming it was to plan the sort of trip I had been on. So with my childhood friend Martyn, who has the same disability as me and who came out to join me on the Californian leg, I put together a newsletter/magazine that we put online, devoted to travel and disability and how to get the most out of it.

It was very well received within the community and that is what got me dabbling deeper into entrepreneurship. As we started to play around more and more with ideas, I realised what a lot of fun it was to build things and then have people use what you make. We were creating content and Martyn and I created a magazine that was focused on accessible travel and how to have a more active lifestyle if you are somebody with a disability. We got great feedback and discovered that when you create something and people gain from it that is a really brilliant experience.

Most people can learn anything from YouTube

When I was doing the MBA at Oxford, 2012, I started to dabble in learning how to code. I was seeing this big thing happening around tech – tech taking off and being the future – so based on what we learned doing the magazine, I started to teach myself some of the basics of being able to create web applications. It was fantastic! I enrolled in an online coding course that cost $49, I had friends that would teach me little bits and answer my questions, and I did a lot of online tutorials that cost nothing.

YouTube is an extraordinary resource, where you can learn about practically anything, and although I find I do need some structure I also really enjoy the unstructured learning that comes with YouTube (and free online resources in general) – you can just try something then if you like it, carry on. You can fill in the exact point where you think you've got a gap in your knowledge rather than go through a whole overarching course which will have so many bits that might not interest you. I believe one of the problems with our education system is it's so designed around exams and grades. Yes, I agree they're important to demonstrate that people understand something, but I *actually* think it is more enjoyable and therefore probably more productive to learn for the fun of it – *Oh, this is something I find interesting, let me go learn it!* One of my philosophies is that if you enjoy learning about something then you'll keep at it. Start that journey because you never know where things will take you, which is what YouTube and other online resources are so good for.

Timing can be everything

During the couple of years from 2013 after I had completed my MBA; I found I was doing more and more and more coding, then starting to freelance as a web developer, then coming in to 2015 my thinking was more, *OK, how can we use these skills to take what we were doing with the magazine to the next level?* We were thinking the content business is just the content business, so how do we turn this into something like a *product*? Ironically we were seeing Airbnb take off, and Expedia and all these big travel platforms, so our thinking was: an online magazine is one thing, but can we do more than simply a content site? Can we actually build an Airbnb-style platform to make this happen?

That was where the nucleus of the thinking around Accomable started – it was really hard to find information about the sort of accommodation and holiday experiences we wanted and we knew other people must have their own knowledge they'd want to share. The internet was the tool that enabled us to think that if it doesn't exist then we could start our own, but it was also an era when it was easier to create what we created than it would be today. These days the internet is a noisier, more crowded place, but in 2010/2011 when we were creating some of our earliest blogs and magazines and online content it was still mainly a hard-copy world.

It was also the beginning of something new in terms of internet evolution and how people interacted with each other on it. The idea of more social-based travel – people recommending to each other – was very new because it was still a bit day one and two of the *social* internet where social media was beginning to take off and people were blogging information. This was around that time when you started finding blogs where people had written 'Ooh, you know this safari centre . . .' or 'I learned to scuba dive and it was great'. People were beginning to share information, and they were all brilliant but before then the internet was a very one-way thing. We were getting in on what I believed was the beginning of the two-way internet, so people were looking for the sort of shared experience thing we wanted to offer.

Would it have been possible five or six years earlier? Probably not. Could the same thing be done today? By no means would it be impossible, in fact it's just as possible to *achieve*, but because there's now a lot more competition you would have to do much more to establish yourself.

A need for a product and a gap in the market aren't necessarily the same thing

There could be a gap in the market because something simply doesn't exist, but that doesn't necessarily mean the *need* for it underpins that gap. Think of it like this: there are eleven different colours but only ten are being sold at the moment – is that eleventh colour a true need? No, it's a *gap* but it's not a need. I believe needs are something a little more fundamental and while sometimes a gap can meet a need I don't think it always has to. Or it isn't always the case.

There was clearly a gap in the market for something like Accomable, and as I found out when I went around the world it definitely met a need.

Perseverance pays off

Establishing Accomable as a platform was brutal! I was glad I did it back then because I was imbued with a certain naïveté! I think as you get older you become just more analytical, more critical, you think *Oh this may not work, that may not work*, whereas if you're a slightly dumb twenty-eight-year-old – bright-eyed and bushy-tailed – you don't see why you can't do anything. I genuinely think you need to be a bit like that because there are so many problems right from the start a certain naïveté is vital to get going and then to keep going after that.

The challenge back then, and I think it's still the problem for people wanting to build stuff within the area of disability today, is that *I* see the gap, I think people who are disabled see the gap, but I still don't think that it's an accepted market opportunity yet. It is really hard to get the necessary stakeholders to believe in what you are doing, which makes it a long and arduous journey because it's still something that people don't truly get.

People just don't take you seriously, and that's not in a malicious sense; I think they just don't understand what you're talking about when it comes to disability. This of course is carried into the world of disability technology – people who may not have any direct relationship with or understanding of the issues someone with a disability faces won't be aware of how tech can specifically help. I think all humans, us included, have our natural biases when it comes to understanding things, and disability as an area is quite anonymous in day-to-day life for most people. If you don't see it you don't understand it and you won't really get the business opportunity compared with somebody who is in it every day.

We just had to push on because there are so many people out there, *somebody* has to get it – there are people who do, but not that many of them! As we pushed irrationally on we got totally lucky and we found some investors who believed in what we were doing; the lead investor had a son who was disabled and so he got it.

Know when it's time to make your moves

I left Airbnb in 2020. A deal was done in 2017 between Accomable and Airbnb who bought us; I first became a regular employee within Airbnb then left in 2020. I felt I'd taken things as far as I could with Airbnb as I'd got things up and running within it, some changes were made, a journey had been mapped out and then it was up to somebody else who enjoyed being inside large corporations to do those next five years.

Of course this involved putting my own ego aside and letting go, which was a really hard thing while I was still working there! All of a sudden it wasn't my baby that I had nurtured and curated, it was part of a very big thing and sometimes there would be people involved who didn't care about it as much as I do. That's a really hard thing to deal with!

Why it came about was I didn't think Accomable could fulfil its potential by itself – remember it was started to fill a need not plug a gap – and we needed a lot of capital to scale up to take us to a bigger audience. It just wasn't viable for it to be a stand-alone business in the long run, although I think we could have survived. Accomable maybe would have washed its face in the sense that it could have paid its bills, but without a really big backer or sponsor behind it, it would have remained a niche business.

I didn't think a partnership would have been enough; it had to be a full-blown acquisition (being bought and owned by another company). A partnership would have been quite surface-level and I don't think people would have taken it seriously enough – even after the acquisition some parts of the company didn't take it seriously! It was as if they went into it naïvely, in the sense they were thinking, 'To much fanfare we've been bought. Everyone gets it, this is going to be really easy.' When actually that was just the beginning. Sure, those that sponsored the deal were very supportive, but then comes the hard work to actually get other people in Airbnb to care as well.

As regards the big picture I was happy with the way it turned out, but did we get everything done that I wanted to get done when I first launched Accomable? No. Again I think that was a bit naïve and overly optimistic about what we could achieve. But I think it can continue to be successful within Airbnb by shifting the bigger company's thinking when it comes to disability. I look on Airbnb as a gigantic oil tanker, and Accomable as a tiny speedboat that didn't have a huge amount of fuel in it, but once we got taken aboard the tanker we made it turn just a little bit.

Lessons

Travel can be one of the greatest ways of educating yourself about new cultures, ideas and ways of being. Travel can really help define who you were born to be. For young Srin his travel experiences led him to successfully building his own company.

As you get older people become more understanding and accepting of the things that make you different.

It's important you know the 'why' behind what it is you are working on. Having a strong enough understanding of why you are doing the work will help you push through all the hard times.

There is value in every experience you have. You just have to ask yourself 'What is this experience trying to teach me?'

Affirmation: Today I will learn something extraordinary.

'The Alchemist'

SHARMADEAN REID MBE

◆

For most of her life Sharmadean Reid has been aware of the power of community. First at school and in church; then in 2003, having just arrived in London to start her degree at Central St Martins with little more than a Mac Mini and a scanner, she launched WAH, a groundbreaking hip hop and street culture magazine for women. WAH then became a physical community with the opening of WAH Nails, a space in London that elevated the notion of the nail bar to, in Sharmadean's own words, 'Somewhere the coolest women in Soho could meet and get the coolest art on their nails.'

Eager for other young women to follow in her entrepreneurial footsteps, Sharmadean's next venture was Future Girl Corp, a bootcamp-style training scheme for prospective female business leaders, delivered through a series of workshops and teaching events. Back in the world of art and beauty, she incorporated a burgeoning interest in tech to develop and launch Beauty stack, a visual app-based solution allowing self-employed beauty professionals to connect with clients and book appointments directly and interact with each other.

The most recent addition to her portfolio is The Stack World, a platform to power women's communities, combining editorial with events and connection tools. In 2022, Sharmadean was selected to join the inaugural UK Black Tech cohort of Launch With GS, a $1 billion investment strategy grounded in their data-driven belief that diverse teams drive strong returns.

Sharmadean Reid was awarded the MBE in 2015 for services to the beauty industry.

Sometimes you are your own best focus group

When I first came to London to do my degree at Central St Martins, my boyfriend at the time was a hip hop DJ, so I'd go to this high-fashion art school during the day, then at night I would go to hip hop clubs and parties. I started the WAH magazine because I loved that music, but I found the whole culture of it very misogynistic. I didn't understand the word 'misogyny' back then, but I immediately recognised that all the women in these music videos or performing were scantily clad – it felt as though the expectation was for me to dress that way too. Whenever I'd go out, there would only be five or six women in a room of about a hundred men, so I know I wasn't alone in feeling this wasn't a very female-friendly culture.

In truth, I started WAH as a process of figuring out my own identity; I was using it to work through my thoughts, coming to grips with what it was like to be a woman who was into traditionally aggressive, masculine music, but who also doesn't want to be hyper-feminine. Looking back, I've definitely taken a path of entrepreneurialism as a way to define my own culture – one free from misogyny, stereotypes and gendered expectations. That's one thing I've learnt from my work in diversity and inclusion initiatives – misogyny in the workplace tends to be a little more insidious rather than obvious. There's a part of me that wonders what other people say when I'm not in the room – how they might be judging me, and whether those judgements are based on my race or gender. But that's the beauty of making your own way in work; you can create the culture and community that works for you while also catering for women across the globe. It's a huge privilege, and I'm eager to empower other women to carve out spaces that redefine the notion of work.

When I made the first magazine, it was pure instinct – I made what I wanted to make and included what felt right. That's how I often approach creativity: I don't think about other people's opinions initially – I make the things I want to, and if other people like it then that's a bonus.

It doesn't have to be perfect, for everybody, all the time. It may have partly been youthful naïveté, but I never thought my creative pursuits could go wrong. I never even considered *What if no-one likes it?* I always trusted my intuition and my taste and gut.

Pay attention to what's going on around you

Part of the reason I know the zeitgeist is through constant interaction on the street with fascinating people. In that way, the nail salon was a constant focus group – they just didn't know it! The salon meant that I had access to a hundred of the coolest girls in Soho and beyond every single day. I'd see what they were wearing, hear what they were talking about, what music they liked. I would observe everything about their user persona. Today I know about women's lives because, as a business owner, I've seen firsthand how various issues stop women from working, what women's anxieties are and more. I've watched how trends come and go, which makes me a better leader because it deepens my knowledge of women – of people. I aim to end every day feeling even more motivated than I was at the beginning, and this type of knowledge consumption, experiences and analysis allow me to do that.

Another crucial lesson that this constant interaction teaches us is that change in the zeitgeist, and when developing ideas, is inevitable. Even though I like new stuff, I find change to be difficult sometimes. Every time we go through a rebirth or regeneration, something has to die in order for something else to be born. It can be a painful lesson, but a necessary one. I've found that the trick is to get out of the weeds and see the bigger picture. Don't be afraid to be a leader. This extends to working with new people and nurturing different relationships. The more you pay attention, the more you realise the different ways in which people are motivated, whether that be through a gentle nudge or a hug; both can be empathetic strategies – you just have to read the person and understand what works for them.

DIY does it best

We always said we had the punk DIY attitude with a hip hop shiny aesthetic. I am a very DIY person, even with my company now. People ask 'Oh, who does your content?' and my answer is always, 'We do our content.'

It's been like that from the very beginning. I made the first issue of WAH in my bedroom on a Mac Mini in the evenings after university – that was all I could afford, but that Mac Mini was brilliant, I even did a TED Talk about it. I would finish my classes, go home and make a magazine. The computer room manager at the university gave me a cracked copy of Adobe InDesign and I used the 'Help' function to teach myself how to use it. It took me about two months to learn it to the point I felt able to make the sixty-page magazine, but it was worth it. Determination, resourcefulness and hard work can get you a long way.

For the magazine, I would go to a club, find interesting women and ask them about hip hop, the scene or themselves. I'd interview them and take photographs that could be included in that issue. For distribution, I firstly took copies to clubs and parties, spreading the word and creating as much noise as possible about the publication. While I was making this magazine, I wasn't quiet about it. I'm not like those people who are secretive about their projects –I'm the exact opposite. I told every single person I ran into that I was making a hip hop magazine for girls and women. Then a few brands got involved. After hearing about the magazine, a streetwear brand decided to pay for ten thousand copies to be made and distributed in a major sporting retailer.

I thought this was amazing. I was only in the second year of a four-year degree and I was already creating a business with connections to one of the biggest brands in the world. It was all going great until the retailer received a printed copy and it had some female nudity in it. I had done this shoot of these girls who had graffiti over their bodies and some shots showed their nipples under the body paint. They were shocked! Unfortunately, that was that – they pulled it.

As it had already been printed, the finished magazines were delivered to me and I had ten thousand copies in my student house. For the next three years, every time I went out, I would put a whole bunch of them in my backpack and give them out to people in the club myself. In the end that really helped me because that's how the magazine got in the hands of the core audience. In a roundabout way, this situation really helped me develop what WAH should be; I was so burned by that first issue that it took me a while to make another one, but I used that time to think about what I wanted to say, and realised that I still definitely had something to say. It wasn't long before I started a blog for WAH. It was essentially all about me, my mates, streetwear, fashion and music – cool things we liked and talked about. It could be about getting my nails done or it could be about feminist history – it was wide-ranging and inclusive. It was also much quicker and more instant than a magazine, so it was easier to express what I wanted to get across.

The blog is what got WAH internationally known. It was quite early on in the blog space in 2006 – they were only just becoming a thing, so people were looking for them and were excited by them. They were finding mine and loving it – people would recognise me from my picture on it and would come up to me in the street: 'Wow! You're the WAH girl!'

Continue to trust your own instincts

A big reason why DIY is still so important for me is because I've had such a unique career and it's been my experiences that make my output really specific – if I outsource something, I'm not going to get those same experiences influencing the outcomes. For example, we just made a film to promote The Stack World app launch; we were picking the song for it and the team wanted this folk song which I immediately felt didn't represent us, and we I ended up getting a licence for the track 'Good Life' by Inner City. With that track, straight away I had a cultural touchstone that will speak to so many people who have had similar experiences, such as raving. My background incorporates art, clubs, fashion, beauty and tech, which I believe gives me a huge amount of cultural knowledge. If I outsource stuff, I wouldn't be able to utilise that knowledge in the way I would like.

Everything I've done has been from the jumping-off point of, *Wouldn't it be cool if X, Y, Z existed?* I know that I could bring it to life because I have the drive and curiosity to see what the outcome would be like. That applies to anything; it didn't have to be a nail salon or a magazine. If I'd run a bakery or a library or anything, I believe I would still have made it interesting.

I'm conscious that this isn't the most commercial path to take, but that's not really the point – sometimes you just have to go for it. I remember with the nail salon, in the beginning, I thought, *Oh wouldn't it be cool if there was a place that looked like an artist's studio because it actually did art on nails?* I never thought, *We are going to have to get this many customers a day so we'd better do this,* I just thought, *Let's do it.* It was only during the process of building the business that I kept refining and learning, exploring different revenue streams so we broke even. With The Stack World, we charged membership from day one, which was one of my biggest lessons. I also realised the importance of making your product or service as visible as possible online, as well as figuring out what people will pay for and why. Throughout the pandemic, it was clear that consumers were used to this model of paying for content that met a need, or remedied a problem – so at The Stack, we followed suit. Now, our other revenue streams include partnerships and B2B contracts.

I look to go forward with things that excite me, which is why I don't think of myself as an entrepreneur, but as a *founder* because I like starting stuff. Thinking about quality and novelty as the primary goal is something I try to keep with me in day-to-day decisions like editorial content too. Throughout my career, I have always trusted myself when it comes to ideas for pieces, because this is what I'm naturally good at. As an example, when we launched our publication, two or three weeks later some of the ideas that we had in the magazine were being picked up by huge magazines, showing we were on the pulse.

We were ahead of the zeitgeist with the things that we did. I had and still have a natural intuition for the mood of the moment, although what I've found as I've gotten older is that we have to justify this with data and customer insight. That's when you slow down and start to look twice at things you would have been sure about before.

It's cool to be smart

A big thing I remember about being a child is that I was always curious. I was just insatiable for information. I read anything I could get my hands on because I hated the idea of being bored. That's why I loved school since it was all about finding stuff out.

I still absorb as much information as I can but growing up, I never really thought about whether it was cool or not to be smart. I just knew that I liked what I was doing. Acquiring new knowledge makes me feel powerful and there's so much information out there, an infinite amount. It was never whether knowing stuff was cool or not, but I guess it is because if you know enough you can make your own mind up about something and that could make your life so much easier.

I never followed; I was never a sheep. If I liked something and everybody hated it, I wouldn't automatically change my feelings to fit in with the majority. I would always be able to make my own mind up because of the stuff I knew. It gives you confidence in your own opinions. I believe it's what sets me apart even today.

It's this skill that allows you to see patterns in things that other people might see as completely random. If you can see these patterns and similarities, you kind of know what's going to be the next big thing because you know what to look out for. It could be something subtle I notice, something that seems inconsequential before a light would turn on in my brain and I'll be like, *Wow! That's important.* Once I see it elsewhere, the little things add up to one big thing. I would see so many random things like a film, an article, or a bag that all had a similar quality to them, although it wasn't immediately obvious, and think, *Oh, they're all a bit squishy, life's all getting a bit squishy right now.* What I'd mean is there was something of comfort and soft touch or cosy familiarity about it all – squishiness – and that would be what was coming next in the mainstream.

My brain absorbs a lot and can hold a lot of information at one time, then after I've processed it when I'm making a decision or forming an opinion, I can call things up that might appear not to be relevant at all. It's like filing stuff away for future use, even if you don't know when that use is going to be – that's what my brain's like, a filing cabinet full of random photocopies and bits of paper.

Do what you know

My motto is 'create what you consume'. Before I did WAH I loved reading other people's stuff, but all the time I was thinking, *Could I make my own?* I loved getting my nails done, but I was thinking *Could I make my own nail salon?* Whatever I'm heavily consuming, I like to create the perfect version of it for me.

Because my media consumption now flip-flops through a range of different things – business information, style and culture information, news – I always look through the different sections and I think, *Hmm, that's interesting – why am I skipping this really vital bit of the paper that's not really interesting to me? What would be interesting to me? What would a newspaper that's not about women's issues as we label them, but is written for half the population, be like?* There's not an equivalent section in a newspaper that's almost exclusively for women, is there?

It's OK to take the easy route

One of the things I would say is that I like to make things hard for myself, and what I'm trying to learn now as I get older is that it's totally OK for things to be easy, be natural and flow. From day one my whole career was based on my love of general media; from a really young age I was obsessed with film, TV, music, music videos, magazines, books and newspapers. I did a degree in magazines when I did fashion and communication at Central St Martins.

I *made* a magazine, I worked at magazines and then I took a completely divergent path and opened a nail salon. It's now taken me fifteen years to get back to the written word with The Stack and although I feel I've never been more at home, even now I'm thinking *How can I complicate this? How can I make it hard for myself?*

We were so ahead of it back then – we were the girls at the forefront of streetwear hi-lo fashion way back in 2004. Sometimes I think about what the magazine could have been if I had stuck with it; perhaps a publishing house and media company for all the millennial women that are into this type of vibe right now. But the minute I climb to the top of something, I force myself to move sideways into a brand-new industry that makes me start again and apply everything I've learned in a new context. Sometimes I wish I had made it easy for myself.

I'm so incredibly proud of what I've achieved over the past fifteen years, and how I've been able to crystalise everything recently into a product – community building, championing women in business, all the curating and creating – that creates value for both myself and others. It was my 'pandemic pivot' in many ways and allowed me to build my resilience while doing something that gave me a lot of joy. We are having a genuine effect on people, with thousands of members who have signed up as business clients or for corporate memberships.

Now, The Stack seems just such a natural fit for where I am and what I've experienced in my life and my career. I've been able to structure my days to work for me: I reserve Mondays for internal meetings and collaborations; Tuesdays for deep work and big picture strategising; Wednesdays are social days for idea generating and being exposed to new challenges and perspectives; Thursdays for external meetings and potential partnerships; Fridays for insight and expectations with investors. I bookend my week with my inner-circle – my community of team members – building, crafting and curating spaces where mission-driven women can make meaningful connections. It is, in many ways, home for me. So I'm going to relax, hone my expertise and enjoy it.

Lessons

Figuring out your authentic identity is a long and complex process. For young Sharmadean that meant starting her own magazine that helped her and thousands of others make sense of the music and fashion culture she loved. Spend time reflecting on what brings you joy so you can marry your passion and wellbeing at work and beyond.

Being of 'founder first' mentality ensures passion is always front and centre of your thinking. Being 'entrepreneur first' often puts profit before purpose and passion.

When you are in the creative industries, observe everything that the world presents to you each day. Just walking the streets with your eyes truly open can give you endless creative inspiration. Don't be afraid to let something go to birth new ideas and regenerate.

If you are running a business, remember to immerse yourself in your community on a daily basis so that you can understand and anticipate their wants and needs.

Don't be a sheep: lead, don't follow!

Affirmation: Today I will lead, not follow.

'ying
and
yang'

RANIA AND TREVOR ROBINSON OBE

◆

In 1992, Trevor Robinson became an advertising industry legend when he created the 'You know when you've been Tango'd' orange man slap TV campaign, which was swiftly banned after a tabloid-publicised rash of playground slapping incidents – although any notoriety was balanced by acclaim as it was voted the third greatest advert of all time in a *Sunday Times* poll in 2000. He founded the Quiet Storm advertising agency in 1995, to bring creative and production under the same roof – it was the first agency to do this – and was joined by his wife Rania some years later as CEO and managing partner. Trevor was awarded the OBE in 2009 for services to the UK advertising industry. Creativity has always been Rania's driving force. Before joining Quiet Storm, Rania worked at two agencies: Billington Cartmell and Exposure, where she honed her pitching skills and creative storytelling. She is the current President of WACL (Women in Advertising and Communications, Leadership), an organisation committed to accelerating gender equality in the advertising and communications industries and was also the Chair of Campaign's Female Frontier Awards from 2021 to 2022. At Quiet Storm, she leads on pitching and ensuring the company continues to impact lives and society positively.

Together, Trevor and Rania have launched a series of influential cause-related campaigns for Operation Black Vote, Project Embrace, the Helen Bamber Foundation and the Women's Equality party. Quiet Storm is also responsible for the Create Not Hate initiative, bringing diverse and underrepresented young people into the creative industries.

Be prepared to be flexible and patient

Trevor: I never intended to go into advertising. I went to Hounslow College then Chelsea College of Art, and I didn't really know what I wanted to do in terms of a career; I just knew I wanted to use my abilities to draw and to create things. I had an extensive portfolio of illustrations and sketchbooks – I used to design things from fashion to furniture and I thought I was always destined to do something in that field. I thought I would be an artist at one stage but I found it too reclusive, if I'm perfectly honest – I found the time alone with myself a little bit boring. I've always liked interacting with people, and solving problems I found to be quite fun, but when I was at college I didn't think I would have the ability to come up with ideas day after day after day.

The main reason I got into advertising was debt. I'd got myself into so much debt because I had to pay for my college tuition and pay for my exhibition; even commuting to and from college was a nightmare financially. I must have been about four grand in debt when I left college after doing my presentations and exhibitions, which at that time was *a lot* of money to me. I thought, *Right, I need to get out of this particular hole.* I had two job offers: one was an animation job where I would have been an apprentice to an animator. I was quite keen on that one, plus it was in Kew Gardens and I thought if this is going to determine where I'm going to end up in life then this is pretty good and with nice surroundings. The other was a below the line agency in Richmond where we were selling cosmetic products and doing leaflets for haemorrhoid cream and stuff like that, and that was the one that I got.

It wasn't at all what anybody could call glamorous, but it was where I met my future creative partner Al Young who was the second of only two copywriters there amongst about six art directors. I was the junior and I used to do all the running around making tea and trying to design these leaflets for piles cream, but it was a place where I realised I wanted to get into advertising and if I was going to do that I wanted to work at a place where you got the opportunity to work on really interesting stuff. The place to do that was Soho, London, so Al and I got our portfolios together and we tried to get into advertising in the West End, which wasn't easy. It took us about a year and a half to break in properly, after going to lots of interviews, and listening to lots of people telling us to change our portfolios.

Eventually the penny dropped, because we got into an agency but were fired after about a year, along with another team, Tom Carty and Walter Campbell who went on to do the Guinness surfer ads, who were a couple of genius guys and they helped us a lot with our portfolio at first. Why the four of us got fired in the space of a week was a little perplexing; our old creative director didn't like us very much although we did win a lot of business for them and subsequent work proved we were actually pretty good. But that's how the advertising industry is.

We eventually got back into a West End agency, Howell Henry Chaldecott Lury, where we went on to do some of the Pot Noodle stuff and the Tango Orange Man slap commercial that was the cause of a few perforated eardrums among people growing up at that time. It was a tough old business to get into but once you're in, you really have to try and make it impossible for people to fire you again by doing work that is not only great but memorable, and making clients seek you out again and again.

Rania: I didn't set out with the intention of running an advertising agency; in fact, I didn't come into it in what would be seen as the conventional way. I didn't have the classic university degree; at school I struggled academically – it was clear my strengths lied in the creative, big picture thinking – and so I didn't follow a traditional path. I started out as a secretary and worked my way up. I had the foresight to know that if I was able to learn secretarial skills, I could potentially get a job anywhere – it afforded me the flexibility and opportunity I wanted. Most of my career has been in media and communications, but I've also worked in the less traditional areas of marketing – I did a lot of experiential music marketing. For example, we would do the V Festival, which is a music festival for Virgin, or music tours with brands – we'd create experiences for customers and so on. At the time that was called 'below the line' as opposed to 'above the line', which is more conventional advertising – Quiet Storm's

227

heartland. I actually met Trev through my old agency because he knew most of my bosses very well.

My biggest challenge at this point in my career was navigating the joys of parenthood with my work commitments. The way I was working wasn't conducive to being the parent I wanted to be, so something had to change. I think a lot of women experience this dilemma – that's why we lose out on so much talent in the industry, which I'm now trying to combat with my work with WACL. It's so important for women to have the right support networks available to them – both on a personal and professional level. The only way I could get the best of both worlds was to go freelance, working as an independent consultant. When the opportunity arose with Quiet Storm, my children were older and the timing felt right – so I made another switch.

Now I'm the Chief Executive at Quiet Storm, so I essentially run the business. I don't get involved in the creative side too much, but I'm part of the team that reviews ideas and decides with Trev which we feel are the strongest. My view is more from a client perspective, not from an overall creative responsibility point of view in the way that Trevor's is. I tend to work on the new business, pitching side; I get involved at the really early stages, when we're trying to win a piece of business and where we have to pitch for a campaign or an account.

Sometimes the only way is DIY

Trevor: I never intended to start my own agency. I never thought, *You know what? I want to wake up and run a place!* It was simply that I'd found myself pushed into a corner more and more as to the kind of work I wanted and the way I wanted to work. No-one else was prepared to do what I saw as being the way forward. I wanted to write and direct my own work, which seems straightforward if you look at the movie business – directors from Tarantino to Spike Lee write their own work and it's been the case for ages – but in advertising it's very compartmentalised and you're either a writer, or an art director, or you're a commercial films director. It was very rare for people to blur the boundaries and when it came to directing, people were more likely to cross over completely and see it as some sort of graduation: 'I was once a lowly creative, then I became a director.'

For me, it always made complete sense to write and direct my own work, rather than give the opportunities and responsibilities to somebody else – after all, who would understand what I've written better that I would, and who better to understand the client as well? Not a director from outside the industry, but someone who's in the industry and in some cases has spent a lot of time working with that client to understand the propositions, to understand the target audience, and who understands what it takes to stand out in that marketplace. Right from the beginning I was keen on being that person trying to make my own ideas stronger,

It's funny because I don't really think there's a real resistance to working this way; it's just that people are creatures of comfort and no-one really wants to do something that takes a step outside their remit. Everybody always says creativity is all about being on the front foot and discovering new things, but in reality it's very much about what they feel comfortable with, or it has been for the last few decades. For an agency, that tended to mean trundling along being an agency and doing what agencies do, because that's what they know they're good at doing, then if somebody comes in and says, 'Well we can do it a slightly different way' that can be quite hard for people to deal with. For creatives and the production crew to think of themselves in a slightly different way seemed to be too much of a risk so what they tended to do was fall back on what they knew. If I wanted to buck that way of thinking, I had to go out on my own.

Maintaining independence is good for more than just creativity

Rania: I came into the business about ten years ago after working as a freelance consultant, and we'd just gone through an acquisition, or more of a partnership than a full-on acquisition. It was with an organisation called Inferno and we partnered with them for about a year and a half before they were bought out by the big American network IPG,

Interpublic Group of Companies. That really wasn't for us, so we went through a management buyout and were fully independent up until last year when we became an employee-owned trust (EOT), which is like the John Lewis model where everybody shares in the profits.

That works perfectly for us, because Trev founded the business twenty-five years ago and I became a partner later, and there is always that long-term desire when you've been running a business and invested in the business all that time, that, ultimately, you want to release some equity. Most people would do that through a classic traditional sale of shares but for us that just didn't sit right; selling to a big operator or a big network agency wasn't for us. We knew from our own experiences of going into the partnership situation with part sale of the business, and through our personal experiences with big organisations we'd worked at that have been sold, what an effect allowing others into your company at that level can have. We knew just how much it impacted the culture, how much it impacted the staff, and we both felt really uncomfortable with the idea of actually selling out in the traditional way – it would be figuratively as well as literally. Then when we found out about this employee-owned option it felt right for us because it just meant that we could put the long-term benefit of the company in the hands of the employees, while at the same time being able to release some equity or some value out of the business.

The best thing was Quiet Storm would continue to run in the way we wanted it to run, remaining true to the values of the business, rather than what happens with most corporate sales when the buyer expects it to be just about the money. The business then becomes all about hitting targets, the bottom line, and if that had happened to us our culture would become massively diluted, and things like Create Not Hate that we're doing as not for profit, and all the pro bono (unpaid) work we do, would be stripped out of the business straight away.

When Trev founded the business, and I'm much the same personality wise, it was as much about him working the way he wants to work as it was about building an empire. For us it was never just about the money – of course you want to release equity, you've built up a business, but if you can find a way to do that whilst maintaining the way you want to work, for us that was perfect as it delivered our values. Also, in the business, we've always been very transparent with our staff, involving them in our decisions and being very open, so really the EOT suited the culture we already had in place. To be able to release equity in a way that our staff could benefit long-term from it too just felt right.

Trevor: It took me a quite a while to get a really strong team together. It's been a lot stronger since Rania came into it; we've had times when we were *almost* right, but it was very much a struggle to find our identity and get the right people in. It was so important to get that right and I'm always amazed when staff will describe somebody to me as 'Oh they're a Quiet Storm person!' That's always quite nice to hear and means we obviously stand for something, hence why we have opted to have our company as an EOT and the people with shares in the company be in the position to run it in a couple of years' time. That for me ensures our agency is going to be relevant in the future, instead of something that is still trying to be this old ocean liner catering for the same crowd that no longer exists, or if they do there's not so many of them.

People say that when they look at our staff on the company website they don't look like advertising people, which means the clichéd idea of advertising people is still present in much of the industry. The EOT allows us to look to the future with our company culture moving forward, rather than looking back which is what I used to feel so much of the industry was doing. I could see why, because the past was the glory days! They tended to always talk about what we did, what we achieved in the heyday and everybody put the past up on pedestals and I always found that a little bit weird – it's like people talking about their school days, hankering and harking to be back there.

With our company continuing to be run by the forward-thinking people that we have put in place, we feel confident it will continue to grow creatively and remain relevant as the world changes.

Be aware of what's going on in the outside world

Rania: What was so interesting about me coming into the business from the other side of it, from a more media-neutral perspective, was that I was looking at where the industry was going. It was becoming much more about ideas that could live beyond TV, could live in any channel, and Quiet Storm were aware of that very early on – the work with the Helen Bamber Foundation, or with Crimestoppers, or with Operation Black Vote was, at the time, pretty unconventional.

Now people don't think of doing a campaign that is just a TV ad, they think about all the different touchpoints along a journey which is something I learned as part of my media-agnostic background. We were having to create activations that were outside TV and the traditional channels, although what was always at the heart of the business was ideas and creativity; now it was ideas and creativity that didn't necessarily live in film or live in TV. What we were able to do was take that creativity and formalise it a bit and put some structure around it, making it second nature for the business rather than something they do specifically on some accounts or projects and not others.

I think it's always been Trev's way, even the stuff he did with Tango all those years ago, with the promotions and the things that went round it. He just thinks creatively and that is not necessarily restricted to a particular medium, it was just that they so happened to do a lot of that stuff for television. So back when I joined they were already doing a lot of work that we would call ambient, guerrilla, experiential. It just wasn't the core of the business; now, growing and expanding campaigns that live across lots of channels is definitely something we'd do more naturally and more organically. I believe it's what's kept us ahead of the curve.

Trevor: Advertising is no longer about putting something on television and people rush out to buy it. Social media and the different platforms have given a lot more people a lot more edge to who they are and what they're buying into. People are able to formulate for themselves, and it's not just about mass followings; instead, it's increasingly a lot of little splinter groups of ideas. In an example outside of advertising, think of those years when a designer would design something from his own creation and it's there for the rest of us to jump on and wear; now people are going, 'No, I've got an opinion on what I want to wear.' Those same people are now going to charity shops and other places to create their own personalities. It's more about the context of the way in which consumers are thinking, they're not waiting for people to show them or tell them what to think or what to wear.

For me, as a creative, this makes life easier because as a species we get bored very easily and we always want to be excited – I couldn't maintain being an illustrator because I got bored with myself and the work that I was doing very quickly. What happens now is that I am always able to jump on the next wave, the next exciting thing, the next new client, the next new set of rules . . . because there will always be a new whatever and it will come at me so quickly. It's as good for me personally as it is for the business, because it keeps me young, it keeps me excited, it keeps me not bored. Not many people at this age in their lives can be like that because most people by this time are very much having to do what they have always done.

That is what I really love about creativity now, it's a bit like TikTok inasmuch as it's swipe, swipe and people want faster, quicker and more entertaining content, and if it's not entertaining then they're moving on to the next *whatever*. The advertising industry has not caught up to that speed yet and a lot of it feels more cumbersome, a little bit more prestige, a little more polished Fabergé eggs as somebody once said. At Quiet Storm we knew we needed to jump on board faster if we wanted what we did to be relevant and not just these accomplished pieces of work that are very behind the times. Just last week we were working with a team of young people, aged 15-22.They were coming up with some ideas and I thought they had just done what they needed to do in terms of formulating a presentation, but within forty-five minutes they had created a TikTok video. They leveraged existing content from all over the media industry – from music videos to memes – put it all in their presentation and played it back to people within three quarters of an hour.

Rania: We can all suffer from default and habitual thinking and behaviour and we have to challenge ourselves as much as anyone else. I think for us, working with these young people for whom it's second nature, is how we can bring that mentality into the agency and keep it very front of mind for people who are perhaps more established, a bit more what you might call old-school. It's almost reverse mentoring – the traditional model would be that newer people learn from experienced people, but we found out that the experienced people could learn from the young people, because they're right at the edge of this new era. I think that for us, the work that we're doing with these young people is keeping us fresh, meaning it does give us the opportunity to be a bit more on the front foot.

Trevor: The great thing about what's happening now is so many different things are erupting every day – different ways of approaching things in different industries. It's so exciting for me, because if you're not seeing it and groaning, like *Oh God! What are the new rules now?* then you're embracing it as *Oh good, the rules have changed. What can we do now? Let's go! Let's see if we can still excite people with what we can do with the new rules.* I do think that is really cool. It's not just technology we're embracing, it's new headsets, it's all about taking on board things we just don't see coming.

Every idea has its time

Trevor: In 2007 we launched the Create Not Hate campaign which was designed to get ethnic minorities and hard-to-reach young people into the creative industries, where people of colour are still very underrepresented, to address systemic racism and gun and knife crime. We reach out to the young people and by running hands-on workshops show them how the industry works with the end result of them producing their own work. These kids had never done anything like an advert in their lives, yet they were creating some really innovative work and within one and two years winning awards and being recognised by the industry. But it didn't really catch, and we've revived it thirteen years later . . .

Rania: I think an important point to make is often it's about timing and in 2007 the idea was way ahead of its time. The industry wasn't ready for something like that and we couldn't get the support we needed to make it work. We both felt a real sense of shame that we let it lie for thirteen years and that it took George Floyd's murder for us to kickstart it again, but that was clearly the right time for it and the mood of the country enabled us to get the support and engagement that we needed that we weren't able to get in 2007. This time around we have been able to make it a sustainable community interest company that is gaining funding, so it felt like it is the right time to get the momentum we need that we couldn't get before.

Trevor: And Rania's right, we just couldn't sustain it before because people weren't interested, they just didn't see the importance or the value of it before. The penny has really dropped with some people, they can see the value and they can see how much more relevant they can be if their products aren't just reflecting the people on their managerial table, they're reflecting the people they're actually trying to communicate and sell to.

Now we're getting the advertising industry interested, but most importantly we're getting clients coming to us and asking how they can bring that form of creativity into their companies. John Lewis has been a big brand for many years, and they've come to us and so we're working with them. It's not just about coming up with advertising ideas for TV commercials, it's coming up with ideas for products or experiences.

Rania: Post-George Floyd's murder we wanted to launch the work in time for Notting Hill Carnival, but that wasn't happening because of Covid. This was such a key moment in the Black community's calendar, for us it was really important to mark what we were doing and to do it at a time that was really significant. So we went ahead anyway and in the space of two and a half months ended up finding the whole youth outreach programme galvanising the industry, running workshops with these young people, developing campaigns, making them and getting them out in the world. I don't know many businesses that could have done that, and I think that is testament to how agile we are. Also, I think working with these young people that just embrace new media and can work with it instinctively will keep Create Not Hate perpetually fresh from an ideas point of view.

Trevor: What's been a real eye-opener to me is how much corporate interest there has been this time. I thought it was a lot to do with lip service at first, with people going, 'Yes, yes, we want to be involved,' and then hearing no more from them, but really they're coming back and we're delivering together. I think *Watch this space* in terms of the work that's coming out. I think it's going to be very fresh and very exciting work you're going to see out there that's sprouted from Create Not Hate.

Working with your spouse? It can be done

Trevor: I've always enjoyed working with Rania. There are lots of things that I'm really rubbish at doing yet they've got to be done and Rania's all over the stuff I'm just complacent about. A lot of punches I just don't see coming and she's in there ducking and weaving and taking them for me. We are a good pairing and when we're working well, we're like a couple of velociraptors able to take down some big old beasts!

Sometimes I know it's bad because I rely on her a bit too much, but that's the difference between having a good business partner and working with your wife – and I wouldn't be so complacent if I didn't have somebody in my company who had my back the way she does because we're family. I think I would have to work a lot harder to still exist. Because it's not everybody out there that you can trust to be bloody good and to be bloody brilliant and we'll both walk out of the meeting and we'll look at each other and we're thinking the same thing about what just happened. That's very hard to have. Full stop.

So for me, yes it can be stressful at times, and we both can get quite heated, but it always comes from the right place. Without ego.

Rania: We've got shared values, we both want the same things and that can make life a whole lot easier, but how we go about it is different, and that's where some of the frustration can come in – even though we've got these shared values and vision, we just go about things really differently. Equally it's brilliant because we complement each other – he's the vision, really, in terms of the big far-ranging ideas, but that's not me, I am responsible for the structures that make those ideas a reality, I make them robust. I make them *work*. In that respect we complement each other beautifully.

When it's great it's incredible, because when good things happen you're celebrating together, but when it's tough it's really tough: you're both bringing home the same pressures and stresses, the same disappointments. But because we're married there's no tiptoeing around each other, we can get straight to the point and we can tell it like it is. We're both big characters and we need each other to tell us about ourselves from time to time. If you're in a more traditional business partnership you *can* have that honesty, but it's not always the case.

We've learned how to respect each other's differences more in the workplace now. I could be thinking about work 24/7, but he needs downtime and doesn't want to be on it all the time, so I've had to learn to pick my moments to discuss things with him. The big challenge is, if we weren't working together he might be able to come home and have a moan about work, I might try to give a bit of advice and it would just be that, and vice versa. With us though it can become very emotional because we're both feeling it, we're both living it, and also it's easier for me to sound off because he's just *there*. I'll chat to him while he's in the bath about a work issue, although I'm learning not to do that unless it's absolutely critical!

Trevor: I need to be able to find time to doodle, to wander off in my mind's eye, going for walks is a good one. Rania's one for going for walks, but I tend to be off on my bike, get a bit of air and just get away from work and life and stuff. It must be working.

Rania: I think it's strengthened us as a couple on a personal level, because we've been through a lot, and when you've been through that much and you've still got each other's back it says something, doesn't it?

Lessons

Careers in the creative industries are extremely competitive. For young Trevor and Rania that meant never ever resting on their laurels. Each creative opportunity they are given means starting fresh.

Manage stress levels through both patience and constant flexibility – think about the long game and what your future self will thank you for.

If you are fortunate enough to run an independent business, ensure that all the decisions that impact culture are values driven. Standing by your values will help you make the decision that's best for you.

Your closest professional relationship is most effective when you are both clear about your differing strengths and how you complement each other to do the best work of your career.

Affirmation: Today I will inspire someone close to me to be creative.

'The Amplifier'

SUKI SANDHU OBE

Diversity and inclusion as a fundamental component of executive recruitment has been what's driven Suki Sandhu in his twenty-year career as a high-level headhunter (someone who finds suitable candidates to fill specific job roles). After joining FTSE250 company Michael Page Recruitment upon graduation, he moved up through the ranks of a far more specialised recruitment operation. However, in spite of the positive steps being made at that firm he realised the degree of focus and effort needed to have any significant impact on 'levelling up' the diversity aspect of British boardrooms required his own company. In April 2011 Suki founded and became CEO of Audeliss, a global executive search firm specialising in diversity and inclusion.

Audeliss is the one of the very few executive recruitment firms to specifically champion LGBT+, ethnically diverse and women candidates for senior appointments; and during 2021, 73 per cent of their total appointments and 93 per cent at board level have been diverse.

Beyond the world of executive recruitment and in partnership with the *Financial Times*, in 2013 Suki founded OUTstanding, an LGBT+ organisation that publishes an annual Role Model & Ally list of LGBT+ business executives and future leaders. This has now been expanded to create similar lists for ethnically diverse and women role models and allies – EMpower and HEROes, respectively. Suki is also a Stonewall Ambassador and supports many charities including the Albert Kennedy Trust as a Patron and Outright International in New York as a Board Director.

In 2019, Suki Sandhu was awarded an OBE by the Queen for services to diversity in business.

Opportunity can be anywhere

I did an internship during two summers in university, where I was selling gourmet frozen food door-to-door. It was very much a student sort of thing, literally going around with somebody else and a freezer in the back of a van, then knocking on doors and selling boxes of fancy frozen food at forty pounds each. I still look back on that and think, *God, how on earth did they get us to do that?* It was probably the hardest thing I've ever done.

However, it turned out that I was really good at it and while door knocking I met a woman who was the MD for a really large recruitment business. She said, 'Look, you're fantastic at this', and gave me her card because she obviously wanted to talk to me some more about my ambitions. I took the card and said a polite 'Thank you very much', but all I could think about was closing the frozen food sale and moving on to the next one. I received commission for every box that I sold, and I was a poor student who needed to make money now.

The summer ended, I came back home and while trying to decide what I wanted to do career-wise I remembered the card that I'd been given and how that woman seemed interesting. I researched what recruitment means, what it involves, what were the different things I'd like about recruitment consulting: it's agency focused, you've got candidates, you've got clients ... My first thought was, *Actually, I could really enjoy doing this*. The idea of sales relationships, and helping candidates find new roles, really appealed to me so I targeted Michael Page Recruitment who offered a really good training ground through their graduate programme. A lot of people say they fell into recruitment, but after researching it I purposely wanted to go into that field, believing that this is something I could do very well.

Out of a thousand applicants I was one of the sixteen people chosen that year to be on the graduate training programme and I found out I had been right – I was really good at it! I had found my niche and I really enjoyed being the go-between, acting on behalf of people and prospective employers, helping them with transitions in their careers and moving them along in their journey. I found it so fulfilling.

I spent a few years at Michael Page where I broke lots of company records and became their top global consultant out of the thousands of people they have around the world. I then moved from there to a smaller boutique firm, where the focus was more on the UK and changing representation at senior levels within companies. This is where I opened my eyes to wanting to level the playing field for diverse professionals and realised the change which could be achieved through focused and fair recruitment.

Just because you've been accepted doesn't mean all is as it should be

I was in my first recruitment job at Michael Page for nearly four years, but because of my experiences right from day one, I was aware there were improvements that could be made to the predominant culture within the recruitment industry. It was very macho, and from the perspective of a working-class lad coming down from Derby like me, it was very intimidating – I hated it when I first started there. I remember I was so excited about moving to London – *Gosh! My big graduate job in this global business!* – so of course I wanted to dress really stylishly and look really cool and trendy coming to London. I bought a suit that was aubergine in colour; I wore it with either a white or a purple shirt and a really colourful stripy tie. And at this time, this is me in the closet, or at least thinking I'm in the closet.

When I got there on that first day, not only was I probably the only working-class graduate, I was the only one who hadn't been privately educated, and they all looked super smart and corporate, wearing a navy blue suit, the red tie, the white shirt, and with me looking garish and very flamboyant. At the end of the day the MD took us all to the pub – there was a very big drinking culture there – and I remember in front of everyone said, 'Suki, what on earth are you wearing? You look like a deckchair!'

You laugh along with it because you don't want to be the troublesome one, but I also remember my manager at the time taking me to one side to give me the 'uniform chat': she said I needed to fit in and I needed to be more restrained in my choices. It was my very first job coming out of university, so I didn't really know anything apart from that environment where I didn't feel like I fitted in, but of course I took notice of what he told me because I didn't want to lose the job.

Then one of the managers took me under his wing and basically mentored me and coached me. It was what we now know as allyship; someone who was very different to me, taking an interest and acting as an ally. He was basically the complete opposite of me, a short, straight South African white guy, but he took an interest in me, developed me and I grew to become the company's top consultant globally. If it wasn't for that support I wouldn't be where I am today because I would have likely screwed up and moved on to do something completely different. I wouldn't have started my own business, I wouldn't have a business in the US, I wouldn't have an OBE.

Even with the coaching it's still down to you

At Michael Page, I might not have agreed with the workplace culture, but it didn't put me off. I put my head down, and I worked my butt off because even though I had really good coaching and advice from an ally, it was down to me. This was almost twenty years ago, when I was twenty-two, and the working world was very different to what it is now. You didn't really have that focus on inclusion and values that we have now with Gen Z coming into the workplace and the purpose they have. Back then you got a job, they made us work our backsides off and that was all I knew because I didn't know anywhere else.

However, when I started earning bonuses that was different. As a previously poor student suddenly getting bonuses, I now felt: *Oh God! I'm making money! I can afford to go out and have dinner with friends and have a fun time!* So ultimately I stuck it out for as long as I could.

I realised I had to work hard and show that I could do a really good job, because they had a culture where you did ten- or eleven-hour days. But I found I *thrived* on that, I loved it. I'm someone that really loves being busy, but busy and effective not a busy fool. So once I get in an environment like that I'm incredibly driven – I want to be the best. I wasn't going to let anybody get better than me at what I had to deliver. I set all sorts of records at Michael Page which still stand, so I am really competitive, but that's also me and my personality – I want to be the best.

It's not just about competing with other people though. One thing I've learned about myself over the years in business is that I'm incredibly self-motivated and I'm someone who competes with myself. I'm not trying to compare myself to others or compare myself to other founders; I simply want to set my own path. As a company I want us to compete, I want us to be innovative, to be provocative, I want us to be *mavericks* in the field of what we do, not follow what others do.

Network, network, network

A key thing is building relationships and networking within a business. Because, unfortunately, life is still a little bit about who you know, so to be able to climb the ladder you have to try and get yourself into networks and communities. That could be networks of other leaders that are similar to you, it could be the LGBT+ community, it could be the Black network . . . get involved in those and be visible, that way you're raising your own profile and opening yourself up for support.

Always look to advance the agenda

I moved on from the boutique firm I joined after Michael Page because although I saw what was possible in the recruitment field, my big thought was, *Actually, I can do it better!* Being in recruitment you see the lack of diversity as you climb the career ladder and that made me think, *Where are the diverse role models that look like me? Where are the LGBT+ leaders? Where are women?* They were just so few and far between. I genuinely believed in what could be achieved through carefully focused recruitment, whereas at that firm it seemed it was all about commercialism and making money. If anything, it was the catalyst for me to want to do more in that space to drive the change that we all needed to see, so I left to set up on my own.

For me, it was about levelling the playing field for diverse talent in the broadest possible sense. By that time, it was a given that lots of Chairmen and CEOs wanted to hire women, but I was looking at a bigger agenda – what about race? You have an entirely white board and entirely white leadership teams. Or what about LGBT+? What about socio-economic diversity? I'm a working-class boy from Derby, so what about the diversity of thinking that people like me can bring? When I started my own company, it was this range of diversity that I wanted everyone to be aware of.

If you roll forward to 2020 and the Black Lives Matter protests, that was a huge catalyst for companies to take the race agenda seriously, but before that it required real persistence. It was where I found my purpose and I believe we have been making a difference and changing the face of business in the UK and the US.

Dress sense is good sense

Part of the reason I set up my own business is because I wanted to create my own path and I didn't want to fit in to the corporate ways of doing things – I haven't worn a tie in about eleven years. Or a business suit! It's almost like my protest to all those older straight white men who are in charge of business wearing the same suits and I'm trying to show that you don't need a suit to be successful. Still, in today's world, I can only do that in my own company.

Obviously dress codes have changed massively from what they were twenty years ago, but in most industries and in most companies guys still wear a shirt and tie, a suit and smart shoes, but I'm a great believer that if you look good you feel good. The way you present yourself can change your mood and the way you relate to other people, so I'm a big fan of fashion. Also, as far as men are concerned, I think they feel quite limited about what they feel they can be creatively wearing and still be smart, so I do a lot of fashion posts on

LinkedIn and Instagram, saying this is what I'm wearing, this is where I'm going, this is the client I'm seeing. That last bit is important, because different clients will expect something different from me.

I didn't push it in the corporate world. Before I left my last firm where I was a partner, I was in a shirt and a tie and suit every day. When I launched my own business I just thought, *I'm not doing that any more! I don't want to wear that.* My clients are largely chairmen and CEOs, and obviously the dress code will vary by industry. We have clients in banking, utilities and real estate where it's still very smart. Although you're quite limited in what you can do, you can creatively dress up the standard uniform to show your individuality. I would do this with some quite jazzy shirt/tie combinations or a little handkerchief in the pocket and jazzy cufflinks, or maybe with the shoes I'm wearing as well.

I never expect employees in my company to wear a tie, unless it's a gala event when it's black tie and even then you can still go for it with an alternative. I'll wear something completely different, like when I got my OBE: I wore this cravat-based shirt from Burberry with a new season Alexander McQueen suit that had a stitched print on the jacket and also on the leg. The other men collecting their awards were obviously all very formally suited and booted and black tie, almost like it was a dress code, and I felt like, *Not doing that! It's my OBE, I'm gonna wear what I want!* It was so funny because the staff in Buckingham Palace were constantly coming up to me, tapping me on the shoulder and saying 'Oh my goodness! You look fabulous!' so I definitely stood out.

But that's it – I want to be unapologetically me. If *you* don't like it, that's your problem, not mine. I think maybe because I've got the confidence – I've been doing it for eleven years, I run a really successful business, I have a really great team – I suppose I'm trying to get others to be brave and be proud to be themselves, and not have to hide who they are.

Of course, I realise how much of this depends on what sort of clothes a person can afford. If you're coming from a more privileged background your parents might get you a tailored suit, but if you don't you're probably going to get something more high street. If you're interviewing candidates, you have to make allowances and be aware that the definition of 'smart' is really hard and it depends on the individual. From the other side, the advice I would give to young people when dressing for interviews, is to wear something you think would be appropriate for the place you are being interviewed by. This would apply to virtual interviews too, even if it is only your top half that is appearing on screen.

If it's financial services, then the guys probably should wear a shirt and tie and a suit, that will probably be expected; likewise women should be very smart. I think you would dress for the industry and the role that you are applying for. So if you're meeting a tech firm I would wear just a cool top, something simple, nothing with a slogan, and not anything that is going to prejudice you in that meeting.

There's so much unconscious bias to deal with, and in virtual meetings you could be getting a lot from the background as well – your prospective employer will be looking into your home and it wouldn't be unexpected for people to form opinions based on what they are seeing in the background. I'm a great believer that if you don't a have good background – neat and neutral – when you're interviewing, then just put the filter on. If it's all blurred out and nobody can see anything then all they can focus on is you and what you're saying in that conversation.

Embrace your performance reviews

Communication is critical. With any person going into a company or a new role, my advice is be really clear about what 'good' looks like. That is to say, what is your manager expecting from you? Be really clear on deliverables and objectives, and you should also be tracking your own success. For example, people normally hate the annual or quarterly review process that looks at their performance as they're terrified they're going to be taken to task over something, but I think you should embrace the opportunity it provides.

The performance review should be used as a two-way thing, as your opportunity to seek feedback and to also give feedback to your manager so you can grow and can grade your own performance. Importantly, it's a chance to seek more projects or new work to do, because I think you always want to lead with your talent and your skills. Yes you might be different, you might be Black, you might be gay, you might be Indian, you might be a woman, but at the end of the day that shouldn't matter: it should be about your performance and how you did a great job. Lead with that, so when you're discussing what you've done you've made sure it's out there. In other words, do a great job because that's what's going to help you get the visibility with other leaders.

If a client doesn't feel right . . .

If I don't like a client, if the vibe is not right or there's not good chemistry when I go to meet them, I don't need the business. I always think that as a recruitment consultancy firm, I don't work for them. I'm not anybody's employee, I'm their *advisor* – I don't need to hire for you, I don't need to find your board for you. I usually say to those clients, 'Actually we're at full capacity, we're too busy, but thank you so much for getting in touch.'

Be careful not to underestimate people around you

I came out of the closet during my time at Michael Page and it was almost as if I wanted to be really successful first, hoping that when and if I came out it wouldn't matter because I was a really great employee. I looked on it as: *I'm a really successful team member, they won't care that I'm gay.* And actually they didn't! To most of the people in the firm it wasn't a surprise, they already knew. I was expecting more tantrums and tears but they didn't arrive; most people were saying things like, 'Yeah, I already knew, can I get a drink now!'

It's the same with my family; you always start to plan for it – coming out – and you naturally start to put up walls. I was in an Indian working-class Sikh household, my mum and dad came over from India with very little – my dad came over when he was six, my mum came over when she married my dad. They were grocery shop owners, and they worked hard for us kids. I've always had that work ethic instilled in me because of seeing my parents work hard for us. Knowing that, you try to create a life where you *are* independent because at that moment when they find out, they might reject you and not want you in the family. I needed to be financially secure and have a friendship circle outside my family that would be there for me if it all came crumbling down.

Also, as a gay man you're always coming out. When I meet people and talk about my husband they hear it's a husband not a wife which means immediately they know I'm gay, or they hear the pronoun 'he' and they know that my partner is a man. So you're constantly coming out as an LGBT+ person but I don't dwell on it, that's who I am. Your homophobia is your problem, not mine.

With my family, my sister was the first one that I told; this would have been in my early twenties because I thought as soon as I tell somebody in my family, there's no going back. This was seventeen years ago so it was a very different world, as there's a lot more acceptance globally now. She's my little sister, we're like two peas in a pod and we've always got on really well. She immediately started crying – she was really happy for me but she was also really worried about how my dad would react.

I told my brother and he was totally fine with it, but I didn't tell the rest of the family and it was only when I met Manuel, my husband, a few years later, that I knew I had to make that decision. We met in Berlin and were doing the long-distance thing for two years, then he moved to London to live with me, and that was when I knew I *had* to tell my mum, because I couldn't have my parents come down to London to see me and feel as though I've got to hide him. So we planned a trip for my mum to come to London for the weekend with my sister when I was going to tell her.

We planned a whole weekend of sightseeing. There was a Hindi film that had come out called *Dostana* that had a gay theme to it – it was a bit of a comedy about two men pretending to live together in a gay relationship so they could rent an apartment. I thought we could watch that on the Friday or Saturday night to start the conversation, because then my mum's got it in her head, and then the next morning we could tell her that I'm gay. This was all because her only view of the gay community would have been what she'd seen on the soap opera *EastEnders* – she didn't know any gay people, or *knowingly* know of any gay people. So we did all the sightseeing on the Saturday, we had a really fun day, came home, had dinner and we were going to put the film on, but then Mum said, 'I'm really tired, I'm going to go to bed.' So we never watched the film.

The next morning we had a really awkward conversation on the big sofa where my mum was at one end, my sister in the middle and me at the other end, trying to tell her that I'm gay. What made it worse was that I'm definitely my mum's favourite and everybody knows it, so it's really hard having this conversation. When it clicked with my my mum she said, 'Well, you can still get married,' and I said, 'Hmmm, I can, but not to a woman!' Which also made me think, *Gosh, how many people does she know that have done this?* People who have wanted to come out and just gone, 'No, I'll just get a marriage of convenience . . . no-one needs to know . . . just get on with it.'

My sister took her for a walk because she was really upset, really tearful. She was saying, 'We'll let you see a doctor . . . get you some drugs, you'll be OK . . . We'll fix you.' That was her reaction, because she didn't really know what gay was.

I couldn't tell my dad. I finally wrote a letter that I had my brother give to him, because my dad is quite a macho man in the family and a well-known person in the local community. When my dad read the letter, he said, 'Oh God I already knew that!' In fact, his first reaction was worry about how my mum would to take it, because he had no idea my mum had known for a few years by then.

Now they call my husband 'son', they see him as part of the family, and they are the biggest allies to the community because of me and my relationship. So there are really positive things to have come out of it, but it took time. That's the healer, and as part of the LGBT+ community you always have your coming-out experience, which is why – if you are LGBT+ – it's really important to be part of that community to share stories. Remember with LGBT+, it's invisible – you can't see it, you need to come out. It's not like my race or my gender which you can see when I walk into the room. With LGBT+, you have to come out.

Why coming out counts

One of the reasons why we did the OUTstanding Role Model List for LGBT+ leaders with the *Financial Times* was because we wanted people to know there are a lot of really successful LGBT+ leaders in business who are openly gay, openly lesbian, openly bi-sexual, openly trans and doing really amazing jobs. We wanted to shatter the stereotypes of what people expect our community to be.

It started first of all as a list of fifty LGBT+ executives. I already had a very good network of LGBT+ executives which is why I had the idea to begin with: I wanted to celebrate business leaders, not just the arts world or fashion, I wanted people in *business*. So I already knew a lot of them, and we did a lot of social media and outreach to companies: 'Hey, come and nominate your openly LGBT+ execs who are doing great things for the community and for your company.' That's how it started, then the year afterwards, in 2014, we did a Top 100 LGBT+ execs and as that was the first of its kind it was all over the media and we reached millions of people globally. That was like a launch pad and it got the message out.

That year, we added the Top 20 Allies list of straight leaders – Richard Branson was the Number 1. Again, that resonated and it just grows year on year: now we do a Top 100 Execs, Top 100 Future Leaders and Top 50 Advocates or Allies for LGBT+. We have also expanded it to do a list for racially diverse executives and future leaders and allies, and also women in business. So we now do three sets of lists a year.

It's how I know Jonathan Mildenhall. He was one of our role models in the LGBT+ list as an executive, and he had an amazing story – a working-class boy, who had a *horrible* journey in advertising and look at him now, he's forged his own path and is doing amazingly. I wanted other people to know that. I wanted other people to read that story and see him and hear about him and think, *I can get there too, and it's OK being gay.*

We need to give the next generation hope, we need to give them people to look up to, we need to inspire them and we need to shatter stereotypes, so that they know that being LGBT+ doesn't mean you have to be an entertainer, or be in the arts, or in fashion. You can be a CFO (Chief Financial Officer), you can be a CMO (Chief Marketing Officer), you can be a partner in a law firm . . .

That's why we did the role model list originally. Now it's grown into this huge movement where we do it three times a year across women, LGBT+ and race, and they're my favourite times of the year because it's amazing to see the change that's happening in business.

If you can, you must

A very long time ago I gave donations to a charity that was called Dress For Success and is now called Smartworks, that was about helping vulnerable women, giving them a makeover and wardrobe to help them with getting a job. There was the male version called Suited & Booted which I've also supported, helping vulnerable men with clothes that have been donated, giving them a makeover and building their confidence to get a job and get a foot on the ladder. I liked the fact that it was about vulnerable people, and obviously as a recruitment consultant we work at the executive level, so it was nice to give back and support grassroots.

I'm involved with a lot of charitable initiatives. I really believe that if you can, you must. I'm able to because I'm in quite a privileged position so I support many charities each year, particularly now because charities are having really tough times. I even set up a fund with an LGBT+ platform called GiveOut, which is trying to get more funds to LGBT+ activists and organisations in Asia.

I'm on the board of Outright Action International, an LGBT+ non-governmental human rights organisation in New York; I've been on that board for three years and I've connected them with some of the corporates that I work with to assist fundraising. I'm a patron for AKT, formerly the Albert Kennedy Trust, which is the UK's largest LGBT+ youth charity – Sir Ian McKellen is one of the patrons – that focuses on homelessness among the young LGBT+ community which disproportionately affects racially diverse youths. If you think about coming out and telling your family, then you layer on race and religion, a lot of the kids get kicked out and are made homeless because the families can't cope with it. I want to be able to support them through the charity by making sure it can help as many people as possible

So charity is really important to me because I just think you *should*. I try and encourage other people to get involved too – having a strong network means I know lots of people who have done very well financially so I'm always pitching for money from them: 'Guys, can you give some . . .' For my fortieth birthday in 2020, everybody was at home because it was lockdown, and I didn't *need* anything, so I decided to support the Asian fund that I set up. I told my friends 'I'd rather you put money into this than anything for me' and we raised £20,000.

Lessons

Opportunity can come knocking at any time. For young Suki, that meant following up on a random encounter with a recruitment consultant who introduced him to the industry in which he now has a leading voice that is driving rapid and purposeful change.

If you want early-stage career success you have to commit to being the very best you can be. Focus on exceeding all the expectations other people will put on you. Do a great job so you get noticed for being great talent.

You must figure out how to harness the power of mentors and allies. Remember to hold on to those who make the biggest impact on your work. We all need cheerleaders along the way.

Professional presentation counts. Dress in a way that suits the industry you are working in but always remember to add your own authentic style. Authenticity matters.

Affirmation: Today I will use my authentic voice to push me forward.

'The Discerner'

MICHELLE YOU

Imagine signing up to a service that thumbed through your music collection, worked out what and who you liked and then alerted you when an act you'd like was playing live near you. Then, better still, it offers you tickets for the gigs before they go on general sale. That was Songkick, developed and launched by Michelle and two co-founders in 2007. Perhaps the most remarkable thing about the launch was Michelle's background as a journalist and editor with an art and culture magazine. Yes, she had built fansites for her favourite band in high school, but other than that she would be the last person to claim a tech background.

However, this has definitely worked to Michelle's advantage, as one of the frequently overlooked aspects of tech-based start-ups is their user experience – what do they want to do, rather than how are they supposed to do it? She believes it was crucial in her so clearly identifying what Songkick should be all about, and in her and her current venture.

After selling Songkick, following a legal dispute with Ticketmaster, she raised funding for, developed and launched Supercritical, a carbon removal marketplace platform that works with corporations to help them achieve net zero by measuring their carbon emissions, providing reduction recommendations, and helping them buy a portfolio of carbon removal offsets. As with Songkick she approached the idea by looking at what was needed and working back from there.

All experiences count

Before co-founding Songkick I came from a background that couldn't be further removed from tech – English literature and philosophy! I got my Masters at Cambridge in literature and I was a writer at a magazine called *Theme*, an arts and culture quarterly. Unfortunately it's not in print any more, but it ran for a few years, based in New York, and I loved doing that because I love culture and I love the arts and music.

To set up a tech company wasn't really such a huge jump for me because I grew up in Silicon Valley where so much of the tech industry is based. Both my parents were software engineers, so I've always been around technology and had a huge appreciation of what it can do. I can remember when the internet first came about and you had dial-up and modems and all of that, and I was fascinated. I just loved the way you could access information, how it allowed you to follow your interests and find things and research stuff – you could learn so much, whereas the opportunity to talk to somebody or go to a library might be limited.

I've always loved the *potential* of the internet and I think, in hindsight, I was captivated by how the internet was shaping culture, although I might not have been aware of that at the time. I still am fascinated as it is shaping how we communicate, how we live, what art we produce, and I think that level of impact in what I do is really interesting for me. Coming from that journalist background, when the possibilities of the internet come together with how I think about people and stories and *why* so much stuff is like it is, I could see so many opportunities for providing information. I've always been a bit of an outsider, so hopefully my background brought me to it with an interesting perspective.

There is no right way to start a venture, as long as you have a good idea

My two co-founders in Songkick were my boyfriend at the time, who is now my husband, and his old university roommate. From college days they had always talked about how they wanted to start a business together. Then they reached that point in their careers where they'd been working for a few years and didn't want to work for anybody else any more and figured that was the time to start something together, but we didn't really know what. Primarily, they wanted to start something of their own, and so the discussion was not 'We've got this great idea but how do we get it going?' but 'What do we want to start?' *Then* we came up with the idea. From there we started brainstorming, and we all loved going to see live music so that was always a big part of the 'What would be really cool to work in?' discussion. Once we'd got to that we started to refine the thinking as to what we would want from it.

I'm not going to say that's a recommended way to get started on a venture, but it's not a *not* recommended way either! It's certainly unusual, but I really don't know if I could say there was one recommended way, because there are so many ways to do it successfully. The process is so personal to who you are. What I would think that everybody needs is to have an idea that they're passionate about because you'll need that to sustain you through so many ups and downs. You'll need full commitment and what I guess would be called total loyalty to the idea. Whether you want to start a company first or do it another way, whatever you choose it's going to be hard, so you'll have to care about what you're doing.

How we came up with Songkick was actually pretty straightforward. I am a huge music fan and I've always loved going to gigs. At that time I was young – twenty-five and childless – and while I would go to as many gigs as I could, I just found it impossible to know everything about what was going on. I lived in New York where every type of gig or genre of band you could possibly want was happening, but there was really no one source of information – or as with most things you have to sort through so much stuff you're not interested in to find something you might want to go to. So when we were coming up with ideas for the company I just asked, 'Could you make something that could scan my iTunes library and alert me when any of the bands I have in my iTunes come to my city?' And that, essentially, was the idea for Songkick.

It is the creative side of innovation and problem solving that has always appealed to me, so coming up with a proposition like that was really my strength. This was pre-iPhone, even pre-Spotify. iTunes was where people had their music and that idea for personalised concert notification was the kernel of the company, and it turned out I wasn't the only one that wanted that service either – there were millions of others out there who quickly found it useful and that's how the company grew.

It moved on from that original idea, because the technology moved what was possible and how people accessed their music. Now it can open up Spotify or your phone's music library, scan through every single artist in there, then crawl the internet for you. Songkick can go to every single country in the world and has the most comprehensive database of concerts *globally*, so if a band you've got music by is going to play a gig near you it will let you know.

Also, it has a database of concerts that are announced that day and as it will know who you like it can send you a personalised notification list – 'You love these 25 bands, this one is coming to London, they've just announced tour dates this morning, get tickets before they go on sale.' That is now used by twenty million people monthly.

Not everybody bearing cash is a fairy godmother

In the beginning we worked with Y Combinator, which was one of the first of what they call Start Up Accelerator programmes – they're sometimes called seed accelerators – whereby prospective companies like ours apply to be taken on. If successful, then the company will receive a little bit of funding before they do anything. At this point the start-up will be put into a group of newbies just like themselves where they will be given mentoring and support around the early stages of starting a company when it will be so fragile.

It's this peer network and advice that is probably more important than the funding, which doesn't tend to be huge amounts. This is why although start-up accelerators are a very good idea they're not always super effective because the quality of the mentorship can vary greatly. So, if you're a successful applicant it's a matter of being sure that you will get the best out of it, because it will become such a big part of your life. We were with a really good programme – Y Combinator was absolutely transformational to us.

I believe one of the most important things about it was just being in a cohort of your peers who are doing the same thing at the same time, because it's so hard and lonely and difficult. Having a support group of people who are experiencing exactly what you are at that point in your development is super helpful – making your first hire, firing the first person you have to, fund raising from venture capitalists – all the stuff that is new and difficult. Being the founder of a company is so lonely, it's very hard to find people you can relate to. I found that among my friends who aren't founders there's only so much they can take on board about what I'm going through, so if you can have people that can understand that it's very helpful.

Y Combinator has now turned out to be one of the best and most successful accelerator programmes in the world: it funded Airbnb, Stripe. Dropbox . . . Some of the biggest tech unicorns of our generation started with Y Combinator. We were part of that programme in 2007, and weren't really anything before then.

Know when to get out

At Songkick we ended up suing Ticketmaster for anti-trust violations. We sold concert tickets through our app and our website, and when Ticketmaster merged with LiveNation they became the biggest concert promoter in the world, the biggest ticket vendor in the world, the biggest venue owner in the world and they started squeezing artists and telling them not to work with us. We weren't alone in this: many, many companies have tried to sue Ticketmaster in the past the String Cheese Incident and Pearl Jam to name but two. We got the farthest along in that process but before we went into court we had to go into arbitration.

They offered us a settlement. Then we ended up selling the rest of the company to Warner Music because we couldn't really go on with it after that. To us that was a safe landing for the product and for the team and it found a great home at Warner Music: the app is still alive, some of the original team work there. Millions of music fans use it every month. I believe it's retained the integrity of what we started.

It was absolutely the right thing to do, but it was a very painful process. You have to be able to give it up and say *I have no control over this any more and they're going to do what they're going to do with it* and not have false hope. So it is a positive outcome that the app is alive and well and updated, but we had a lot of ambition for the company and at that point we hadn't wanted to sell, we wanted to make it a longstanding thing that would be useful to the public, in perpetuity. I don't think anybody starts a business with the intention of ending in a lawsuit. It felt like we didn't get our David and Goliath moment, we had to accept the outcome and walk away which was very hard. It took me many years to get over it.

Do something you believe in

I left Songkick in 2016 and didn't start Supercritical until January 2021, nearly five years later. I had just become a mother and I took time off to be a parent, so there were a lot of life changes. Pretty soon after I left Songkick I read this book, the Patagonia founder's company values handbook, *Let My People Go Surfing*, by this man who'd started an outdoors company that became much more than that – it's looked at as a great company with a lot of influence and impact in terms of how he ran the business. I read it because I was curious about his story. It's part memoir, part company values book, and the whole thing is about climate change. I remember reading it and thinking, *Oh my God! I didn't realise we were so fucked!*

I knew that climate change was happening, I recycled and did the things responsible people do, but after reading this I realised we're not doing anything about it, this is really bad and it's nearly too late. I was really scared! *'What am I going to do about this?'* I had my son about a year later and about a month after he was born the report came out from the IPCC, which is the UN body of scientists that report on climate change. That report was about staying below 1.5 degrees Celsius of warming and what we need in order to do that, and if we don't get to net zero emissions by 2050 we're going to see increased warming and disasters. Having a son made that timeline very real – I could look at him and think: *2050? You're still going to be a thirty-something young man. It's really terrifying to think about you trying to live on a planet that's basically unlivable.*

That urgency became a lot more real and I went through a real period of depression about it as I just felt so terrible and helpless. I came out of that thinking *I don't know what I can do, but I need to do whatever I can.* I started a mobile app, Songkick, that has twenty million users so I must be able to do something useful on climate change?

I joined a venture capital fund in London that was founded by one of my early investors, and they encouraged me. They said, take the time to explore and learn while you're working with us and see what's going on around tech in climate – just learn. I was there for a couple of years, I got to know climate companies, I met scientists, I had meetings with people in government and economists, just getting my head around it. That's how I found the space to think up the idea for Supercritical.

What is unique about what we do is we focus on carbon removal – carbon removals are the technologies that remove carbon dioxide from the air and then sequester it permanently. The best-known example is something called Direct Air Capture which is literally fans that filter the air, absorb carbon dioxide and sequester it in the ground. These technologies have been around for less than twenty years, so they're quite early and new, and we've created a marketplace that aggregates all these removal solutions and makes them available to companies that want them. It's almost like a brokerage that puts carbon removal together with the customer.

In 2018 the IPCC report I mentioned talked about getting to net zero by 2050, which was the first call to net zero globally. That's when the UK decided to put the net zero target into law — it was the first G7 nation to make that a legal commitment. Quickly that idea trickled down into the business community and now companies are making net zero commitments. But with this idea of getting to net zero carbon emissions there's so much confusion and doubt and uncertainty, so we basically help businesses cut through all that. Our software measures their carbon emissions automatically, then we can take some data inputs and we can spit out, automatically, something that tells them, 'Here are your global carbon emissions — here are their sources: they come from Cloud computing, they come from your team lunches, they come from online advertising, they come from heating et cetera.' Then once we've done that we can help them figure out the best way to reduce those emissions over time and finally the last step is to actually lower those emissions by carbon removal.

We've raised capital, we're building the product, we have customers . . . we just want to unfuck the planet and sell as much carbon removal as possible.

Don't go back to the fray until you are sure you are ready

I do think we could have done something really great with Songkick if it hadn't been for that lawsuit, and it was very painful to swallow, so after that I took a year off and travelled around the world with my husband. We backpacked for six months straight. We just packed up our backpacks and went on the road which was amazing, then when we got back we continued travelling for basically a year.

Sadly we weren't actually sitting on a pile of money — even with the settlement and the exit from Songkick, the way all the agreements were constructed meant we didn't walk away with enough money to retire by any means. But we were lucky enough to have enough cash to give ourselves the space to figure out what came next, so it was really important that we had that time out of tech or out of business, because I was really lost after that whole experience of starting a company and leaving it before I felt properly ready. It's not a common experience at all – what do you do after you leave a company that you started? It's a very difficult process and I was lucky enough to have a couple of friends who had gone through the same experience and I could talk to them about it. Even so, it's such a loss because my whole identity was bound up in Songkick and what I did there, so when I left I felt like, *Who am I? What do I care about? What do I want to do next?* That process of searching I found really frustrating, and in spite of giving myself the freedom to explore, I did not handle it well.

However, it was going travelling like that I believe offered me an amazing opportunity – here we were, living out of a backpack with very little, we were *incredibly* frugal, and it really made me question: *What matters to me? How much do I really need to be happy? What do I need to be happy?* Also around that time we were doing a lot of outdoors sports – before that trip I'd never been hiking or camping or anything like that, but we started surfing and climbing and really falling in love with nature. I believe that kind of exposed me to a different lifestyle and pace of life.

My big thing was figuring out: *Am I going to start another company? Am I a founder? Am I an entrepreneur?* I believe I kind of accidentally became an entrepreneur – I've never been somebody who's had a *plan* or a ten-year career path, I just go with my own instincts, so finding out where my instincts were leading me was hard, but I am glad I gave myself that time.

I guess this wasn't like redefining who I was, it was more like *discovering* who was in there. I think that impact and mission was always there, we had such a mission to make it easy to discover gigs – we really believed in the value of live music and the experience of it. Supercritical is also mission driven, but focused on a more existential impact like climate change. By that time I was sure of what I wanted to do, so by then it was quite easy for me.

265

It was as if I was shaking myself up and no longer being in this high-powered, fast-paced start-up world. I think it gave me the ability to see what was possible in a different way and I hope I've carried a lot of those values into what I do today because it's really easy to lose sight of them when you're back in your normal environment.

Give yourself the time and space to experiment

One of the great learnings I've had as a founder is 'Ideas are cheap'. If you think you've had this original idea then twenty-five other people have had that idea at the same time, because it's in the zeitgeist. It's the execution that's really hard – giving an idea life, making it stick and making it grow is what's really difficult. That's the beauty of venture capital; it's capital that gives you that foundation to invest in making the idea happen, and that investment will largely be in the people you hire because things don't happen without people doing them. Hiring the right people to create them is vital. You're also giving yourself the space to fail – you try stuff out, it doesn't work, because you don't know what's going to work, so you try something else – that's all about time, really, which in itself will be about money at this stage.

So often the dividing line between making a company work or not making it work is having a very experimental mindset as to what you try out, and being open to being wrong. That and thinking about the fastest way you can test an idea and get feedback on whether it's right or wrong. I know I'm not the first person to say that because it's something I learned the hard way at Songkick – in the early days before I was experienced enough I would build something, design it, it would take months, I would launch it and then the market didn't want it!

It's another great learning that other than Steve Jobs no-one is a genius who can predict what the market wants, and you need to learn by putting something out there and getting feedback so you can keep doing this while you're getting to the right idea. I believe it's that approach and that mentality that determines whether people and companies will succeed.

You don't need to be a coding nerd to succeed in tech

I'm probably the biggest charlatan in the tech world, because I never learned how to code! Well, that's not entirely true at a very basic level – when I was in high school I taught myself to code so as to build a fan website for my favourite band. So I did that, but that's not the only skill you need to build an app, so at Songkick I was never a contributor to the code base, let's put it that way! I've needed to hire and lead the people who are good at the coding,

With my background in literature and philosophy I was bringing this storytelling element to why we're doing what we're doing, which is necessary to lead a team. It's not just a case of telling them what to do! I worked with them to figure out what to do and then I made sure that everybody was on the same page as we were building the thing. You can never tell people what to do – you have to convince them that your idea is the right thing and then get their buy-in. One of my key skills is communicating and explaining concepts, making the arguments as to *why* something is a good idea.

The other thing that I actually loved doing at Songkick was on the user research side, which I saw as very similar to my previous life as a journalist. You sit down with customers and you show them the product, you ask them questions and then you learn how they feel. What do they feel? How do they feel when they think about this? Those skills were the same as when I was reading novels or interviewing subjects for my stories and looking for those kinds of empathies.

If you want a certain sort of investor you have to go and look for them

One of the things I'm proudest about with Supercritical is that when we raised some funding for the company over half of our investors were women, which definitely wasn't the case with Songkick. In this instance I made a real effort to find female investors to bring on board, because what people don't realise is that a situation won't just happen naturally, you have to make it happen.

Having been a venture capitalist and looking at all the investors, there are so few women who invest and I probably doubled the length of my fund raising, timewise, because I was committed to having 50 per cent women. You have to make the commitment and then say you're not going to stop until you've done it, because if you just do it the same way as everyone else and wait for them to come to you, then you won't end up with half women on your panel.

Lessons

Understanding the value of your outsider perspective is critical. For young Michelle that meant having confidence to build a tech platform even though she was a tech novice; she knew what her customers wanted.

Look for the potential in everything you do and are passionate about. The status quo can and will evolve with your creativity and focus.

When you are starting a venture, think about the biggest problem you feel most capable and passionate about solving. Passion is power.

Network with peers who are at the same stage as you. Peer-to-peer learning can be transformational for a young business.

Affirmation: Today I'm going to do my bit to protect the planet for current and future generations.

'The Advocate'

MOHSIN ZAIDI

♦

Mohsin Zaidi won a national Penguin Books writing competition, resulting in the publishing of his memoir, *A Dutiful Boy*. It is the poignant story of a Muslim boy growing up in a religious, working-class household in London's Walthamstow, coming to terms with his sexuality and being the first from his school to go to Oxford university. The book was critically acclaimed, won the US Lambda Literary Award and the UK Polari Prize and was featured on several Best Books of the Year lists including the *Guardian* and the *Newstatesman*.

While writing *A Dutiful Boy*, Mohsin was a criminal barrister with a strong sense of social justice, following a globe-trotting spell as a corporate lawyer with leading international law firm Linklaters. He has worked at a UN War Crimes tribunal in The Hague and as Judicial Assistant to Lord Sumption and Lord Wilson at the UK's Supreme Court.

Deeply involved in community issues, Mohsin actively campaigns for increased diversity and minority representation among Britain's decision makers, for greater social mobility and for LGBT rights. He was on the board of Stonewall, has been listed by the *Financial Times* as a future LGBT leader and, at the time of this interview (from which the following text is based), was regularly writing and commenting on issues of diversity and inclusion for outlets such as the *New York Times*, Sky News, the *i* newspaper and *Newsweek*.

What you sound like matters

I grew up in Walthamstow in a council house. I've always been well-spoken, which makes people assume I'm either middle class or I've changed my accent. I can remember when I was in reception class in the first year of school, the teacher said to my mum, 'He's like a little public schoolboy!' It's not something I'm proud of, in fact there's something uncomfortable about your voice betraying its origin.

People often assume that when I went to Oxford I changed my accent to fit in, but I always sounded like this. When I used slang words people would laugh at me because they sounded odd coming out of my mouth. Then I got to university and I was nowhere near as posh as everybody there; people would say, 'Oh, you're quite urban!' I thought, *Wow! That's the first time anybody's ever called me urban.*

I think, overall, my accent has been a bit of a Trojan horse because it has allowed me to exist in spaces where people have assumed I'm something I'm not. People think I'm privately educated, that I'm middle class, and that comes with certain assumptions about my politics and the way that I look at the world. For example, I was once at a dinner party where someone was talking about how they wouldn't want to live in the same building as council-house tenants. I pointed out that that would mean me and my family and the person was shocked.

I remember I was short-changed recently, and the person assumed, I think because I'm a brown guy, that I'd try to pull a fast one, but as soon as I started speaking he could tell that I was articulate and I wasn't going to back down – my voice became my sword because then it's suddenly, 'Oh, he doesn't sound brown, he sounds white! Better treat him like a white man!'

While the way I speak invited relentless bullying when I was at school, for the rest of my life it's been quite helpful.

Otherness isn't always a bad thing

My parents had made it clear, *You are going to university*, but Oxford was never, on the cards, even when I did surprisingly well in my penultimate year at school, getting three As when I really wasn't expecting it. It was my parents who said I should apply, because I had the brains, but I thought it would be a waste of time. Oxford was the sort of place our then Prime Minister Tony Blair or Bill Clinton had gone to, or Benazir Bhutto and Imran Khan, these rich Pakistanis I had heard of, so it wasn't something I ever thought I would be able to achieve. When I applied it was because my parents made me, and when I got the offer letter, I called Oxford because I thought they might have made a mistake.

That's how much I didn't believe I belonged there, and, at the same time, this unbelonging became something of a theme in life: when I was younger I knew I was gay, but I was from a religious family so I didn't think there was any space for that. I worked hard at school, I sounded so middle class and I was top of my class and people hated me for it – *I* hated me for it – so I didn't feel like I belonged. I took this to university, where suddenly people were asking me what school I had gone to, as if they would have heard of it, and I would have heard of their schools. They were talking about second homes and going on ski holidays, when the only place I had been on holiday to was Pakistan.

In many ways, though, that played to my advantage because there was an English etiquette that I didn't know existed. For example, I didn't know you couldn't talk about money, or that there were certain questions you weren't meant to ask. I always behaved the way I thought was best and fairest to everybody. I was never embarrassed about being the stupid one either, I had no problem saying, 'Look, I'm sure this is a stupid question but can I please ask it anyway?' Because I wasn't afraid to ask, I learned a great deal that might have otherwise passed me by.

I was honest about it and I think that that honesty helped to endear me at university. It meant that I made friends – there was no judgement. I didn't know there was a class system, let alone how rigid it seemed, so I didn't have a chip on my shoulder; in fact I have more of a chip on my shoulder about class now than I did when I was at Oxford. That ignorance was an advantage, because I hadn't known so much about the world; I was this bright-eyed person who just wanted to learn lots.

I went through a mental breakdown because I felt lost. In some ways, though, otherness has always been and will continue to be a superpower, and like all superpowers it's not always perfect. There's got to be some flaw, otherwise it's not an interesting story. I believe the same is true with human beings: our strengths are sometimes born from our weaknesses. I was bullied at school and this has helped shape me and the path I took. One of the reasons I became a lawyer is because of injustice. When I see bullying in whatever form it takes, I'm outraged and there is power in that outrage.

That feeling of unbelonging stayed with me for most of my life, although I believe that after publishing the book I've been able to put it down because I feel able to say, 'Actually I don't need to feel like I belong'. Getting to that point, though, took time.

Understand the relationship between success and failure

Particularly since I published *A Dutiful Boy* – and I'm really pleased that it's doing so well – I'll go to a speaking event and get an introduction on stage about how wonderful I am and here's what I have achieved, and I think, *no!* It gives everybody this false idea that somehow I'm superhuman and perfect, which can make other people feel like failures. It would be much healthier if we were able to reflect on failures and weaknesses. I'm terribly impatient, I'm insecure, I'm quite a strong personality . . . all of those things are things that I know that are good in some respects and they have helped me achieve, but they're also things that I'm working on and I'm not proud of all the time.

In some ways, failure can be easier to deal with than success because failure can be safer. Failure has always given me something to strive for. When I was younger life felt easier to navigate because there were all these hurdles put in front of me and I had one job – to get over them. I don't have to worry about being from a council house, or not being middle class, or being gay, or being from a Muslim background because I've managed to find a way of reconciling the different parts of my identity.

Although that reconciliation feels like success it's also the more uncomfortable way to be because suddenly there's this blank space in front of me and I'm thinking, *OK, what hurdles do I jump over now? What's next?*

The generation gap between immigrants and their children can be a chasm

It's a common immigrant mentality that their born-in-Britain children are going to do well for themselves, otherwise why are they – the parents – staying in this country? As Pakistani immigrants my parents believed that becoming a professional, being a doctor or a lawyer, was the single most important thing because it was a route to safety and security. I wasn't good at science so I chose the law.

Linklaters, one of the biggest and best law firms in the world, offered me a job and I discovered that I would immediately be earning more than my parents combined. That was a weird experience, because I suddenly found myself considering where it placed me in the family dynamic. Did it change anything? My sense of guilt started to creep in, about the things that life was giving me because my parents had sacrificed so much. With Linklaters I lived in Paris, Brussels, Madrid and I travelled the world. I remember wishing that my parents could have had this life.

I used to feel guilty and I still do sometimes; I acknowledge that they wanted a better life for me and so the best thing I can do is lead that life. I believe it is very important to make sure that other people that come behind me can lead that life too. I'm a governor at my old secondary school so I'm going back and telling the kids there that there is more to life than what they are told by society is for them; it's about them knowing they're allowed to dream. That's my way of knowing that I'm doing for them what my parents did for me.

On a more domestic front, being the successful child of immigrant parents brings its own issues. I grew up in a traditional Pakistani household and – leaving aside my sexuality– as I got older and started to form my own opinions my dad didn't know how to deal with it. Here was a child that wanted to be treated like an adult and to have his views and thoughts given the same respect as an adult's would be given, and that was complicated.

At some point all children and parents go through this dynamic of 'You can't tell me what to do any more, but you're still my dad so I have to figure out how to navigate this', but for *us* it felt more pronounced because I had gone from being in a council house in Walthamstow to being an Oxford-educated lawyer.

In the end my mum and dad surprised me – as you get older, you soften and you realise just how right your parents are about so much. When I was in my twenties I was battling with them a lot because of my sexuality, then once that battle was over it was much easier to acknowledge the ways in which they had been right. When you're a kid your parents are your parents and I guess through this battle of acceptance over my sexuality I was forced to see their humanity, good and bad. When they found a way of loving and accepting my partner, I was reminded of their superhumanity as my parents again. So it was a lovely full circle.

That chasm may not be so wide after all

They had to make a massive concession over my sexuality – it was something they wanted nothing to do with and they were entrenched for ten years. Pakistani culture comes with certain expectations about what the children will do and for us that was getting married to a person of the opposite sex, having children and living near my family – I wanted all of that, but I wanted it with a man. My parents had this dream for my life, then I got into Oxford and the dream just got larger, then I got into Linklaters and the dream got even larger, to the point it felt like this massive bubble that I was going to come along and burst.

I decided it was important to do it sooner rather than later, because I had to leave home. I had to get out, or at least I thought so then, because there was no way I could live there as a young gay guy. But the last thing I wanted my parents to think was that leaving was about me becoming western – or becoming middle class. I understood there were reasons they wouldn't be able to accept me, but it wasn't fair that I should have to leave and also let them believe that I've done it because I was rejecting the value system in which they'd raised me.

Eventually I told my mum and at first she was devastated; she took a week off work. It wasn't until a few years later I told my dad. I wanted to tell him on the same day, but my mum was worried he'd kick me out. I told my dad when I was about to start at Linklaters because I knew I'd be able to afford to pay rent somewhere if he did kick me out – I actually had my bags packed upstairs when I told him. But he didn't kick me out. He told me he loved me and I was his son, and that I wasn't going anywhere. It was remarkable, although some complications came later.

There's no reason to stick with something if you fancy a change

When I started at Linklaters, I did mainly corporate litigation – big companies fighting each other in court – then I switched and became a barrister, prosecuting and defending crime.

I don't think life is about doing the same thing forever; we have so little time on the planet and I'm excited by trying something new and the opportunity to learn more about the world. That's why I'm not a barrister any more; I now work for a consultancy called Hakluyt.

Be as open as you can about things, upfront

When I won the writing competition and knew I was going to write the book, I went to my mum and dad's house and told them about it. I didn't think there was any point in writing the book if they were not going to be on board. I told them they would have the right of veto, so at any point they could pull the plug on it. And I would let them read it before I sent it to my editors. So, on that basis – on the basis that they could pull the plug whenever they liked – they gave me the green light.

Once I'd finished the first draft I sent it to my mum and my brother and they had a couple of comments, but they said they were proud of me .

Lessons

When you are unafraid to ask questions, you have the opportunity to learn a great many things that might otherwise pass you by.

Being honest about who you are and what you believe in helps to build authentic relationships.

Life is short; it is OK to try new things and move your career forward in surprising non-linear ways.

Affirmation: Today I will remember that I am not alone on this journey.

ACKNOWLEDGEMENTS

When we started TwentyFirstCenturyBrand, my co-founder Neil Barrie and I had just left TBWA/Chiat/Day and Airbnb. We set out on a mission to challenge all leaders globally to create a positive cultural legacy and, in doing so, build the most influential brands of our time. As a company, we live and breathe this with our amazing clients, such as Netflix, Pinterest, Headspace, Lego, Peloton, Depop, Bumble, Zalando, LinkedIn, Mars Inc. and many more. *A Colourful View From the Top* is just another expression of this mission.

This book has been a beautiful labour of love. For the past two and a half years, we have partnered with numerous wonderful people to make this book a reality. Back in 2020, when Neil and I decided that we wanted to bring this collection of stories to the world, we had no idea how much time, energy, passion, creativity, generosity and resilience it would require.

It would not have been possible at all without the unwavering support of many people:

To our luminaries, thank you for your generosity, time, commitment and for living life boldly and with a sense of legacy.

To Little, Brown, it has been an absolute pleasure to partner with you from the very beginning. Thank you for understanding the vision and chiselling this into an editorial gift. From Holly Blood and Claire Chesser on the editorial side, thank you for your guidance, accountability and encouragement along the writing journey; to Duncan Spilling, Jess Gulliver and Abbi-Jean Reid on the Creative, PR and Marketing teams, thank you for helping us to communicate these stories to the world, in visuals and words.

To Sam Adefe, our phenomenal artist whose vision has captured the inner child and wisdom of each luminary, we are honoured to be in your portfolio of work and we can't wait to see where the future takes you. You are a star!

To Matthew Hamilton, our writing agent, thank you for all of your support, for brokering such special relationships to key people in the industry and for your reassurance, patience and expertise.

And, last but very not least, thank you to the whole team at TwentyFirstCenturyBrand, including Fauzia Musa who editorially contributed to the reprint of the book. But in particular, two people who are already striding like the giants portrayed within this book, Stephanie Nicolaides and Isaiah Wellington-Lynn. Throughout this entire process, you two have worn the most hats from pitching to editing, curating to designing, and everything in between. Thank you!

In loving memory of the incredible Abbi-Jean Reid (13/10/1994–22/12/2022), whose unrelenting warmth, generosity and positivity are – and will continue to be – hugely missed. Thank you for making the world a more colourful one.

Once energy is created, it cannot be destroyed. Rather, it transforms.